REAL MOVING PICTURES!

'HOLLYWOOD SCANDAL"

1¢

☆ HOLLYWOOD BABYLON II ☆

Every Man and every Woman is a Star.
—ALEISTER CROWLEY

We all have the strength to endure
the misfortunes of others.
—LA ROCHEFOUCAULD

ARROW BOOKS

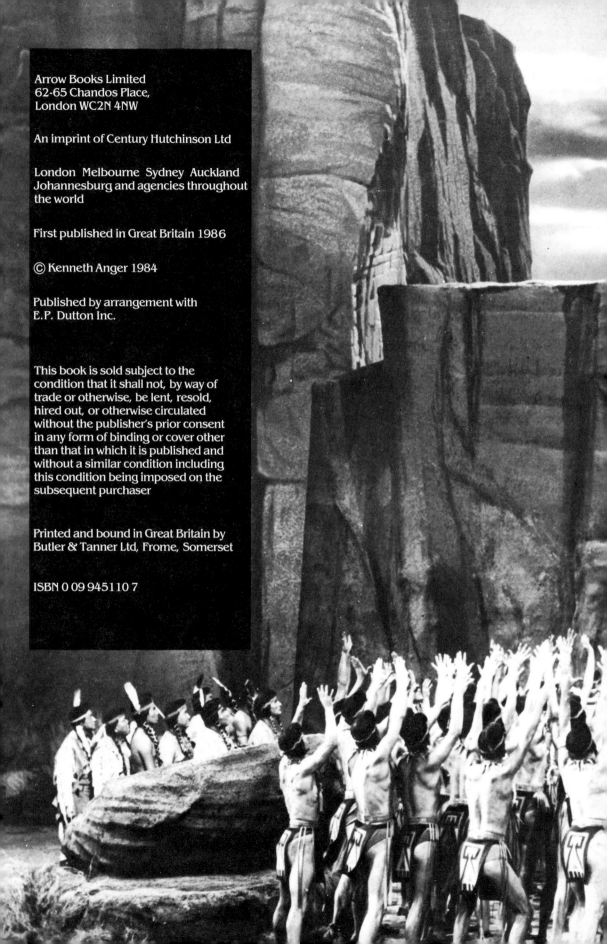

Arrow Books Limited
62-65 Chandos Place,
London WC2N 4NW

An imprint of Century Hutchinson Ltd

London Melbourne Sydney Auckland
Johannesburg and agencies throughout
the world

First published in Great Britain 1986

Published by arrangement with
E.P. Dutton Inc.

Printed and bound in Great Britain by
Butler & Tanner Ltd, Frome, Somerset

ISBN 0 09 945110 7

For

J. Paul

Getty, Jr.

☆ CONTENTS ☆

1	A Walk on the Dead Side
13	Getting Gloria's Goat
15	Killer Kelly
29	Why Be Good?
39	Bootlegger Joe
49	The White Legion and the Purple Poodle
65	Gangland Goes Hollywood
71	Dangerous Curves
87	The Two Faces of Tinseltown
105	Stumpfinger
113	Witch Joan
127	The Trouble with Jimmy
141	Odd Couples
155	Closely Watched Blondes
161	Babylon Boozers
183	Lost Boy
189	Attila the Nun
195	The Magic of Self-Murder
261	Indiscreet
279	Hollywood Hospital
291	The Purple Princess
295	Hollywood Drugstore
305	Death Valley Days
316	Index

AN ODE TO HOLLYWOOD

City of stertile striving,
Where brains have not begun,
I sing thy Idiot Faces,
Thy leaguèd Commonplaces,
Bright in thy silly Sun!

Thy ballocks have no Semen,
Thine Udders have no Milk;
Ever thou seekest Bliss
With Hard-ons swoln with Piss;
Thy Gods are Bunk and Bilk.

Fertile in naught but faking,
Futile each season passes;
And scrutiny discloses
Thy most prodigious Roses
Are really Horses' Asses.

Strange Cults are thine, strange Cunts,
Dry Nymph and arid Venus;
Or should a cundum bust
'Tis but a puff of dust
Powders the satyr's penis.

Diffuse, wide desert reaches
Where no Mind ever wrought!
Peer from thy cloudless skies
Demons with lidless eyes,
Scorching the buds of Thought!

Thy passions all pretended,
Thy pulses beat for pelf—
But should more Irrigation
Bring dustless fornication,
Go fuck thy Suffering Self!

—DON MARQUIS

☆ A WALK ON THE DEAD SIDE ☆

I confess: Growing up in Tinseltown, my childhood hobby was visiting cemeteries, seeking the resting places of my heroes, those with the fabulous faces of Hollywood in the Twenties who had "passed on." My grandmother had given me *her* habit of using that genteel euphemism, and I didn't know any better. For a long time, like Grandmother, I didn't believe in death. It was just a transition, a special-effect lap dissolve, and I *really believed* that when it would be my turn later on, I'd finally get to meet Mabel Normand, Barbara La Marr and Rodolfo Valentino. Me, I wouldn't approach them with autograph book in hand. Oh, no! That was for the proles from Venice and Redondo High. *I* firmly intended to approach my idols—Mabel, Barbara, and Rudy—as their equal. After all, I too had once acted in a Hollywood movie! Not by a long shot a star—I conceded that to Mickey Rooney (Puck Forever)—

◀ Kenneth Anger in *A Midsummer Night's Dream*   Mabel Normand: substance and shadow

Sincerely,
Barbara La Marr

but a decent little walk-on. I was proud of my Changeling Prince in Warners' *A Midsummer Night's Dream*.

When I found Valentino's tomb, it proved a disappointment. It was nothing special—not at all like the marble wedding cake that *Photoplay* had announced Pola Negri was going to erect. Just a space on the wall with two dinky flower vases, like those in an old-fashioned limousine, with Rudy's name spelled out in bronze in the long version. Still, I was drawn back again, and *again,* and *again.* These visits were charmed—there was never anyone else around. I had Rudy all to myself.

I confess: I'm a loner. I think I got to liking solitude in that flatland Hollywood cemetery. It was peaceful, quiet. I liked that. It was so quiet I could hear the mourning doves, their soothing dirges

▲ Barbara La Marr: beckoning from Beyond   Rudolph Valentino ▶   Valentino puzzle ▶▶

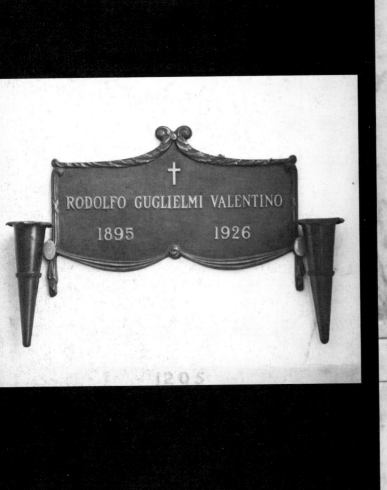

RODOLFO GUGLIELMI VALENTINO

1895   1926

broken only by an occasional mockingbird. So quiet, I could hear a distant lawnmower manned by a Mexican vassal way off amidst the flatland of tombs. So quiet, I was startled when a warning recording horn honked out from nearby Paramount: a star was spouting dialogue into a backlot mike. (When sound was recorded inside the big blank stages, they just turned on red lights—"whorehouse lights," I'd heard them called—on the stage doors. They didn't bother to honk.)

The warning honk from the backlot soundman invariably broke into my Valentinian reveries—my musing abruptly switched to the studio next door, where the Austrian cat-trainer, Von Sternberg, was putting Marlene Dietrich through her paces. *Dietrich next door!* They could have been on take fourteen of *Caprice Espagnole,* the loveliest S and M drama ever turned out in the mills of Tinseltown. (Adolph "Whispering Jesus" Zukor insisted on retitling it *The Devil Is a Woman.* Its distribution was cut short by Zukor, who caved in to Franco—another authoritarian—who saw the movie as an insult to Spain's honorable fascist military.)

Did I ever seriously consider a career in Hollywood? Of course—if I could have had my own studio, like Charlie Chaplin.

I knew damn well I'd never have one— no illusions on that score. The likes of me and the likes of the front-office men—the Mayers, the Balabans, the Warners, or the Cohns—would never have got along.

When I graduated from Beverly High, instead of knocking on the doors of the employment offices of "The Industry"— that nauseatingly self-important monicker they use in Tinseltown—I stole and sold my family's sterling flatware and solid silver tea service, bought a Greyhound ticket *and* a ticket on the *De Grasse,* pride of the fabled French Line, and hightailed it to Paris. There I met a dictator, not of front offices or backlots, but of something more fabulous: Henri Langlois, Grand Pasha and Sultan of the *Cinémathèque Française.* I worked ten years for the Terrible Turk, a consensual bondage, since Henri loved movies more, much more, than I ever could. Let me make it clear, though, that, in my own way, I do *adore* the movies, although they disappoint in that they promise immortality, but don't really deliver (you listening, Bernhardt?); they get folded, spindled, and mutilated, and grow scratches like wrinkles. Their blooming colors fade—as people do. And like lovers and people in general, a lot of 'em explode in flames and disappear without a trace.

What have I to tell that I haven't

Condom named for Valentino's "Great Lover" notoriety ▲

already told in Holly Baby 1? Some more dish, dirt, or if you will, more maverick movie history. Gents and ladies, let me take you on another walk on the Dead Side. Call it Hollywood's Walk of Fame, or Walk of Infamy—the expression used by Jane Withers when Hugh Hefner bought *his* star on the slippery sidewalk.

And be sure to take along some Black Humor batteries. You can, if you will, take the tour with your favorite High. I don't mind.

I promise to deliver you back to your hotel. At dawn.

KENNETH ANGER

Funeral for Thelma Todd ▲   Kenneth Anger and Samson De Brier at the Tomb of the Unknown Starlet ▶

☆ GETTING GLORIA'S GOAT ☆

DING, DONG, THE WITCH IS DEAD! If Tinseltown ever had a witch—a *witchy* witch, not a play-pretend witch like Margaret Hamilton, the Sweetheart of Gramercy Park—that real, bona fide, black-magical witch was none other than that flower of Chicago's stockyards, the *late* Gloria Swanson.

DING, DONG, THE WITCH IS DEAD! And not her maid, not her secretary, not her effete sixth husband can bring Old Gloria back to life again.

Gloria's *gone.*

Sic Transit Gloria Mundi!

◄ Gloria Swanson: topsy turvy   ▲ Queen Bee

☆ KILLER KELLY ☆

SOCK! Stage and Screen were battling it out in a Hollywood apartment that spring evening, and Stage was down for the count. Screen had had a few drinks too many, and in a fit of frenzy dragged Stage along the rug, knocking over a Spanish Revival table. He then proceeded to thump Stage's head against the wall.

It was April 16, 1927. In the Screen corner: Paul Kelly, twenty-six, 180 pounds, a lean tough six-footer with an athletic build, a redheaded and red-blooded Irish-American movie star who had grown up on the streets of Brooklyn. His dad had owned a saloon named Kelly's Kafe, which was located near the Vitagraph Studio. Vitagraph scenic workers who were in the habit of dropping in for a drink at Kelly's soon also got into the habit of borrowing furniture for their sets from Mrs. Kelly. One day in 1907, in return for the favor, she insisted that her son be given an acting job at $5 a day. He was given one—and a career was launched. Kid Kelly worked on several Vitagraph films—one of them appropriately entitled *Fit to Fight*. The moppet actor befriended the top studio stars of the day—John Bunny and Flora Finch—and was soon headed for Broadway, where he appeared opposite Helen Hayes in Booth Tarkington's *Penrod*. In 1926, Hollywood beckoned. His most

important film to date (*Slide, Kelly, Slide,* in which Kelly appeared with the popular young "lavender" leading man, William Haines) had been released just three weeks before this deadly brawl. His next film (*Special Delivery,* with Eddie Cantor and William Powell) was scheduled to come out the week after this stormy evening, but the young Irishman would be unable to attend the premiere. By then, his life and career would be complicated by a slight case of manslaughter.

In the Stage corner that fateful night was Ray Raymond, thirty-three, 155 pounds, five-feet-eight, a wiry song-and-dance man, who, after appearances in *The Ziegfeld Follies* of 1918 and 1919 was featured in *Blue Eyes,* a 1920 Broadway show. When he met a lively seventeen-year-old redhead in the cast named Dorothy Mackaye, it was love at first sight for Ray. They married.

Dorothy had been born in Scotland. At the ripe age of four, she had toured the British Isles as a dancer. She later turned to drama, and received fine notices for her work in a production of *Peg O' My Heart,* which ran for two years. But the young girl was plagued by a slight lisp, and, self-conscious about it, decided this might impair her career in high drama. Little Dottie decided to concentrate on farce and musical roles, in which she might use her lisp for comic effect. She had two of her biggest successes in *Head Over Heels,* and later as Lady Jane in Oscar Hammerstein II's *Rose Marie.*

The Raymonds had recently arrived in Hollywood. Sound was in the works—in a few months' time, *The Jazz Singer* would startle the world. Everyone was already talking about the Talkies. The prospect of a singing and "audible" movie career had drawn the musical Raymonds to Tinseltown. They appeared in a Vitaphone short that recorded one of their vaudeville acts, and were soon known as one of the most high-spirited and hard-drinking young couples around town.

The fisticuffs in Ray's apartment were over the affections of Mrs. Raymond. It was a classic triangle. Kelly was a good friend of Ray's—but an even better friend of Mrs. Ray. The town had been nattering about the dalliance of

handsome, thin-lipped Kelly with petite, "hot stuff" Dorothy. Kelly had learned that Ray had been complaining to their friends about "that son-of-a-bitch Irishman who has been trying to steal my wife!" Earlier that evening—he had already gone through half a quart of Scotch—Kelly called up Ray, who had just returned from an engagement in San Francisco. A shouting match ensued over the phone—Ray was already half blotto, too—and Raymond dared Kelly to come over to his house—if he was a man!

By the time Kelly got there, he was nine-tenths blotto. This was the Hollywood of the "Roaring Twenties" (the title of one of Kelly's later films), when gin came in bathtubs, not bottles. Paul and Dottie "partied around" a good deal with their movie friends. There were parties in Paul's apartment, at the Raymond home, at Lila Lee's, at John Bowers', and at the house of director Lewis Milestone and actress Nancy

The victim: Ray Raymond ▲   ▲ The *casus belli*: Dorothy Mackaye

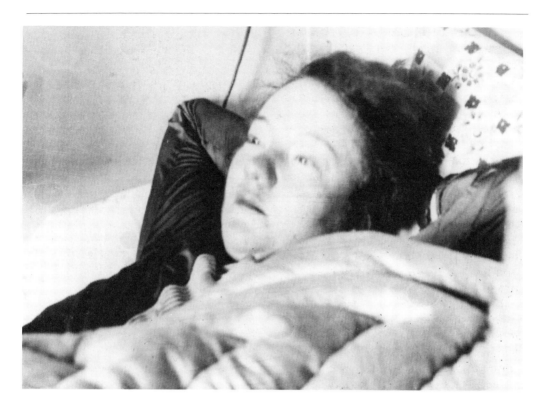

Carroll—gin wingdings where everyone gathered in the kitchen with the shades down and mixed the booze with anything available that would camouflage the taste.

If Dottie had been there, she might have been able to separate the two enraged studs. But if you went to "cherchez la femme" it would have been in vain—later, in her testimony at the trial, she declared that she had been downtown, "shopping for Easter eggs."

There *were* three witnesses to the mortal brawl, and they made an odd trio: Ethel Lee, the panicked colored maid, whose main concern was to "save the furniture"; four-year-old Valerie Raymond (who was later brought up as Mimi Kelly and had a brief career in the Fifties in Broadway musicals); and Dottie's dog Spot, who barked away and added to the general confusion (even in the Hollywood of the Twenties, where members of the gay set dyed their pooches purple, *this* was a mutt that

Dorothy recovering from collapse after questioning ▲   ▲ Paul Kelly: fat lip from fisticuffs

attracted all eyes wherever it went—the heroic fox terrier sported a wooden leg. One front leg had been bitten off when Spot defended Dottie's niece from a police dog that had attacked the child.)

With maid, child and pooch as audience, Ray kept coming back for more punishment. Kelly held him by the throat with one hand and smacked him in the face several times with his other fist. After the song-and-dance man had had his head rapped against the wall by Kelly a few times, he was hearing birdies. Having made his point—or whatever he thought was his point—Kelly staggered on home.

Dottie arrived soon afterwards with her Easter eggs to find the apartment in a shambles. She helped her husband to his feet, and propelled him to the bedroom. He dropped into bed, fully clothed, made a joke with the maid about the fight, then passed out.

The next morning, Dottie and Ethel Lee found him unconscious. Two days later he was dead.

Dottie called a doctor friend—Walter Sullivan—who knew as well as she did that if word of the brawl got out, Dottie's and Paul's careers might be ruined. Dr. Sullivan declared that Ray's death had been due to complications resulting from past illnesses. Ethel Lee did not, however, hold up very long under intense police questioning: the maid gave in and described the donnybrook, remarking on how furiously Kelly had kicked Ray when he was down, and how he had slammed his head against the wall.

The actor was arrested. In a statement to Police Captain *Slaughter*, he confessed that he loved Mrs. Raymond, but said that his love had never been returned. He was charged with manslaughter. Dottie and Dr. Sullivan were charged with compounding a felony by attempting to conceal facts as to the death of Raymond. (The charges against Sullivan were later dismissed.)

The trial of Paul Kelly was a maudlin melodrama that played to a full house. The prosecution produced dozens of his letters to Dottie. The maid had found them, hidden, ironically enough, under the conjugal mattress. In one of them, he wrote: "I'm crazy, cray-zee about you." He even tried his hand at pig Latin: "I-ay uv-lay oo-yay, arling-day . . ." The letters were read in court while Paul changed color and sweat glistened on his forehead. The "sob sisters" of the tabloid press had a ball with the story. One front-page item in the *Herald-Examiner* clucked that it would have been far more tasteful if Paul had said it with flowers instead of in silly pig Latin. (This was the first eruption of this nutty lingo into Tinseltown consciousness—six years later the fad climaxed with the opening of Busby Berkeley's film *Gold Diggers of 1933,* in which Ingergay Ogersray sang "We're in the Money" in pig Latin.)

The courtroom vibrated with excitement when Dorothy took the stand as the star witness for the defense. Necks were craned to permit eyes a better look at her. Some of the craners were disappointed. Dottie was not glamourous; she did not square up to anyone's image of a *femme fatale.* She was of medium height, with shingled red hair and odd Oriental eyes—for a lassie born in Scotland. Her face was pert, sensitive and intelligent. She refused to play to the gallery: in spite of her troubles, her demeanor was proud and aloof, preventing the jurors from taking her to their hearts.

She did not admit to loving Kelly—he was a good friend, that was all. She was trying to help her lover, in her own way, but her attitude was almost one of disdain for the court. She glared defiantly at the district attorney as he cross-examined her.

"So, Miss Mackaye, you 'partied

around' as you say, with Mr. Kelly. Did you consider his attentions proper?"

"Why, yes. Nobody thought anything of it."

"And why not?"

"Well, you see, Hollywood is different. We accept violation of convention because it is all right for us—that is, professional people are less conventional, more sophisticated—"

"So unconventional"—the D.A. promptly nailed her—"that you *kill* when someone is in the way?"

Tension at the trial was temporarily broken when some comic relief arrived in the person of Teno Yobu, Kelly's Japanese houseboy, who was nicknamed "Jungle." When Jungle was called to the stand, he brought down the house with his account of the "prijama patties" that had often taken place in Paul's apartment. He told of serving breakfast in bed to Dottie and Paul—garnished with aspirins and Alka-Seltzer for their hangovers.

Jungle's testimony was of no help to his boss—Paul and Dottie had steadfastly denied any intimacy. Other

Paul Kelly and his lawyer in court ▲   Kelly in San Quentin: model prisoner ▶

19

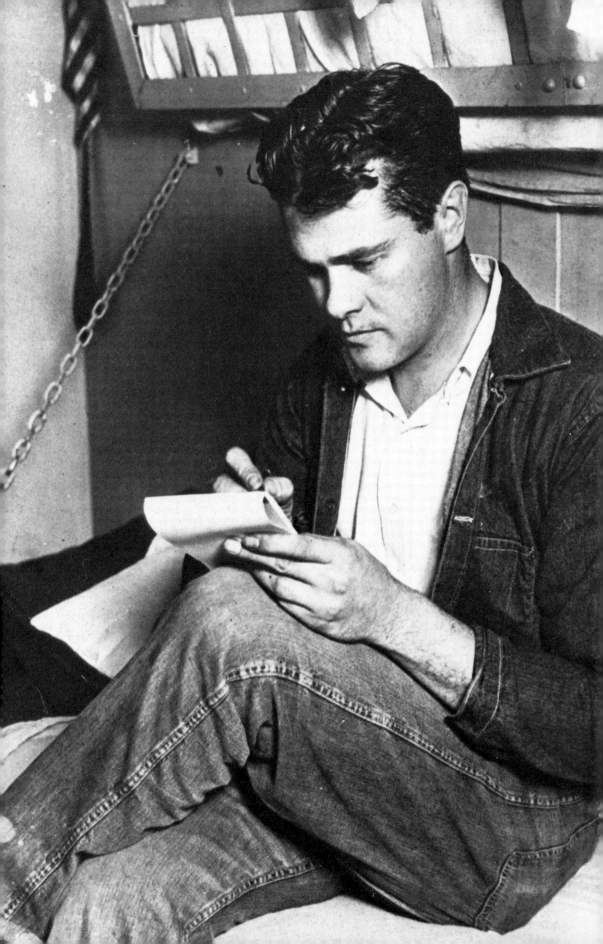

testimony did appear to be helping Paul's case a bit, however: many Hollywood friends were called in as character witnesses—James Kirkwood and Lila Lee (parents of James Kirkwood, Jr., the author of *A Chorus Line*), director Lewis Milestone, Nancy Carroll, Marguerite De La Motte. They gave the impression that Kelly was a good egg, with loyal friends—but the jury still arrived at a verdict of manslaughter. The actor was sentenced to serve from one to ten years in State's Prison—San Quentin.

Dorothy was in a downtown hotel room, surrounded by newshens, when a phone call informed her of Paul's sentence. She looked as if she were about to faint, then caught herself, straightened up and whispered, with a trace of arrogance: "Well, that's that."

Her casualness about the verdict led the print cacklers to headline their columns the next day with "scoops" about a rift between Dottie and Paul.

They were disabused, a few weeks later, when she risked a great deal by going to see Kelly before he was taken to San Quentin. Paul had been let out of the L.A. jail in the custody of a sheriff in order to arrange his business affairs. This was to be done at the home of a friend, Ben Wilson.

Behind her cold mask, Dottie was at heart *une grande amoureuse.* She was out on bond, pending the result of her own trial. The jury's good impression of her was vital to her defense—yet she risked everything to go and see her lover. While Mrs. Wilson gave the sheriff a tour of the house and grounds to distract him, the couple sat down on the couch and held hands—and were in a sense, then and there, married—though not legally. They had been through hell together, but it had not turned them against each other. Both had matured considerably and their love had survived the ordeal: it was stronger than ever now. It was all really like a movie script.

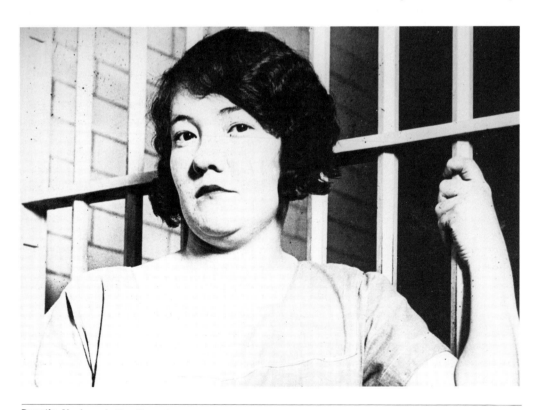

Dorothy Mackaye in San Quentin ▲

The next day's headlines blared the news of this "clandestine tryst." Then, after deliberating only two and a half hours, the day before Kelly left for the Big House, the jurors on Dottie's case found her guilty as charged. Judge Burnell sentenced her to one to three years—also to be served at San Quentin Penitentiary.

A sob sister visited her soon afterwards in the L.A. jail. She was asked why she had gone to see Paul, knowing full well that if news of her visit got out, it would hurt her case. She replied, "I had to do it. I couldn't let him be sent up like that without trying to make him see that whatever has been done is done— but there is still a future for us. Perhaps his career is finished. Some people think so. But he's still young—he's a fighter and I think there's a good chance that it isn't. I wanted him to realize that. I wanted to give him hope and let him know that if I get out before he does, I'll be waiting for him."

Though she had lost everything, she was not thinking of herself for once, but of Paul.

After their conviction, a story appeared about them that began with a poem:

Once they had a penny,
Yellow as the hay,
Now they haven't any—
They heard the piper play. . .

Kelly did not even wait in the L.A. County Jail, as he was entitled to, in order to appeal the sentence. "I want to get it over with," he declared. He proved a model prisoner at San Quentin. The Talkies came in with a bang—and Kelly read everything he could about the technique of sound films. He took courses in elocution and voice projection. He sensibly believed that keeping busy, planning for the future, was the best way for him to avoid going bananas.

Dorothy did wait in the L.A. County Jail for seven months, but when she lost her appeal, and was then denied clemency by Governor C. C. Young, she was transported north to the grim confines of California's Big House. She did not idle there either. She took notes on the condition of the women prisoners and listened whenever she could to the life stories, real or invented, of her fellow inmates. In later years she would put her prison experience to good use. She organized a drama club for women prisoners and directed plays in the pen—one of her productions had an all-killer cast, featuring the notorious "hammer murderess," Clara Phillips, and Dorothy Ellingson, the "Jazz Slayer."

A visitor received Dottie's version of the manslaughter case: "After the fight, Paul apologized to my husband. Ray accepted it and told him that all was forgiven—they could remain friends. Ray died two days later. The inquest showed he died of kidney trouble and cerebral hemorrhage—induced, not by the fight with Paul, but by acute alcoholism. We were all crazy to be drinking so much—all of us, we were silly pigs. I was horrified to find they had been fighting over me. Ray had been mean to me since he found out about Paul, but I still cared for him. Why, Ray would have been the first one to come to Paul's defense—if he had survived, they would have remained friends. They fought like two kids, but those guys really liked each other. And before Ray died, he pleaded with me not to let Paul's name be dragged into the case. 'I've had lots of fights in my life, Dot dear,' he told me. 'This thing was just another stupid brawl—it was as much my fault as his. Keep Paul's name out of it.' And because I kept the promise I gave to my dying husband, a jury convicted me of compounding a felony!"

Dottie was afraid that prison would

Tuesday.

Darling Mine :—

Oh I am so terribly
in love with you — so terribly —
I'm miserable here without you —
I love you love you — love you — love
you —

I thought I'd die last
week — I hadn't a civil word for
any one when they spoke to me —
was always thinking of you and
dreaming of you — oh God it was
awful —!

When I couldn't speak to
you on the phone your wires took
it place — but since I haven't
received any more I didn't know
what to think — then your first
letters nearly drove me crazy —

Jesse Smith's birthday party — our
producer — at "Montmartre" all
dressed up — wish you were
going with me — I'm going stag —
I miss you so —

please — please — please try
and call me before Saturday —
even if you are out some place
just so I can talk to you
once again before I go to
Arizona — please — any time
of the morning — I don't care — as
long as I can hear your voice —

well good night sweetheart
mine — I want to hear from you
soon —

Valerie — Etta + Helen send their
love — and mine always +

my adorable —
Paul ?

---

mar her looks. She held on to her dream
of making a stage comeback when
released. She remembered the rave
reviews she had received when she
appeared with Richard Bennett in *The
Dove* (Bennett, the father of Joan and
Constance, had been a popular matinee
idol in his prime—he can be seen as old
Major Amberson in Orson Welles' *The
Magnificent Ambersons*). She took care
to maintain her self-respect by making
herself up carefully every day in her cell.
She soon discovered that other women
prisoners, in the midst of the horrors of
captivity, attempted to cling to their
smartness and beauty. Quentin was one
of the nation's toughest jails—but in
those days, women inmates were
allowed a few privileges. They were
permitted to fashion their own clothing,
and garnish their blue denim uniforms
in a style suitable to their personalities.
Dottie became a fashion advisor for the
girls. They loosened up and unburdened
themselves to her. Her time "in stir" was
an extraordinary learning experience for
the actress.

Dorothy Mackaye was out in a year,
paroled for good behavior. Kelly was
released for good behavior after twenty-
five months.

They were married in 1931. It was a
good marriage and lasted until death
did them part.

Women in Prison, a play by Dorothy
Mackaye, was produced in 1932 and
attracted much favorable attention. It
was bought by Warner Bros. and
brought to the screen in 1933 as *Ladies
They Talk About,* directed by William
Keighley. It starred Barbara Stanwyck as
a hard-boiled gun moll. The fine
supporting cast included Preston Foster,
Lillian Roth, Maude Eburne and Ruth
Donnelly. (It was lensed by the great
cinematographer John Seitz, who had
been the masterful cameraman of
Valentino's *The Four Horsemen of the
Apocalypse.*) The script of this effective
prison comedy-melodrama was very

◀ Dorothy at her prison sewing machine: style behind bars　　　　▲ Love letter from Paul

strong, and marked by both humor and compassion. The movie had several brushes with the Hays Office, and Warners was eventually obliged to trim a few scenes concerning the lust of the man-hungry women inmates. These scenes were based not only on Dottie's observations of her fellow prisoners, but on her own frustrated body's knowledge that her lover was just a few dozen cells away.

Ladies They Talk About was remade by Warners in 1942, as *Lady Gangster,* with Faye Emerson, Julie Bishop, Ruth Ford and Jackie Gleason. Dottie never got to see the second film version of her play. "Brat Face," as she was affectionately called by Kelly, was driving home to the Kelly-Mac Ranch, the couple's home near Northridge, in the San Fernando Valley, on January 5, 1940. The car skidded on a soft shoulder, and turned over three times. She was pinned under the wheel. Dorothy Mackaye, dead at thirty-seven.

Hollywood, which can be cruel and hypocritical, can, on occasion, be kind— if *real* talent is involved, accompanied by real drive and ambition. After his release, Kelly returned to the screen and enjoyed a successful career for another quarter of a century. He appeared in several hundred movies, and scored heavily in his 1933 "return" film, *Broadway Thru a Keyhole,* based on a story by Walter Winchell, in which he appeared with Constance Cummings, Russ Columbo and Texas Guinan. After that, he worked continuously, often making more than five movies a year. It is bizarre that this ex-con (although he was occasionally seen as a mobster) was often cast as an authority figure. He played a prison warden; in *Torchy Blane in Panama* he was a police lieutenant; in *Fear in the Night* and *Side Street,* he was a police officer. (The hard-bitten quality that he emanated made him equally creditable as slouch hat cop or slouch

hat gangster.) In Cecil B. De Mille's *The Story of Dr. Wassell,* he was a Navy officer. He worked for every one of the major studios, alongside Judy Garland and Lana Turner in MGM's opulent *The Ziegfeld Girl,* and on dozens of B pictures at Republic and Monogram. He appeared with the big names—Gary Cooper, John Wayne, Cagney, Bogart, Stanwyck, Bette Davis. His best film of all was probably Raoul Walsh's *The Roaring Twenties,* one of the greatest of all gangster movies. It was made at Warners, and although Kelly did not work there more than at other studios, there was something of the typical Warner Bros. actor about him. Most actors at Warners—during the great years of the studio, now long since past—looked like "just folks," not like movie stars. And Kelly was never a glamour boy; he was a solid, believable actor with a believable presence that lent credibility to whatever sort of film he appeared in. (Although he was friendly with Cagney, Pat O'Brien, and Frank McHugh, off the set he did not run around with Warners' famed Irish Mafia. He spent most of his leisure hours with Dorothy and a few close friends.)

His most memorable performance was as Gloria Grahame's strange boyfriend in RKO's *Crossfire.* And, believe it or not, this ex-con played in *two* movies at Warners written by prison wardens: *Invisible Stripes,* based on the memoirs of Warden Lawes, and *Duffy of San Quentin,* based on Clinton T. Duffy's *The San Quentin Story.* In it, Kelly starred as Warden Duffy—playing the warden of the very prison in which he himself had been a prisoner for over two years!

Dotty never lived to see Paul's two greatest theatrical successes. In 1947, he made a triumphant return to the Broadway stage in Kermit Bloomgarden's long-running production of William Wister Haines' *Command*

Decision. For his magnificent performance as Air Force Brigadier General Dennis—outwardly hard-boiled, but inwardly compassionate—Kelly won the Donaldson Award, the Variety Critics' Award, and the Tony for Best Actor of 1948. He returned to Broadway in 1951 and scored another triumph as Frank Elgin, the alcoholic actor, opposite Uta Hagen in the Strasberg production of Clifford Odets' *The Country Girl.* Unfortunately, when these plays were made into movies, the studios opted for big star names in the leads—Clark Gable played Dennis in MGM's version of *Command Decision;* Bing Crosby was cast as Elgin, opposite Grace Kelly, in Paramount's version of *The Country Girl.* Neither of them matched Kelly's stage performances.

On November 6, 1956, Paul Kelly died of a heart attack in his California home, shortly after returning from voting—for Stevenson.

Killer Kelly cast with future wife-killer Tom Neal in *Within the Law* ▲

☆ WHY BE GOOD? ☆

This one took place *at* the movies.

The first great Art Deco movie palace was the Hollywood Pantages (1930) at Hollywood and Vine, designed by an inspired theater architect, B. Marcus Priteca. It is still in operation and is now mostly used for road shows of Broadway musicals. Nine years earlier, Priteca had designed another theater for the tycoon entrepreneur, Alexander Pantages, a beautiful eclectic Beaux Arts edifice in the heart of downtown L.A., at the corner of Hill and 7th.

In the downtown theater, on the fateful afternoon of August 9, 1929, a plump teenage girl, wearing a low-cut red dress, ran screaming out of the janitor's broom and mop closet on the mezzanine. The audience could hear her hysterics above the music score of the feature picture.

A theater employee raced to the scene of the shrieks; the girl collapsed in the youth's arms. She screamed: "There he is, the Beast! The Great God Pan! Don't let him get at me!" She pointed to a middle-aged man with silvery hair, stumbling about in the office adjacent to the mop closet. It was the boss— Pantages. A traffic policeman, summoned from the street, arrived. Pantages bellowed: "She's trying to frame me!"

Thus began an affair which would not only result in several sensational Hollywood trials, but would establish new legal principles which would come to bear on future rape cases.

Pantages had been born in Athens. He came to this country before the turn of the century. He shined shoes, sold newspapers, then operated penny arcades and nickelodeons. He made his way to Alaska during the Klondike gold strike, amassed a pile of nuggets and returned from the wilderness in 1902. He bought a run-down theater in Seattle, and with his natural flair for showmanship kept the place packed. Soon he acquired another vaudeville house and gradually added movies to the bills. He eventually owned sixty theaters—most of them designed by the great Priteca—which extended from Mexico up to Canada. All of the big variety stars from the East Coast vied with one another to be booked for Pan-time. (His only competitor on the West Coast was the Orpheum Circuit—later gobbled up by RKO, the Radio Keith Orpheum conglomerate which had sprung from Joe Kennedy's parent movie company FBO.) By 1929, Alex Pantages was worth $30,000,000.

The yelping damsel in the red dress was Eunice Pringle, a stage-struck school dropout and would-be dancer from Garden Grove, California. She claimed she had come to see the theater owner to get him interested in an "act"

◄ Alexander Pantages: the Great God Pan goes to jail

of hers. She sobbed to the cops that he had tossed her into the mop closet, wrenched her underwear loose and raped her.

Little Eunice had an agent, Nick Dunaev. Rumor had it that he was a shrewdy, and that his client's casual visit to Pantages had been part of a scheme of his—in connivance with "higher powers." She had bought a ticket to the show, had gone up to Pantages' office on the mezzanine level unannounced—the rest was rape or frame-up.

The papers went to town with the case. Hearst's *Herald-Examiner* described Eunice as "the sweetest seventeen since Clara Bow." The *Los Angeles Times* called her "a full-blown beauty."

Pantages claimed that she had "raped herself"—she had torn at her clothing and ripped her garments so that it looked as if a crew of sex-hungry sailors had had their way with her. He stated what was common knowledge—that sex was available every few feet in Hollywood, and there was no need for him to molest a moppet in a mop closet.

Unfortunately for Alex, when he came to trial, his broken English and foreign airs made a poor impression, whereas sweet-toned Eunice was an instant hit with press and jury. Public opinion was outraged at the goatish Greek millionaire who had deflowered a native daisy from Garden Grove.

By the time the case was over, it was apparent that the star of the trial was neither goat nor daisy, but an unknown lawyer named Jerry Geisler, whose

Art Deco masterpiece: the Hollywood Pantages ▲   Los Angeles Pantages: framed on the mezzanine ▶

brilliant defense of Pantages earned him a reputation that turned him into the "Lawyer of the Stars."

Eunice was most demurely dressed during the preliminary hearing. When questioned by the D.A. she stated: "He said he wanted me for his sweetheart. I told him I was not interested in sweethearts, I was interested in work, but he continued his advances. . . . He seemed to go crazy. . . . He clapped his hand over my mouth. . . . He bit me on the breast." She claimed that she had fainted, and regained consciousness in the mop closet to find that her dress was up and Pantages' private parts were out. Alex maintained that she had been to see him several times before, and on each occasion, he had refused to book her act—it was "too suggestive."

When the case came to trial in L.A. Superior Court, Eunice wore a Mary Pickford girlish frock and flat shoes. Her hair was in a bow at the back. She looked thirteen.

After her preliminary testimony, when the court recessed, Geisler requested that when she returned to court the following day she wear the same clothing and hair style which she wore at the time of the alleged attack. When she did, she looked like a seductive twenty-year-old.

Despite Geisler's stubborn defense, Pantages was found guilty and sentenced to fifty years in the jug.

Geisler was convinced the verdict could be overturned; he filed an appeal which left its mark on jurisprudence. He argued that it was prejudicial to Pantages to exclude testimony about the

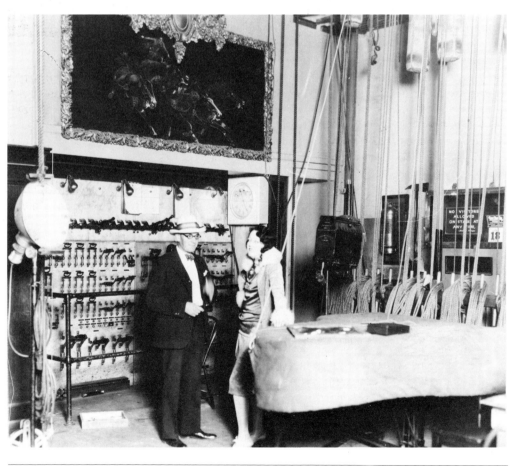

Marble switchboard of the Los Angeles Pantages: the Great God Pan and the showgirl ▲

morals of the plaintiff, although she was underage. Prior to this, judges had barred such testimony on the grounds that the morals of a minor were not an issue because a minor was legally incapable of giving assent in a sex case.

Geisler carried the case to the California Supreme Court. It granted a new trial in a forty-page ruling which created a precedent for the adjudication of California rape cases. The Court commented that "the testimony of the prosecutrix was so improbable as to challenge credulity," and ruled that any relevant evidence—to the effect that an allegedly damaged party in a rape matter might have been pre-damaged with her own connivance—was admissible.

The case was re-tried in 1931. Geisler built his case on the contention that Eunice had conspired with her agent/teacher to compromise Pantages. Pringle admitted on the stand that her dancing skills included the ability to do

a full split. Jake Ehrlich, Geisler's associate, had no difficulty in convincing the jury that an athletic youngster such as Pringle, capable of doing a full split, could easily have fought off an attack from a small middle-aged man such as Pantages.

To clinch the matter, Geisler and Ehrlich re-enacted the rape in court. The portly Geisler played Pantages—Jake played Eunice. The two men "performed the scene with realistic finesse right up to the climax." The lawyers made their point: it would have been inconceivable for a rape to have occurred in the mop closet in the fashion described by Eunice.

Ehrlich turned up with a surprise witness: an old lady who managed the Moonbeam Glen Bungalow Court, where Eunice and her agent had lived as man and wife, although they were not married. At first, the old lady, an avid reader of Hearst papers and a member of the "Gospel Truth Assembly," would

do nothing to help Pantages. She declared: "I wouldn't help that rich despoiler of women if my life depended on it. They had men like that in Babylon before the Fall. The *beast!*" Ehrlich quoted large passages of the Bible to her at great length and persuaded her of the moral obligation she was under to appear in court. There, she picked out the former tenant of Bungalow 45—and saltily testified Eunice's case right out the window. The verdict: Not Guilty.

The party most disgruntled by the verdict was not Little Eunice, but Joseph P. Kennedy, bootlegger to the film colony, head of FBO Pictures and pater of a future President of the United States. Kennedy had hoped to destroy Pantages, and in the process gobble up the Pantages theater circuit. On her deathbed, Eunice confessed that it had been Kennedy who had masterminded the frame-up.

The downtown Pantages theater was later taken over by Warner Bros. Ironically enough, most of Errol Flynn's movies were shown there, for it was the court case hatched in the mop closet of this theater which established legal principles which would save Flynn's neck when two underage girls accused the Warner Bros. star of rape.

In the 1960s, the theater was acquired by the International Church of Compassion, which replaced much of Priteca's original design with gaudy Fontainebleau Hotel Revival decorations. The church went out of business; when last I saw the place, it had been turned into a Jewelry Exchange. Pantages' original solid marble lightboard with its gold frame— the only lightboard of its kind in any theater in the world—was still there. The historic mop closet is no more.

The movie that was playing at the

◀ Lawyer and client: Jerry Geisler and Alexander Pantages   ▲ Eunice Pringle and parents at the trial

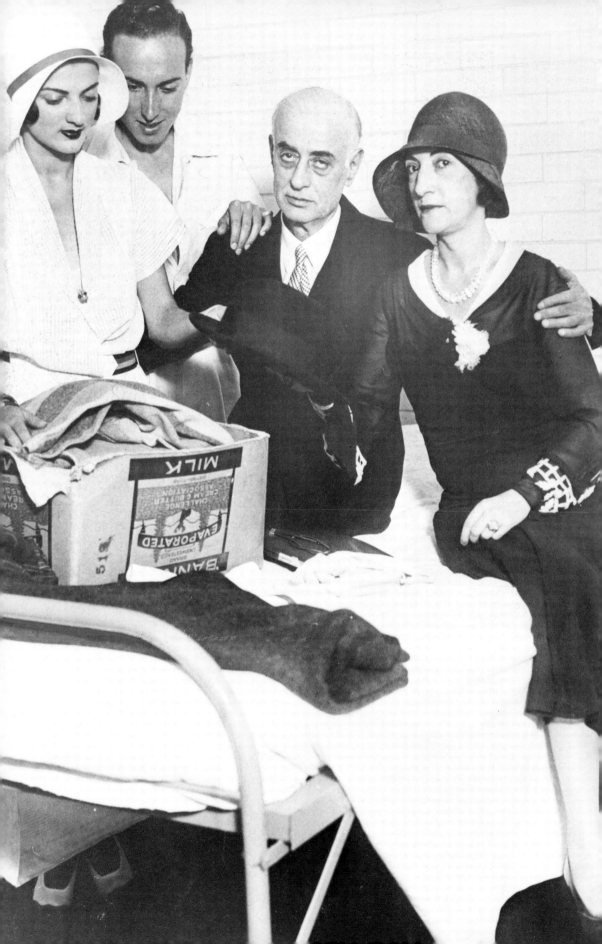

theater when shopworn angel Eunice Pringle assumed the role of a chaste colleen brutalized by a Greek in heat was William A. Seiter's *Why Be Good?* It is concerned with the misadventures of a virginal young woman, Colleen Moore, who pretends to be a wanton in order to attract a little attention.

◄ Daughter, son, and Mrs. Pantages bring Papa a CARE package   ▲ A brass band to celebrate his release

☆ BOOTLEGGER JOE ☆

JOSEPH PATRICK KENNEDY, BANKER, was Boston's lace-curtain Irish contribution to Hollywood history, thanks to his takeover bid on Miss Gloria Swanson, Star—another Irish scrapper. The cast of characters in this drama of sex and moolah included Rose, Joe's wife, a quiet saint, and a roster of kiddies, some of whom would grow into fame, several struck down by tragedy.

Joe Kennedy's character was clear from the start: no fair-minded sportsman and gentleman, he—Joe was a tough competitor who loved to win and *hated* to lose. The Kennedys *would* win; what he couldn't do himself, his phalanx of sons would accomplish. That's why he had them. *"Go for it!"* was Big Joe's lifetime motto.

The class yearbook at Boston Latin, his boyhood school, predicted that Joe Kennedy would make his fortune in "a very roundabout way." This was a farsighted prediction, if the routes of Wall Street, bootleg Scotch, and Hollywood's Gloria Swanson could be considered roundabout.

At Harvard, Joe applied his yell of "Go for it!" to the challenge of sports. In no time at all, he was captain of the baseball team, driving it on to victory. And, like all else he touched, sports yielded useful lessons for his career. "Remember," he liked to say, "if you can't be captain, don't play."

After he graduated from Harvard and was in possession of a small nest egg, he decided to be a millionaire by age thirty-five, and he made it. Never mind how; he made it.

At twenty-five, he was Boston's youngest bank president. "It's no crime to be young," he commented. Joe Kennedy operated as a lone wolf, alert to tips on Wall Street, keeping his ears perked for gossip that might provide useful information, yet secretive about his own dealings. With the advent of that Great Folly, the 18th Amendment, his Irish good sense told him that human nature would overcome silly legislation. Clandestine boatloads of the finest Scotch and Irish whiskies and French champagne soon crossed the "Big Pond," bound for Kennedy's secret warehouses on both coasts. "Bit of a gamble" that paid off handsomely: Joe Kennedy, dynasty-founder, was, during the Twenties, Hollywood's top-drawer booze connection, the "Real Thing" bootlegger. And he multiplied his investment of a few million in booze into a family fortune of many millions, a fortune based on hooch that continues to flow to this day.

Kennedy was not, however, a gambler. He analyzed the difference between gambling and speculation: "The prime motive back of most gamblers is the excitement. Gamblers

◄ Joseph P. Kennedy: movies and moonshine

want to win, but the majority derive pleasure even if they lose. Whereas, the compelling force behind speculation is the desire to win, rather than the excitement." Joe was only happy when throned beneath an Arch of Triumph.

One of Kennedy's acquaintances was a small-town banker who had invested $120,000 in one movie—*The Miracle Man,* with Lon Chaney—and made three million. Hollywood, it was apparent to Joe, was a prime plum to be picked. His first gambit in the realm of the Silver Screen was the takeover of a chain of three dozen New England movie houses. His ambition did not stop with the thirteen colonies. Kennedy planned to take over movie houses across the country: the Balaban and Katz chain in the Midwest would be his when he ferreted out their Achilles' heel. Alex Pantages, that illiterate Greek peasant with his fancy movie palaces on the West Coast, was also ripe for the picking. Find the weak point—and go for the jugular!

As the Twenties began to roar, movie-going became a national obsession. Hollywood's Satanic mills churned out miles of celluloid weekly. Escapist dreams were a growing market, abetted by the lore of fast living and the glamourous, loose women that accompanied it. (By the end of the decade, sixty million Americans would go to the movies in 21,000 theaters across the country.) Bigger, grander picture palaces were springing up every week.

Yes, there was no business like the infant picture business. Many doubted that it was a rational business at all. Each picture involved fresh problems and different risks. Individual and organizational fortunes swayed dizzily from year to year.

The men at the corporate heights who tried to guess the whims of millions of movie fans were an odd assortment of upstart petty entrepreneurs, recent immigrants, hungry and ambitious Jews on the make, still outsiders in the country's ethnic melting pot. They included the former furrier, Adolph "Whispering Jesus" Zukor, like his future star, La Swanson, a dwarf; Marcus Loew, wholesale fur trader; ex-ragman, ex-scrap iron dealer, Louis B. Mayer; one-time glove salesman Samuel Goldfish—changed to Goldwyn. Only a few, like vaudeville producer Jesse Lasky, had actually been showmen. Haphazard, intuitive, uninhibited, the founders of the movie business were a new breed of self-made mogul. Irish Joe was up against some tough competition. Always a quick study, though, "Go-for-it!" Kennedy caught on faster than most.

Kennedy's timing was perfect. He came on the Hollywood scene at the right time, arriving on a flood tide of prosperity. With his quick grin, open manner, and direct speech laced with profanity, exuding a sort of contagious

sexual energy, he was refreshingly unlike the usual aloof, cold-eyed gents from Wall Street. He looked and behaved like a picture man.

He bought out the floundering British owners of the Robertson–Cole Studios, with some help from the Prince of Wales. In February 1926, Kennedy became the head of FBO Pictures—the Film Booking Offices of America, Inc., buying the Hollywood studio, sight unseen. After moving from Boston to New York, he went to Hollywood for the first time to have a look at his new property.

He discovered a studio that lacked the prestige of the majors, but was doing good steady business grinding out a feature a week at a bargain basement cost of $30,000 per picture. The lot's biggest asset was Fred Thomson, the first movie cowboy to give his horse star billing. (This was Silver King, a stallion who traveled to work in a deluxe Packard van.) Kennedy signed up Thomson for a new contract—fifteen grand a week, almost twice his former salary.

Although FBO's product was popular in small towns, it had not yet cracked the urban markets—and their big box-office receipts. Kennedy went to see "Roxy" Samuel L. Rothafel. Two of America's titan salesmen looked each other in the eye. "Try a Fred Thomson picture," Joe urged. Roxy demurred— his audiences wanted "flesh and the devil" and plenty of both, not horseflesh. "It won't cost you anything," Kennedy coaxed, and won his point. When *The Sunset Legion,* a Thomson Western, had proved a hit at Roxy's fabled "Cathedral of the Motion Picture," Joe could remark with some disdain, "Roxy didn't know his own audience. Now he plays Westerns all the time."

Further proof of Kennedy's flair for showmanship involved Red Grange, the "Galloping Ghost" of University of Illinois football fame, and later a star

attraction as a professional. Grange had made his availability for pictures known, but studio after studio had turned him down. Kennedy went to his favorite potential audience and put the question: "Would you like to see Red Grange on the screen?" His sons Joe and Jack screamed an instant affirmative answer. Grange starred in *One Minute to Play,* and, ably directed by Sam Wood, the movie proved a big moneymaker.

As my dear devoted readers have already learned from perusing Holly Baby I, all was not wine and roses for the dream factory during the Twenties. After a series of unsavory scandals, Hollywood, in the eyes of Middle America, appeared to be a veritable modern Babylon, with Sodom for a suburb. The magnates undertook to clean house by installing Will Hays, Harding's former postmaster general, as the window-dressing "czar" of movie morals.

In a move to upgrade Hollywood's respectability, Kennedy hatched the idea of sending some Tinseltown leaders to lecture at Harvard's business school. Harvard was willing; the speakers were sent. It's a shame there is no record of their discoursing—they must have been priceless. The guest lecturers were functionally illiterate and most had never graduated from high school.

Kennedy gobbled up the theater empire of aging E. F. Albee, offering a price for the vaudeville house circuit that the old man couldn't refuse. At the time of the takeover, shares in the Keith-Albee-Orpheum circuit were selling for $16 each; two weeks later, they were going for $50. Again, the golden Kennedy touch. (Later, after a few more Kennedy-inspired mergers, the letters would finally settle down into RKO, trademark of an eventually famous major studio.)

Meanwhile, La Swanson, most glamourous of movie queens, returned

to her Hollywood turf after an uppity sojourn in France filming *Madame Sans Gêne* in authentic locales. When she returned, with her fancy new title, Marquise de la Falaise de la Coudraye, Gloria sent an advance order to Paramount: "Please arrange ovation." Kennedy and Gloria the Marquise then met in the crowd of "ovationers," beneath a barrage of flowers. It was a surefire chemical click—the attraction of opposites, short and tall. Kennedy was charmed by the tiny creature; Gloria cast her net. The vamp batted her mascaraed eyes and cooed, "Joe, you're the best actor in Hollywood."

They became lovers, with the added spice of a secret trysting place for the horizontal arrangements of their illicit affair. Kennedy, besotted with lust, lost his good business judgment in the perfumed purple satin sheets of his Hollywood Hills love nest. He undertook to finance independent pictures for his mistress under the vanity banner of Gloria Productions, Inc. Gloria would soon know the price of hubris. The Clock of Comeuppance was ticking fast.

Their daring artistic production was to be called *The Swamp*. This enticing quicksand would be helmed by Erich von Stroheim, an undisputed genius, but an erratic one. His movie-making method was to expose miles of film,

Joseph Kennedy and censor Will Hays ▲

improvising as he went along, with uninhibited attention paid to every sexual kink. In *The Swamp,* he told the tale of a convent-bred girl who inherits a string of African bordellos. The climactic scene would show the once-innocent Irish convent girl, who had become a prosperous Madame, on her deathbed, receiving the last rites from a humpy young priest. A strong suggestion of necrophilia was the kicker.

Gloria learned what it meant to be appalled: "Von" kept changing the script daily, a ploy with which he hoped to trap her at the production point of no return. The film was not really "dirty"—it was merely that, in 1928, it was unreleasable.

Gloria screamed over the phone to her lover in New York: "Joe, there's a lunatic in charge here!" Kennedy the Catholic was equally appalled; he knew Czar Hays would never pass this bouquet of Venus's-flytraps. Genius von Stroheim was fired. Kennedy arrived in Tinseltown and, with his rattled paramour, attempted to salvage the mess. First of all, the film was retitled: it became *Queen Kelly* (although the reason for the lady's royalty was that she queened it over a chain of cathouses!). The botched, unfinished movie was never shown in this country; Kennedy saw eight hundred grand—in 1928 big bucks—go flush down the drain.

It was his first big business loss; he took it like a bad loser and was of sour disposition for weeks. During this sour spell, Gloria lost a good deal of her appeal for him. The bloom was off the peach. Though he backed his mistress in her first Talkie-singie, *The Trespasser* (1929), and in an Art-Deco turkey entitled *What a Widow!* (1930), they parted company with some bitterness, with Gloria accusing Joe of leaving her with a mountain of unpaid bills.

Putting Gloria and *The Swamp* behind him, Kennedy threw himself into a

nefarious business scheme. He set about to destroy the reputation of Alex Pantages, in order to swoop in and take over the chain of Pantages movie palaces when the old man was down for the count.

Joe Kennedy's demon had one last

◀ Gloria Swanson and pearl perfume holder: a gift from Joe   ▲ Gloria "presented by Joseph P. Kennedy"

joke to play—on Kennedy. Exit Swanson in black satin; enter Eunice Pringle in red satin. The seventeen-year-old Miss Pringle was dispatched to the Pantages Theater—but her mission was not to see a movie. She accused Pantages of having sexually outraged her in his theater when she applied for a job. A jury eventually found him not guilty.

When his Satanic plot backfired, Kennedy finally gave up on movies. The last refuge of a scoundrel is politics.

Another Kennedy presentation ▲   Joseph Kennedy and wife, Rose—Gloria was also on board ▶

☆ THE WHITE LEGION AND THE ☆
PURPLE POODLE

On February 13, 1939, all Hollywood was stunned by the announcement that George Cukor, one of the most respected and professional directors in the business, had been fired from *Gone With the Wind* (a few days later he was replaced by Victor Fleming). Latter-day film historians commenting on producer David O. Selznick's decision interpreted it this way: although Cukor was known and admired as "a woman's director," brilliant at handling Vivien Leigh and Olivia de Havilland, Clark Gable had insisted on replacing him with his buddy Fleming, "a man's director," who would devote more attention to Gable. This explanation is piffle—the *real* reason for the affair did concern Gable, but it was of such a scandalous and highly confidential nature that all copies of Selznick's memos concerning the firing of Cukor were destroyed.

Gable was the key to the affair, but the real reason concerned a fifteen-year-old incident in the sex lives of Gable, "The King"—and "The Queen." "The Queen" was William Haines, a popular MGM star of the Twenties who had nothing to do with *Gone With the Wind.* He had been fired by MGM in 1933 when his out-of-the-closet gayness became an embarrassment to the prissy studio.

William Haines was a "child of the century." He was born a few minutes after midnight on January 1, 1900, in Staunton, Virginia. He attended the military academy there, studied drama, and after graduation got a job as an office boy on Wall Street. Bored with his job, he entered a "New Faces" contest sponsored by Samuel Goldwyn in 1922, and won it. Casting Director Robert McIntyre, who was in charge of the hunt, selected Haines from thousands of applicants in New York. Hollywood beckoned and he entered pictures as an "artistic ward" of the Goldwyn Company. When the Metro and Goldwyn companies merged and MGM was formed, the new studio inherited Haines. He averaged six movies a year at MGM for the following six years, appearing opposite Joan Crawford, Marion Davies, Mae Murray, Norma Shearer, and Mary Pickford, and was directed by Victor Seastrom, Clarence Brown, and King Vidor.

His early films were a varied bunch. The versatile six-footer played comedy or drama with skill and a lively pantomimic style. By the late Twenties he was one of the most active and popular stars in the MGM constellation and became typecast in the sort of role his fans preferred: a breezy, charming, but often arrogant wise-cracking young man, a sort of male "flapper," always ebullient and peppy—he usually acted as if he were on speed—who is generally brought down a peg or two by the girl he

loves. In *Slide, Kelly, Slide,* a baseball comedy, he was a swell-headed pitcher; in *Spring Fever,* a stuck-up champion golfer; in *West Point,* a conceited football player; and in *The Smart Set,* a brash sportsman who referred to himself as "America's gift to polo." In the last reel, once his arrogance was scratched, he was always revealed to be "a true blue good egg."

The New York Times review of King Vidor's *The Wine of Youth* curiously remarked that Hal, the character played by Haines, tried "to make it a gay adventure." In *Tell It to the Marines,* one of his more interesting movies, Sergeant Lon Chaney and New Recruit Haines have what can only be described as an odd love-hate sado-masochistic love affair.

Haines was the first MGM star to face the ordeal of the microphone in *Alias Jimmy Valentine* (1928). The film was completed as a silent, but with other studios coming out with sound pictures, Irving Thalberg ordered it back into production, and Haines and co-star Lionel Barrymore repeated their parts for the last two reels—with sound. Techniques were still clumsy and the mikes were hidden in bouquets of flowers or under tables. The film was a big hit, but Haines described the coming of sound to MGM this way: "It was the night of the Titanic all over again."

Haines was as breezy and wise-cracking off screen as on, and quite popular, not only with Tinseltown society, but with crew members, property men and studio grips—whom he often greeted with a friendly pat on the butt. He was a popular and relaxing court jester at MGM—which certainly needed one, for it was the stuffiest of all the studios.

With the advent of sound, L. B. Mayer ordered that all contract players who had not had extensive stage training should receive elocution lessons. One afternoon, the voice teacher was giving lip exercises to a group of actors, and asked Haines to recite quickly the phrase, "Sweet sister Cecilia seated ceremoniously 'neath the sun-kissed spruce." Haines got bored with repeating this tongue-twister and started to mumble. The teacher chided him: "The trouble with you, Mr. Haines, is that you're *lip*-lazy!" Haines (whose reputation for giving good head was legendary in Hollywood) replied, "I've had no complaints!"—which broke up the onlookers.

At first, Thalberg took a liking to Haines and approved of him as an escort around town for his sister Sylvia, who had been given a nepotistic, well-paying job in MGM's script department. Haines often accompanied Irving and Sylvia on weekends to Lake Arrowhead.

However, the boy wonder producer detested physical contact with most people, and Haines lived to regret his prankish familiar ways. After his marriage to Norma Shearer, Thalberg and wife arrived at a party given by Marion Davies at San Simeon, the palatial "Xanadu" built by her lover, William Randolph Hearst. The Thalbergs were dressed identically—as West Point cadets. Haines goosed Thalberg, then said, "Excuse me, Irving, I thought you were Norma!" The producer took umbrage at this harmless goosing, never forgave Haines, and was of no help whatsoever to his former friend when L. B. Mayer decided to "fire the fagelah."

The storm broke in 1933. Under Mayer's iron hand, Howard Strickling, the head of publicity at MGM, made sure that the press reports on the activities of the studio's stars conformed to a strict image—an image as scrubbed and controlled as anything about the Third Reich coming out of Hitler's Ministry of Information. Romances were encouraged or destroyed, elopements provoked, abortions arranged in Tijuana—all according to what Mayer and Strickling decided would best feed the voracious box offices of Loew's Theaters around the country. The male image at the studio was extremely important: he-man Gable, the sporty outdoorsman; the great lover, John Gilbert; Wallace Beery, the big folksy slob with a heart of gold (in real life Beery was a real turd of a toad). When a few blind items—obviously referring to Haines—appeared in the columns intimating that the actor was a pansy, there was panic in MGM PR land. A ton of press material was immediately fabricated to provide the "news" that Haines had suddenly fallen in love with Pola Negri. Photos of a king-sized bed, selected by Pola and Billy to be shared by them after marriage, were distributed to the fan mags.

Things went from bad to worse. Haines loved his boyfriend, Jimmy Shields, his ex-stand-in, but like most gay men—like most *men*—he liked to play around a bit from time to time. He had a thing about uniforms. He had

William Haines and Hedda Hopper in *A Tailor Made Man* ▲

worn them himself in *Tell It to the Marines, West Point,* and *Navy Blues.* He liked wearing prop uniforms—but even more he enjoyed making out with the real thing in downtown L.A.

They met in Pershing Square—the Hollywood star who impersonated servicemen on screen, and an honest to goodness cutie-pie U.S. sailor ten years his junior, on liberty from his ship docked at San Diego. The babbling fountain surrounded by palms was a notorious gay pick-up spot; from there, the horny, newly formed couple repaired to the no-less-notorious downtown YMCA, where Haines rented a room on the seventh floor. The tryst in this seventh heaven was not of long duration—it was rudely interrupted by a house dick and the vice squad. As handcuffs snapped, two careers were terminated—the sailor's in the Navy, and Haines' at MGM.

L. B. Mayer was informed of the bust at once—and exploded. It had only been a few weeks earlier that, provoked by the gossip column items, the weasly, straight, lecherous mogul had given the handsome gay leading man an ultimatum: ditch Jimmy Shields and acquire a wife in the form of Pola Negri or another respectable actress, or give up his career. On learning of the arrest, Mayer fired Haines instantly. In any case, the weasel decided it was not a bad business move. Recent polls had shown that the thirty-three-year-old actor— the oldest college boy in North America—was slipping at the box office. (Mayer's morals were as flexible as the rubber band around a roll of two-dollar bills. A decade later, when another male MGM star was entrapped in a similar fix, Mayer had the morals charge quashed— in a company town like L.A., it wasn't hard to do—and continued to employ him. The blond star was still an assured box-office draw at the time.)

The majors were a Mafia—Mayer made sure that Haines was not employed at any other studio. He made two programmers at Mascot, a Poverty Row studio, and never appeared in another movie. Film books often cite Haines along with John Gilbert as a victim of sound. Nonsense. His voice was fine; it accorded well with his screen personality, as all of his sound films attest. He was purely and simply pansy-purged.

In 1950, at the height of his second career as a decorator, Haines was offered a cameo role in *Sunset Boulevard,* appearing in the company of H. B. Warner and Buster Keaton. He refused, and told Billy Wilder, "I'm content with my work. It's clean, no mascara on the face."

Shed no tears for Billy Boy. He had a good life and a sensible one. He hedged his bets—and his beds—carefully. As early as 1930, when straight-as-a-rod silent male stars and popular divas of the silent screen who had been cursed with screechy voices were falling by the wayside, Haines laid the basis of his second career. He had always had a passionate amateur interest in decorating and had excellent taste. In 1930 he set up his "secretary" (i.e. lover) and stand-in, Jimmy Shields, in the decorating business, with himself as silent partner.

The firm did moderately well for a few years. Haines, still busy with picture work, never had time to decorate an entire house. When his movie career was shattered, three great stars who became lifetime friends, who appreciated his talent, his polished good nature and gossipy ways, and for whom Haines was a brother/sister surrogate—Carole Lombard, Joan Crawford, and Marion Davies—gave him immeasurable help in starting his second career.

In 1934, after her divorce from William Powell, Carole Lombard went

looking for a home of her own. She bought a simple medium-sized house and engaged Haines to "do" the entire place. Haines decorated Lombard's home to match her personality and created a gay, feminine, and slightly screwball interior. While they were discussing the work to be done, Carole would often walk around stark naked in front of Haines. He described one session this way: "She was late for a tennis date, but she wanted to continue our conversation while she changed. I was startled when she stripped completely, staring at me all the while, going on about Hepplewhite and Sheraton. She never wore a bra; oftentimes she didn't wear panties either, and this was one of those times. She saw my surprised look, and I remember her saying the cutest thing: 'I wouldn't do this, Billy, if I thought it could arouse *you.*'"

(Years later, during her marriage to Clark Gable, Gable, noting that his wife seemed to be palsy with every male in Hollywood, remarked annoyedly, "Don't you have any girlfriends?" She rejoindered, "Sure, I have two great girlfriends—Mitch Leisen and Billy Haines.")

Lombard's house was Haines' first big personal commission—it had his name on it. He refused the check offered to him by the delicious blond star. "I offered to do her house without charging a fee, knowing that if people liked what I did, I'd have a business foundation."

For Lombard's home décor, Haines went against the grain of the "Hollywood modern" style with its accent on white,

---

Decorator Haines and clients the Fredric Marches ▲   Carole Lombard in a Haines decor ▶

which had become a Tinseltown cliché. He made her house a riot of color, against which her blond loveliness stood out. The drawing room was a sea of velvet, in six shades of blue, with French Empire furniture. He plunked a huge bed down in her bedroom and covered it with plum satin, with a mirror screen on each side. Soon everyone in Hollywood was chattering about the Lombard house, and Haines, whose finances had recently become shaky, was besieged by clients. Every rising starlet wanted a mirror screen on each side of her overworked bed.

Next, he designed a new modernistic office for himself in brick and spun-glass in Beverly Hills and employed a staff of six. His clientele eventually included Nunnally Johnson, Claudette Colbert, William Seiter, Joan and Constance Bennett, Jack Warner, and Lionel Barrymore. He was particularly adept at solving the problem of reconciling private projection room practicality in the home with domestic aesthetics. Haines concealed the projection equipment of producer William Goetz behind a picture collection in the drawing room. *Chez* Nunnally Johnson, the projectors were hidden behind rows of dummy books. He cleverly arranged Jack Warner's eighteenth-century English library so that it would do double duty as a screening room. Leila Hyams' luxury yacht was built to Haines' designs. The Mocambo nightclub was one of his most striking commissions: it contained dozens of birds behind glass, a Venetian carnival décor, and a nearly pitch-black lighting scheme that flattered aging stars with crows'-feet.

Haines and Marion Davies became great friends in 1928, during the shooting of *Show People,* in which she played Peggy Pepper, a spunky girl who arrives in Hollywood in an old Ford and is romanced by Billy Boone (Haines), a young, slapstick Mack Sennett actor. Haines gave his best and (under King Vidor's careful direction) most restrained performance. It is one of the few great screen comedies about the movies, and Marion Davies' best film as well as Haines'.

Haines and Jimmy became frequent guests at San Simeon. Hearst was shy and a bit stuffy with Marion's friends—Haines, the charmer, and writer Gene Fowler were among the rare few who could successfully break through his reserve. Haines adored the Hearst estate and its nutty agglomeration of priceless antiques, wild and tame animals, and classy kitsch. After the purge, Haines remarked to Hearst, "You know, you and San Simeon really got me started in decoration. I didn't know a jardiniere from a peepot until I started studying all the relics you have here."

Only a few of Marion's chums were invited to the funeral of her mother, "Mama Rose" Douras—Haines was one of them. He was also present at the memorable soirée in 1933 at which Hearst played host to George Bernard Shaw, during Shaw's only visit to the United States.

Haines' finest hour at San Simeon occurred during a party for Elinor Glyn. (She had written *Three Weeks,* one of his earliest movies, but her greatest claim to fame had been the invention of "It." She had decided that Clara Bow was the epitome of "It." A film called *It* was hastily produced, starring Clara, who went down in screen history as the "It" Girl. Miss Glyn even appeared in the film, to explain what "It" was. She defined it as "A strange magnetism which attracts both sexes." Having or not having "It" immediately became a big deal in Hollywood.) The self-important Miss Glyn was standing near the swimming pool, holding court and handing out marks, when she turned to Haines and announced to the assembled guests that he definitely did *not* have "It." At this very moment, Jerry, Hearst's pet chimpanzee, who had been listening to Glyn's discourse, defecated and threw some turds at her. As she frantically attempted to brush the monkey-do from her trailing scarves, veils, and turban, Haines turned to her and remarked, "Well, we all can see that you have 'It.' "

Haines had befriended Joan Crawford (or Lucille LeSueur as she was then known) when she first arrived at MGM in 1925. He introduced her to the power boys, and gave her pointers on how to deal with them. Through Haines she met Carey Wilson, who cast her as Miss MGM of 1925 in a short promo film for the annual exhibitors' convention. They appeared together in four films: *Sally, Irene and Mary, Spring Fever, West Point,* and *The Duke Steps Out.*

One evening in 1932, Haines was seated near Franchot Tone at a dinner party *chez* Tallulah Bankhead. Tone repeated a few raunchy stories about La Crawford that were going around town. Haines bawled him out: "Never say another word about her until you meet her. When you do, I bet you'll fall in love with her." Sure enough, they met, appeared together in *Today We Live*— and were married. They secretly lived together several months before the

The Smart Set: Bob Montgomery, Noel Coward, Joan Crawford, and Bill Haines ▲

57

wedding in Joanie's Brentwood house, which had been decorated by Haines in a combination of modern and antique English furniture.

Joan's home became a set where she could play Mommie Dearest for the fan magazines and photographers. One room, designed for her by Haines, was intensely private—the largest room in the house, which she called "my workshop." It looked like a hospital operating room, done in chrome and glass, with glaring light, but it was Mommie's dressing room. It contained massage tables, a hair dryer that disappeared into the wall, vast circular racks for clothing, glass drawers, and shelves to contain her two hundred pairs of shoes. Haines had created a deliberately cruel lighting system—the sort of harsh lighting flashed on by bars at closing time to drive customers back on the streets—so that if her makeup was correct there, it would pass muster under any light. Many of Joan's favorite private hours were spent in her "workshop" creating Joan Crawford—with a little help from Bill Haines' appurtenances.

Haines often visited Joan with his lover, Jimmy (their pet name for Crawford was "Cranberry"). Many "Uncles" turned up at the Brentwood house—generally to ball Mommie. "Uncle Willie" and "Uncle Jimmy" were only balling each other, and were great favorites with Christina Crawford. Mommie often told her that Uncle Willie and Uncle Jimmy had the best marriage in town.

June 3, 1936, was a night in the marriage of Uncle Willie and Uncle Jimmy that they would never forget—a night that was no honeymoon.

The Twilight Men—as homosexuals were then dubbed in Hollywood—led largely closeted lives, even in the studios, where they worked as actors, dancers, designers, hairdressers, dressmakers, makeup artists. Closets were for survival in the film industry as elsewhere, and gay caballeros, faced with homophobia among the populace and constant vice-squad raids led by the authorities, were obliged to tiptoe with care through the tulips of Tinseltown.

Haines and his coterie of friends had taken to avoiding the better known beaches of Santa Monica and Malibu. Haines rented a house on Moonstone

The White Legion: spooks in the night ▲

Street in the hideaway beach town of El Porto, just south of Manhattan Beach. Taking the lead from Haines, a few "lavender" buddies were also in residence there for the season. It was a perfectly harmless and peaceful pocket of poofs, a relatively discreet but swishy microcosm—nothing like the full-scale suck-and-fuck gay communities in latter-day Fire Island. Children were not molested; local husbands were not seduced. But Orange County, even in the Thirties, was a cesspool of right-wing reaction, and middle-class El Porto was home base for the White Legion—Southern California's version of the Ku Klux Klan. And it was obvious to many of the local compulsive-haters that a fairly

Franklin Pangborn and Marcel Silver, co-director of the Hollywood Ballet: houseguests ▲ ▲

large ball of alien fluff had landed on their beach—it was almost perceived as a menace from outer space.

Bill Haines' toy poodle, who answered to the name of Lord Peter Whimsy, had been dyed purple by its owner in a moment of gay abandon earlier that year at Easter. The purple pooch was a sort of surrogate child for Jimmy and Billy—closeted like themselves, he had nonetheless been trained to camp it up at home, and the curious canine queened it over Haines' private bachelor parties like a four-legged Franklin Pangborn. El Porto Beach seemed safe enough. The flamboyant poodle was often seen romping in the sand, accompanied by a gaggle of sand-kicking flaming creatures, who startled the sea gulls and eventually aroused the locals to action.

That evening, after dinner, as Haines and friends left the house and approached their cars to start back for

Lord Peter Whimsy ▲   ▲ The White Legion: mob action

Hollywood, they were approached by a group of hooded white-robed men who warned them not to come back. Haines and Shields were knocked down, their car smeared with tomatoes and eggs.

Later, new hostile figures appeared in the night—a veritable lynching party. Get the fruits! Bash the fags! Lord Peter was kicked senseless. Haines received two black eyes. His nose bleeding and lip cut, the actor, Jimmy, the poodle, and three shaken guests were shoved into their car. They drove out of town amidst hoots and jeers. The Queens' Retreat from El Porto Beach was a nightmare tableau that none of them ever forgot. (For the rest of his decorating career, Haines shied away from white sheets and introduced the first color-coordinated designer bedsheets for his celebrity bedrooms.)

The incident that precipitated the mob action was absurd. Earlier that day on the beach, a six-year-old local boy had befriended the colorful bunch of Haines' houseguests, playing with the poodle and tagging along after them all afternoon. When the bright little boy, whose name was Jimmy Walker, followed them back to the beach house, Jimmy Shields gave him six cents and told him to run along home. Parental paranoia construed this innocuous incident into a charge of molestation, which roused over a hundred of the townspeople to don their White Legion gowns and storm the Haines party. The next day the Walkers brought little Jimmy to the police to testify, but the case was dismissed for lack of evidence. Haines never returned to El Porto Beach.

On November 22, 1969, *The New York Times* ran a large story covering half a page and headed MILLION-DOLLAR SPARKLE ADDED TO ENVOY'S RESIDENCE. The article reported that the newly decorated

residence of the American ambassador to Britain, which took nearly a year to finish and cost its tenant, Philadelphia publishing magnate Walter Annenberg, a million dollars, now looked so grand that it hurt to use an ashtray.

For an entire week, Annenberg led reporters from many countries on two-a-day hour-long tours of the great house. "We operated as a team under the Haines flagship," the ambassador said. Haines and Annenberg had first met when Haines undertook the decoration of the Annenbergs' desert house in Cathedral City near Palm Springs—a job that took five years. The desert house, called Sunnyland, was conceived by Haines as "a great solarium, with orchids, lava stone out of Mexico, floors of pink marble from Portugal, rooms divided by plants."

Winfield House, in Regent's Park, the London ambassador's residence, had been given to the United States government by Barbara Hutton in 1946. The place was filled with Monets, Gauguins, Cézannes, Van Goghs, Renoirs, and Toulouse-Lautrecs. Its magnificent decoration by William

▲ Jimmy Shields and Bill Haines testify after the assault

61

Haines was the finest hour of his brilliant second career.

Haines died of cancer in December 1973. He left everything to his two sisters and to Jimmy Shields. Shields killed himself a year later. His suicide note read: "It's no good without Billy."

In 1937, George Cukor gave a memorable party to honor William Haines after Haines had finished decorating Cukor's splendid house. *Le tout* Hollywood was there—and everyone remembers the moment, late in the evening, when a blind-drunk John Barrymore puked all over Cukor's antique satin couch.

Cukor and Haines remained close friends. Cukor never seems to have suffered professionally for his homosexuality. Though not closety, he was relatively discreet, and during most of his career avoided discussing the matter—for publication. Toward the end of his life, he did let a whopping cat out of the bag. He revealed that he had been taken off *Gone With the Wind* by Selznick and replaced by director Victor Fleming because Clark Gable knew that Cukor was a close friend of Billy Haines, and assumed that Cukor was aware that—when still a bit player at MGM—he had let himself be serviced on several occasions by Haines in order to further his career. He hated Cukor for this knowledge, and could not look him in the eye or bear the thought of taking direction from him during the long months of filming that were involved in the making of *GWTW*. Thus, one of the great directorial shifts in film history took place in 1939 because of a few blow jobs given by Bill Haines—who certainly was not lip-lazy—in 1925!

◀ Little Jimmy Walker is brought to testify ▲▲ Cukor and Gable: old secrets not gone with the wind

☆ GANGLAND ☆
GOES HOLLYWOOD

Few of the millions of people who yearly gawk at the tasteless and boring Academy Awards ceremonies are aware of the ignominious *raison d'être* of the Academy of Motion Picture Arts and Sciences. The Academy was the brainchild of Louis B. Mayer, who gave the monster dinner party in 1927 at the Ambassador Hotel in Los Angeles which launched the Academy. Mayer founded the Academy as a "company union" to combat the legitimate unionization of directors and actors and to block the emergence of screen talent guilds. Mayer and the other studio heads intended the Academy to be the contract arbitrator between the studios and the talent groups. Since it was totally a creation of the studios, its arbitrational impartiality can well be imagined.

During the 1930s the struggle to create legitimate craft guilds in Hollywood was bitter and prolonged. One of the results of the studios' anti-labor stance was the scandalous IATSE affair. In 1934, the International Alliance of Theatrical State Employees (the union that encompasses theater projectionists, art directors, makeup men, gaffers, grips and stagehands) fell into the hands of two racketeers from Chicago. These two supergoons were George Browne, the new IATSE president, and his associate-in-crime, Willie Bioff. Bioff was the more aggressive of the pair and

had the entire motion picture industry by the balls for nearly seven years.

It began in the Windy City, early in 1934. Browne and Bioff, an ex-pimp with the physique of a burly Greek wrestler (he had been arrested a few years earlier for running a whorehouse) were moving into the "union business" and putting the squeeze on the Balaban and Katz theater circuit. Balaban, head of the circuit (he was later to become president, then chairman of the board of Paramount Pictures) had offered Browne, the union representative, a measly bribe of $150 a week to ensure that Browne would forget about an agreement to raise theater employees' wages. Bioff, on behalf of Browne, spurned the offer and demanded a flat $50,000. Balaban refused. His refusal triggered a series of mishaps at B and K movie palaces: the Oriental, the Uptown, the Tivoli; film was run backward, *One Night of Love,* a Grace Moore musical, was shown without sound, the image blacked out during the motel scene of *It Happened One Night.* All over town, angry patrons were demanding refunds. B and K began to realize the extent of Bioff's clout. The payoff was paid. Within days, booze and blondes had loosened the tongues of Browne and Bioff. Their independent new racket and newfound fortune came to the mob's attention.

◄ Willie Bioff: the man who stole Hollywood

Frank (The Enforcer) Nitti, a crony of Al Capone, was intrigued—especially when he learned that Browne and Bioff were about to make a real killing, creaming a small fortune from Balaban and Katz by *not* calling a projectionists' strike which would have closed down most of Chicago's movie theaters. Nitti was an organizer; he immediately sensed that the racket could be organized on a national scale, which would deliver the entire movie industry into his hands.

Nitti sent "Cherry Nose" Gioe and a few other picturesque thugs to the office of the IATSE stagehands' local, of which Browne had been business manager since 1932. The message to Browne and Bioff was clear: Nitti was cutting the syndicate in for half of their labor racket. To emphasize the message, two contracts were sent out: T. E. Maloy, head of the projectionists' local 110, and Louis Alterie, president of the Janitors' Union, were riddled with shotgun blasts. The syndicate was promptly cut in.

Nitti's next step was to push George Browne into a figurehead presidency of the national union. If it could be done in the Windy City, it could be done on a bigger scale. Plans to rig the next union election at the IATSE convention in Louisville were hatched in a series of conferences between Nitti and such notorious underworld figures as Paul (The Waiter) Lucca, Lepke Buchalter of Murder Inc., and Lucky Luciano. Luciano guaranteed that the New York delegation would tilt to Browne. Bioff imported a squadron of goons from Chicago to ensure Browne's election.

The new president immediately appointed Bioff as international representative. Bioff went straight to Tinseltown. From then on, Browne faded into the background and Bioff became the syndicate's chief negotiator. Bioff sent to Chicago for beefy goonsquad reinforcements; opposing unions were quelled by threats and beatings. Dissident craftsmen in the studios were "persuaded" to join IATSE.

The studio heads were soon given to understand that if Bioff didn't get what Bioff wanted—*money,* and lots of it— the film industry would grind to a halt because of projectionists' strikes all over the country.

Bioff and Browne soon went bi-coastal and were paying call on Nick Schenck, president of Loew's Inc., which controlled MGM from New York. Bioff demanded a cool $2,000,000—or else. Schenck held a hurried conference with Sidney Kent, president of 20th Century-Fox. They decided to make a united stand against the gangsters. It was soon made clear to them that Bioff's threat to strike shut every studio in Hollywood was not an idle menace. The following day, Kent and Schenck paid call on Bioff at his room in the Warwick Hotel. Schenck brought $50,000 in cash in a brown paper bag; Kent brought $25,000.

At the height of his power, Bioff ordered studio moguls about like office boys. On one occasion, when the

Union under a cloud ▲

gateman at Warners refused to let him in without a pass, Bioff phoned Jack Warner and ordered him to come down and usher him inside personally. On another, when Bioff refused to negotiate with Paramount, studio head Ernst Lubitsch felt obliged to pay him a personal visit.

Bioff forced the studios to appoint him their "agent" for the purchase of raw film stock. Jules Brulator, distributor of Eastman stock in Hollywood, was obliged to accept this extortion or risk a bomb in his warehouse. Bioff received a 7% commission on all film stock bought by MGM, Fox and Warners. By this means, the syndicate raked in over $150,000 a year.

Bioff took huge bribes in return for keeping down wages for IATSE members; he then upped their dues $1,500,000 yearly. These sums were all split with the syndicate.

The beginning of the end came for Bioff when he alienated the feisty and scrupulously honest old editor of *Daily Variety*, Arthur Ungar. Ungar could not be won over—not by bribes, not by threats. He soon began campaigning against the excrescence from Chicago.

Ungar found an ally in Robert

Hollywood and the Underworld: too close for comfort ▲

Montgomery, president of the Screen Actors Guild. Montgomery was alarmed at Bioff's attempt to move in on SAG. He hired a private eye to delve into Bioff's past, uncovered evidence of Bioff's sentence for pimping and offered the information to Ungar for use in the pages of *Daily Variety*.

Ungar and Montgomery's campaigns began to hit home. Westbrook Pegler, syndicated Hearst columnist and muckraker, joined them and published stories excoriating the pimp IATSE leader.

The fat really hit the pot when the federal government, which had been waiting for an opportunity to pounce, became alerted through tax inspectors to a $100,000 check from Joseph M. Schenck, made out to Bioff. Schenck, chairman of the board of 20th Century-Fox and president of the Motion Picture Producers Association, claimed—and then later testified—that he had given Bioff the money as a loan. When the facts of the payoff were revealed, the veteran Schenck (he had produced most of Buster Keaton's great silent films) was convicted of perjury and sentenced to a year in prison. His citizenship was revoked. (Schenck, however, who had habitually been a hefty contributor to Democratic Party campaigns, was soon granted a pardon by President Truman; his citizenship was restored and he returned to Fox as an executive producer.)

One studio head after another came forth to confess their hanky-panky with corporation books in order to bribe IATSE's distinguished "international representative." Bioff and Browne were charged before a federal grand jury in New York on May 23, 1941, of extorting huge sums from Fox, Warner Bros., Paramount and MGM. Bioff was sentenced to ten years in prison; Browne got eight.

Bioff was sent to Alcatraz—and blabbed. He named seven Chicago mobsters as the gang who had set up his shakedown of the movie industry. One of the seven was Frank Nitti—Al Capone's ex-Enforcer. The day the

▲ Smashing the rackets: plot twists from the real thing

68

indictments were returned, Nitti shot himself in the head on a railroad track in a freightyard in a Chicago suburb.

When Bioff was released from prison he settled in Phoenix, Arizona, as Willie Nelson, stock investor. On November 4, 1955, he was preparing to go to the Phoenix brokerage to check up on his stocks. He got in his car, turned the key and was blown sky-high. Who put the bomb under the hood's hood has never been discovered—or if it has, it has not been revealed.

The most memorable residue of the entire sordid affair can be traced to a meeting of the Motion Picture Producers and Distributors of America which had been called to discuss coming to terms with Bioff. On that occasion, Samuel Goldwyn, the prince of Hollywood malapropisms, uttered his most ineffable one-liner. "Gentlemen," he said, reaching for his hat, "include me out."

Bioff and lawyer: moment of levity in court ▲

☆ DANGEROUS CURVES ☆

Busby Berkeley was the undisputed Genius Numero Uno of the Hollywood musical. He is the only Hollywood director whose name is a dictionary entry. He had the boldest imagination in the history of Tinseltown. Before his arrival on the movie scene, musicals were stagebound. Berkeley ripped away the proscenium arch. He sent his camera up to the roof—sometimes through the roof—then craned it down to within an inch of a beautiful girl's eyeball. His numbers did away with time and space—they became more than song and dance routines. He made surrealistic, voyeuristic, erotic musical dream fantasies which made eyes pop and pricks stand up around the world. He saved Warner Brothers from bankruptcy during the Depression and turned the geometry of girls' legs into art. Yet, this great original talent was also a Mama's boy and a bit of a monster. He was a neurotic alcoholic who killed three persons with his roadster and later slashed his throat and wrists in a bloody suicide attempt.

Although he married five times (one wife was Merna Kennedy, Chaplin's leading lady in *The Circus*—she can also be seen in Buzz's *Wonder Bar*) the Big Lady in his life was Gertrude Berkeley— Mama. Ma and Buzz were closer than Hamlet and *his* Gertrude. His mother was a stage and screen actress who appeared for many years in plays and films with her close friend the Legendary Lesbian Alla Nazimova, who had worked with Stanislavsky. Buzz made his stage debut—as a child—in a production of *A Doll's House* in which his mother was appearing with Nazimova. In 1914 he was graduated from the Mohegan Lake Military Academy; during World War I, he directed parade drills in France. This work influenced his later feats in Hollywood where he presided over armies of scantily-clad chorines and combined the skills of choreographer and drillmaster.

In 1923, Berkeley scored his first success on stage in the role of "Madame Lucy," as an effeminate fashion designer, in the musical *Irene*—opposite Irene Dunne. During the 1920s, he became known as one of Broadway's top dance directors. The man who was later to become the greatest choreographer in the history of motion pictures never had a day of formal choreographic training.

In 1930 he was brought to Hollywood by Sam Goldwyn to do the dance numbers for the screen version of *Whoopee,* starring Eddie Cantor, produced by Flo Ziegfeld. Among the first girls Buzz chose for the movie were Betty Grable, Virginia Bruce and Claire Dodd. (B.B. had a great eye for female talent—he also gave Paulette Goddard,

◀ Busby Berkeley

71

Veronica Lake, and Lucille Ball their first important breaks.) In *Roman Scandals,* made for Goldwyn in 1933, he concocted a lascivious Human Bondage number with completely nude girls—they were only wearing long chains and blonde wigs which fell down to their snatches.

When Darryl Zanuck asked Buzz to create the musical sequences of *42nd Street* at Warner Bros., the studio was deeply in the red. *42nd Street,* a landmark film, proved such a triumph that it saved the studio from bankruptcy. Buzz shot to fame and glory—his career moved into high gear, with one boffo musical after another. (He did not direct his first complete musical—numbers and plot—until *Gold Diggers of 1935*— and later directed a number of non-musical films, the best of which is *They Made Me a Criminal.* But he is indisputably the *auteur* of all the films he dance-directed. No one goes to see *Flying High* because it was directed by Charles Riesner—no one goes to see *Dames* because of the plot.)

During all his peak years, Gertrude was his mentor and his solace. He installed his mother in royal splendor in a Beverly Hills mansion where she could indulge her antique-collecting mania.

Buzz's attraction to violence and his ambiguous attitude to women are evident in his dance numbers. In *42nd Street,* there is a shooting and a stabbing during a production number. In his masterpiece, (it was his favorite sequence of all his dance numbers) the "Lullaby of Broadway" in *Gold Diggers of 1935,* the heroine, Wini Shaw, falls from a skyscraper, screaming as she twirls down to her death. During the tango in *Wonder Bar,* Dolores del Rio stabs Ricardo Cortez. And in a kinky dance scene in *Small Town Girl,* Ann Miller dances among a few dozen disembodied mens' arms. His numbers obviously have more to do with his own inner fantasies than they do with the plots of the movies.

At the height of his success, violence and tragedy appeared in his real life. On September 8, 1935, Buzz attended a party given by William Koenig, production manager at Warners, to celebrate the wrap of *In Caliente.* By the time he left the party, he had certainly had one for the road and one too many.

Berkeley and his girls: the sound of taps ▲ ▶

In addition to the booze, Buzz was suffering from nervous exhaustion—he worked on five movies that year, and the Brothers Warner were hard taskmasters. As he speeded down the dark and twisting Pacific Coast Highway towards Santa Monica Canyon, he lost control of his white roadster and careened into the path of oncoming traffic. He was driving on the wrong side of the highway when he hit one car, then smashed into another one. Three of the occupants of the second car were killed: William von Brieson, his mother Ada von Brieson and his sister-in-law, Dorothy Daley.

Buzz was charged with second degree murder. For Warners this was secondary to the fact that their successful director was locked into a nonstop shooting schedule—three films in a row, two of which he was to direct in their entirety. Since he was obliged to appear in court during the day, the studio would change the schedules so the films could be shot at night—even though he had suffered head and leg injuries in the accident. To hell with Buzz's shut-eye and mental and physical health.

The defendant was brought into court on a wheeled stretcher. Warners had

◀ Buzz rehearsing Mickey Rooney   ▲ Busby on his beloved crane

75

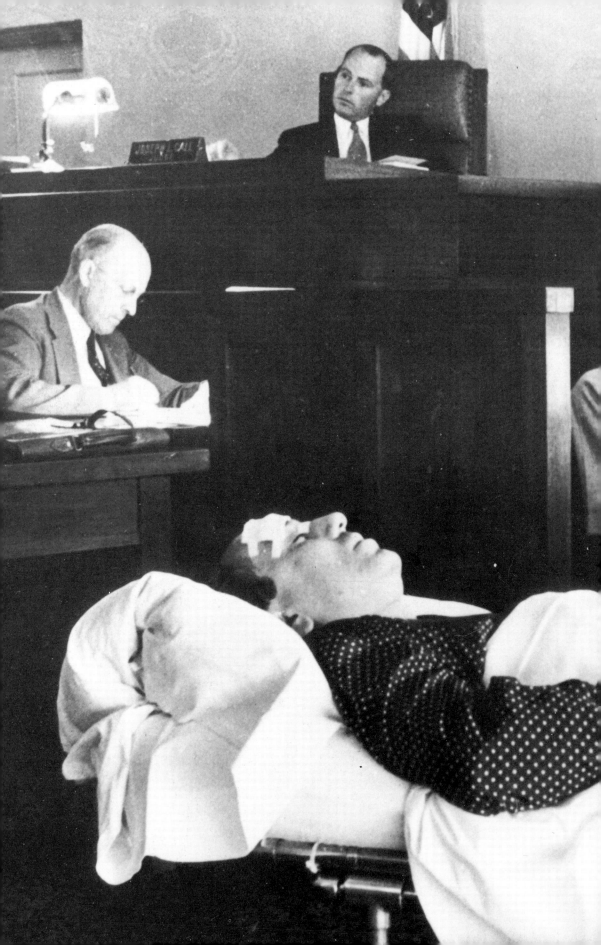

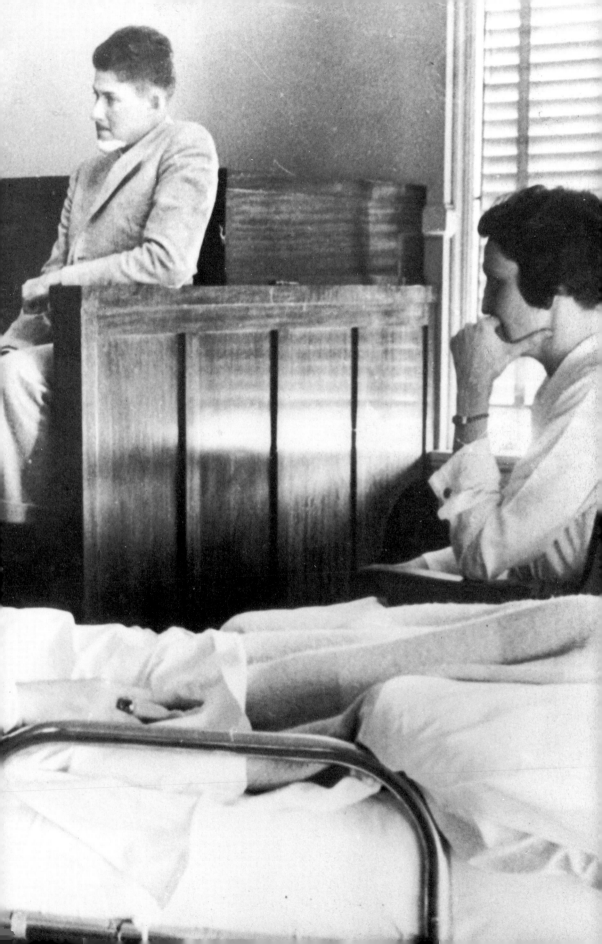

hired Jerry Geisler to defend their star director. Geisler, "the lawyer of the stars" (he pleaded for Chaplin, Errol Flynn, Robert Mitchum, Pantages) managed to confuse the jury by exhibiting the blown-out left front tire of Buzz's car—he claimed *it* was the cause of the accident. Several personalities who had been guests at the party— Frank McHugh, Pat O'Brien, Glenda Farrell, Mervyn Leroy (all of them under contract to Warners) testified that Buzz had not been blotto when he left the festivities. The first trial resulted in a deadlocked hung jury. A second trial ended in a seven-to-five vote for acquittal. A third trial took place in September 1936—at this one Geisler got his client off.

During these trials and tribulations Buzz was building up for a nervous breakdown. Up all night manufacturing movie madness—he would work until the wee hours on a Dick Powell sequence for *Stage Struck*—and have to appear at court at 9 A.M. for his murder charge. Later, he commented: "Even though I was found innocent, it was a shocking and depressing thing to have been involved in the death of three people. I was lucky that I had so much work—it probably saved my sanity."

Berkeley was later involved in a brouhaha over the affections of blonde and bouncy sexpot Carole Landis. They had met when he selected her to appear in the chorus of *Varsity Show* at Warners, and gave her—as he had given so many other girls—her first break in pictures. He later pulled strings to get

◀ Berkeley in court: horizontal testimony ▲ Busby, his mother, Gertrude, and his lawyer, Geisler, in court

her a contract. In 1938, Landis's spouse, Irving Wheeler, sued Buzz for a quarter of a million, claiming that he had wheedled Carole's affections from him. The suit was thrown out of court. (Her affections did not have to be wheedled very hard by anyone. At Fox, she later became known as "the studio hooker"—she was the most constant visitor in attendance in the back room of Darryl Zanuck's office, servicing the potent mogul who regularly balled a female studio employee at 4 P.M. every working day.)

Buzz's mother died of cancer in June 1946, after a long and expensive illness. His beloved "Queen Gertrude" was gone—she who had been his pillar of strength. His long overdue breakdown finally caught up with him. He had a drinking problem; his career was in a shambles; he had recently been divorced again. In 1943, he had directed one of his greatest films, *The Gang's All Here,* a delirious, wildly imaginative musical with Carmen Miranda. It was followed by the so-so *Cinderella Jones.*

At the time of his Ma's death, he had not made a movie in over two years. He accepted an assignment to stage a Broadway musical—*Glad to See You,* starring Lupe Velez. His luck continued bad—the show never got to Broadway. After negative notices, it folded in Philly.

Buzz slashed his throat and wrists a few weeks after Gertrude died. His Japanese houseboy, Frankie Honda, found him lying in a pool of blood on the bathroom tiles. Frankie tore up a sheet and bandaged up the boss. When he recovered from surgery, Buzz stated: "I'm a has-been and know it. I can't seem to get myself straightened out for any length of time. Each time I get married it seems to turn out wrong. I'm broke. When my mother died, everything seemed to go with her."

He was later admitted to the psychiatric ward of Los Angeles General. This is his description of that snakepit: "It was a nightmare. I was thrown in with dirty, disheveled, bedraggled creatures. They were so short of space my cot was placed in the corridor, where these

"The Shadow Waltz" number from *Gold Diggers of 1933* ▲

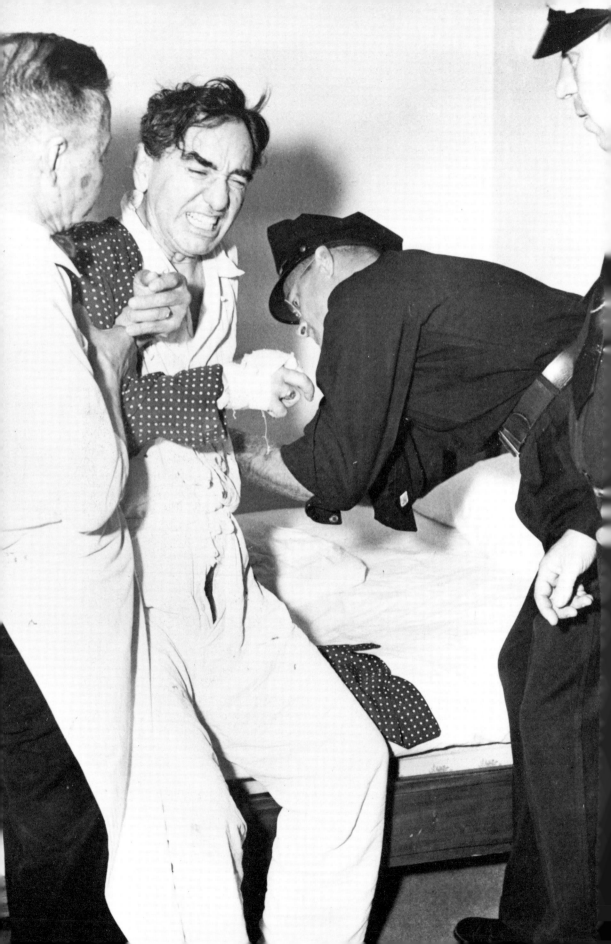

horrible characters passed me day and night. I knew that if I wasn't already mad, I soon would be."

He spent six weeks there. During that time his weight dropped from 170 to 107 pounds. He found out he had $650.00 to his name. In 1948, his old boss, Jack Warner, hired him to supervise the musical numbers on Doris Day's *Romance on the High Seas.* It was a slow trip back up again, especially since Buzz's big enemy at this point was the bottle. In 1949 he convinced Arthur Freed to let him direct again at MGM. The result was the delightful *Take Me Out to the Ball Game,* starring Frank Sinatra and Gene Kelly—Buzz had lost none of his directorial ability. It was, however, to be his last film as a director; he worked on eight more pictures,

creating and directing only the musical numbers. They include some of his best—the water ballets in *Million Dollar Mermaid* and *Easy to Love,* the nutty "Totem Tom Tom" sequence in *Rose Marie* and the aerial trapeze ballet in *Jumbo.*

Jumbo, Buzz's last movie, was made in 1962. He died in 1976. But his final years were not shadowed by oblivion. Major retrospectives of his films were screened at the *Cinémathèque Française* in Paris and at the New York Cultural Center. Several books on his work were published. He was in demand for interviews and for speaking tours of college campuses—a whole new generation had become acquainted with his work through television. He became an entry in slang dictionaries. A Busby

◀ Busby being subdued after suicide attempt　　　　▲ Lining up the legs for *Footlight Parade*

Berkeley is, of course, "a very elaborate musical number."

The highpoint of Buzz's resurgence arrived in 1970, when the producers of a revival of *No No Nanette* hired him as supervising producer of the show, which starred Ruby Keeler, star of several of his greatest films at Warners during the 1930s. At seventy-five, he was back in business auditioning chorines—looking at 350 pairs of girls' gams in order to select a chorus line of 22. The show was a great hit. The opening night of *No No Nanette,* January 19, 1971, Busby Berkeley was again receiving a standing ovation.

◀ In the swim   ▲ Military maneuvers: Berkeley diagrams the action for his water ballet

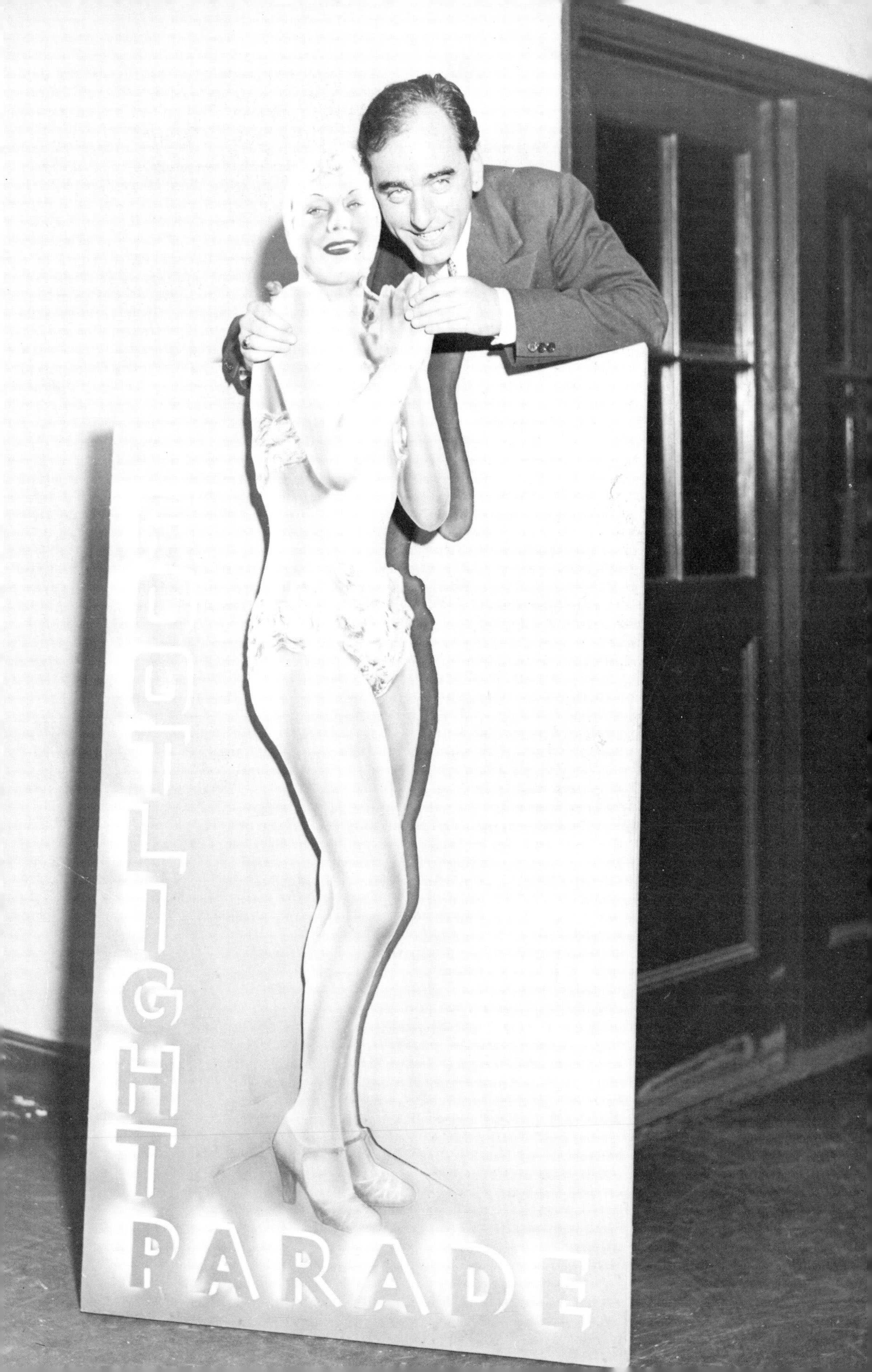

LIGHT
PARADE

☆ THE TWO FACES OF ☆ TINSELTOWN

"*See*—one side of my face is gentle and kind, incapable of anything but love of my fellow man. The other side, the other profile, is cruel and predatory and evil, incapable of anything but the lusts and dark passions. It all depends on which side of my face is turned toward you—*or the camera.* It all depends on which side faces the moon at the ebb of the tide."

These amazing words of Lionel Atwill once described Lionel Atwill's own amazing face for an interviewer. An alpha and omega of angel and devil, that disturbing face was a godsend for an actor who brought to life on screen a certain urbane, suave, and ineffably sinister gentleman: Mister Lucifer. Try to hear those words caressed by Atwill's dulcet, organ-toned British baritone, a voice that could speak low and deeply of truly terrible things in nuanced tones of careful shading, with impeccable enunciation. Listen again, and try to hear the authoritative baritone that later, in real life, in 1941, on the witness stand, lied like a gentleman: "Not guilty, your honor."

Guilty of what? Of being the perfect squire of his manor, the exquisite host? Or of throwing wild parties at which lewd movies were shown, and contributing to the delinquency of a pregnant teenager from Minnesota who cavorted with celebrity guests on a tigerskin rug? No— surely not this distinguished

Englishman who had played opposite the greatest ladies of the stage in Ibsen, Shaw, and Shakespeare, and whose chilling good looks and resonant voice—invaluable in the early days of talking pictures—had brought him a Hollywood contract at the beginning of the Thirties! Not this man of culture who prided himself on his art collection and who, with every film, acquired a new Old Master: after *Dr. X,* Sir Henry Raeburn's *Lady with a Shawl;* after *The Mystery of the Wax Museum,* a Lawrence portrait; and much of his paycheck for *Murders in the Zoo* spent on a Gilbert Stuart.

Atwill came from a wealthy Croydon family, which wanted him to pursue architecture. He took to the boards instead and was embarked on a successful career as a young leading man in London's West End theaters when, in 1915, he was persuaded by the legendary Lillie Langtry (the idol of both Edward VII and Judge Roy Bean) to accompany her on a tour of the United States. After the tour, he played the title role (a character based on Jack the Ripper) in *The Lodger* in New York, appeared with Billie Burke (Mrs. Ziegfeld), and was chosen by Nazimova to perform with her in a season of three Ibsen plays. He worked for David Belasco, starred with Katharine Cornell, and then appeared opposite Helen Hayes in *Caesar and Cleopatra.* In

◄ Lionel Atwill: two faces

Another Man's Shoes he enacted the role of a man with a dual personality.

In 1928, Atwill and detectives raided an apartment at 59 West 68th Street, New York, and discovered Mrs. Atwill (actress Elsie McKay) and *his* protégé, Max Montesole, together. The actor sued for divorce and soon married Louise Cromwell, an heiress to the Philadelphia Stotesbury fortune, who had recently divorced General-to-be Douglas MacArthur.

In 1931, Atwill toured the country in *The Silent Witness,* and when the Los Angeles run of the play was over, he starred in the movie adaptation, his first Hollywood film. He played the role of a man who perjures himself in court—a strange omen of things to come in real life.

His next film was one of the most bizarre chillers of the Thirties. In 1931, Universal had made a fortune with *Dracula* and *Frankenstein.* Then, as now, hard times proved a bonanza for horror films. The masses were feeling the pinch in the depths of the Depression, but tens of thousands preferred to skip a meal in order to be scared out of their wits by imaginary monsters who helped them forget the economy and their own troubles for a few hours. Not to be outdone, Warners starred Atwill in *Dr. X* (1932). This eerie film engraved Atwill's screen persona on celluloid once and for all time. Cinema historian William Everson aptly described Atwill's eyes as lighting up "like Satanic neons" in *Dr. X.* There is something for everyone in this picture:

Broadway beginnings: Atwill with Fanny Brice and Leon Errol ▲

cannibalism, dismemberment, rape, and necrophilia—and a piquant kinky bonus when Atwill displays erotic arousal at the sight of Preston Foster unscrewing his artificial arm.

Atwill was stark raving again at Warners the following year as a mad disfigured sculptor in *The Mystery of the Wax Museum* (1933). Like *Dr. X,* it was directed by Michael Curtiz, with sets designed by Anton Grot; these experienced Europeans conspired to give the film a properly spooky and suggestive German Expressionist atmosphere. It was shot in luscious yet restrained two-color Technicolor, and its memorable climactic scene occurred when Fay Wray, the Great Screamer of the Thirties (she had to cope with King Kong that same year) recoiled from Atwill and hit his face in self-defense, breaking his mask to reveal the burnt distorted visage of a monster underneath.

By now Atwill was typecast as Hollywood's best and quintessential mad doctor. As the nutty Doctor Von Niemann in *The Vampire Bat* (1933) he gave Fay Wray further cause to shriek, and that same year in *Murders in the Zoo* he played a man who uses animals to kill off his wife's suspected lovers. (In *Zoo* he first appears sewing up a victim's lips in the jungle and leaving him to be devoured by the wildlife.) Atwill not only made the most of every psychopathic line of dialogue; his chilling voice added nuances of depravity that the script writers had never dreamed of.

Mr. A was bonkers in *The Sun Never Sets, Man Made Monster, The Mad Doctor of Market Street*—right down to his last completed feature, *Genius at Work* (1946), in which he played a notorious murderer called The Cobra.

Although mad doctoring was his stock-in-trade, and he amply endowed his bank account through such roles over the years, he was also capable of superb performances in relatively non-lunatic characterizations. Josef von Sternberg's *The Devil Is a Woman* was based on Pierre Louÿs' S and M novel *La Femme et le Pantin.* In it, Atwill plays Don Pasqual, an Army officer who has been emotionally crushed and ruined by his affair with Concha (Marlene Dietrich), and in the masochistic part, which he made extremely sympathetic, the actor bore an uncanny physical resemblance to Von Sternberg, Marlene's real-life mentor. Likewise, in *Son of Frankenstein,* on the right side of the law for a change, Atwill was unforgettable as Police Chief Krogh, who had had his arm torn out from its roots by the monster. Krogh's masturbatory playfulness with his prothesis throughout the movie—until the climax when the artificial arm is also jerked off by the monster—oddly prefigured Kubrick's Dr. Strangelove.

The wages of the fear he inspired in

Atwill: Hollywood's Mad Doctor ▲

audiences soon enabled Atwill to purchase a perfectly splendid, comfortable, spacious, and properly secluded Spanish Colonial Revival home in the affluent, conservative community of Pacific Palisades, situated between Malibu and Santa Monica where Methodist churches rub elbows with quaint Anglo-Norman cottages, chic International Style houses, and elementary schools topped with Moorish towers. It was a fellow Englishman, the dapper, dandy director James Whale (*Frankenstein, Bride of Frankenstein, One More River,* in which he directed Atwill, who played the lawyer of a sadistic husband in a divorce action against his submissive wife) who found the property for him. Whale was already settled in a neighboring Pacific Palisades palazzo. Whale's off-the-set hobby—the pursuit and disrobing of young men—would later crown the local Boy Scout troop with some fleeting eminence, but the breath of scandal was first to blow on Mr. A.

His marriage to Louise Cromwell was apparently happy and successful. She came supplied with the greatest society credentials. The Atwills became well known in Tinseltown society and were often the guests of Hearst and Marion Davies. Louise's brother was soon to be named Ambassador to Canada. Mrs. Atwill herself was a direct descendant of Oliver Cromwell, through her father,

Atwill co-starring with Marlene Dietrich in *The Devil Is a Woman* ▲

Oliver Eaton Cromwell, who had died in 1909. Her mother, Eva Cromwell, had then set her cap for one of the wealthiest men in the States—and hooked him: Edward Stotesbury, international financier, and associate of J. P. Morgan. (Although he never read a book in his life, through the good auspices of the art dealer Duveen, he acquired one of the greatest private art collections in America.)

Stotesbury built Whitemarsh Hall, the stateliest Old Philadelphia Palladian palace ever constructed, for Eva Cromwell and her children. Eva personally oversaw the design and construction of Brooklands, a large Georgian mansion Stotesbury built as a "little present" for Louise in Maryland. (When she married MacArthur, she renamed it Rainbow Hill.) Henrietta Louise Brooks Cromwell MacArthur Atwill was a lady of many parts: one of them was obviously to the manor born.

The Atwills' appetite for sex had drawn them together; a snake was the source of the first serious squabble in their domestic Eden. Lionel lusted for the exotic, for thrills touched by danger. His favorite pastime, between pictures—one

Atwill in *Murders in the Zoo* ▲   ▲ Lionel as the artificial-armed constable in *Son of Frankenstein*

Atwill and friends, including Rita Hayworth at far left

which Louise did not share—was attending murder trials in Los Angeles. While working on *Murders in the Zoo* he became infatuated with a fellow player: Elsie, a movie-trained, house-broken, and human-loving fifteen-foot kinky python! Louise etc., who had not objected to the occasional addition of a parlor maid or chauffeur to the conjugal bed, drew the line at Elsie. When all fifteen feet of potential I. Miller costly snakeskin slippers moved in, Mrs. A threatened to move out.

"All women love the men they fear," Atwill epigrammatically and revelatorily informed an interviewer. "All women kiss the hand that rules them. . . . I do not treat women in such soft fashion. Women are cat creatures. Their preference is for a soft fireside cushion, for delicate bowls of cream, for perfumed leisure, and for a *Master!*"

TIFFANY THAYER WOULD RATHER ACT THAN WRITE, BUT NOBODY IN HOLLYWOOD WILL GIVE HIM A CHANCE.

LIONEL ATWILL'S HOBBY IS ATTENDING MURDER TRIALS.

▲ *Murders in the Zoo:* Atwill and Kathleen Burke

In 1939, Lionel Atwill's cat creature had finally had enough of her master's bowls of cream. She moved out for good, separating from her spouse, blaming his "surly character." She moved to Washington, D.C., and soon had many fans of her own as the hostess of a popular radio program of political satire that razzed government officials (she called it "Mrs. Atwill's Dinner Party").

Meanwhile, back on d'Este Drive, left with a lonely libido in his spacious hacienda, along with his python-mistress, Elsie, a half-dozen bed-trained Dobermans, a talking macaw named Copulate, zoo-keeper Lionel maintained a rigidly disciplined work schedule as a cog in the studio-factory wheel during the week. He did, however, more than his share of unwinding on weekends.

In Hollywood's hothouse solarium, Atwill's erotic imagination blossomed florid fantasies that could now become realities. Just as Rudy Valentino, after the separation from *his* fata morgana, Natacha Rambova, staged orgies to distract himself from the loneliness gnawing at him within the splendor of Falcon Lair, the solitary mad doctor of the screen was now able to use his home freely as the setting for libidinous weekend parties. Directors Eddie Goulding and Joe von Sternberg, and actor Victor Jory were among the best known Tinseltowners who regularly piled their peckers into these *partouzes*.

The early Forties movie public, secretly salacious and hypocritically envious because *it* had never got invited to a Hollywood gang-bang, quickly learned through a crash course of headlines that a single married couple in the missionary position was not the be-all and end-all of sexual delight. When the Atwill scandal broke, the papers evoked the orgies of ancient Rome and the Arabian Nights when the "heathens" usually seemed to be off on

many-course sexual picnics. Headlines around the country echoed the accusations voiced in the Los Angeles courtroom: Lionel Atwill was the erotic equivalent of Maestro Leopold Stokowski—a flamboyant conductor, not of a battalion of skilled musicians and pulsating symphonies, but a baton waver at frequent, flamboyant, aesthetic, and artistic large-scale saturnalia!

As it was for the immortal Mae, sex was Lionel's principal hobby. His criteria in preparing the guest list for those who would enter the doors of his wrought-iron and oaken fortress were fairly rigid: not only good bodies and endurance, but that special blend of a taste for ritual, role playing, and sexual highjinks that are the basic ingredients of fantasies of a truly erotic imagination. He went as far as insisting on hygienic screenings of the guest list to keep VD

from his door. The gatherings at Casa Atwill never generated outbreaks of clap, which might have caused gaps in Busby Berkeley's chorus line. Far worse finally occurred: two tarts talked. Aleister Crowley, the English mystic, once remarked, "In every gathering of thirteen, expect one guest will turn out to be a Judas!" Fatally, twenty-six guests attended Atwill's memorable 1940 Christmas Party, and Crowley's insight proved certifiably true: two Judases in skirts did their best to drag their host by the short hairs all the way up the hill to Golgotha.

One ill-omened day in early December 1940, a man named Carpenter, bit

Mystery of the Wax Museum: preserving pulchritude ▲

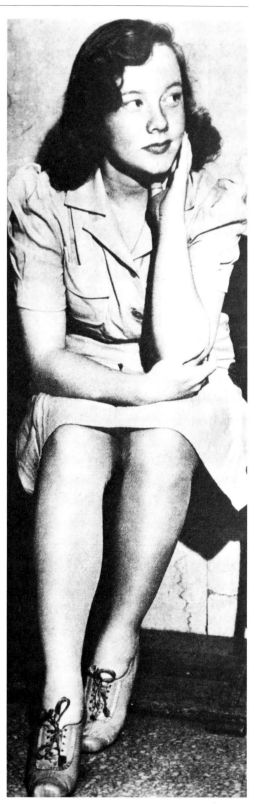

player, used car salesman, and part-time pimp, an acquaintance of Atwill's, drove up to the actor's palatial home at 13,515 d'Este Drive, on the edge of Santa Monica Canyon, just as Atwill was finishing a tennis game. He was accompanied by Virginia Lopez, a dress designer from Havana, and her "protégée," named Sylvia, a chubby sixteen-year-old corn-fed blonde from Hibbing, Minnesota, who had left her masseur father to come to Hollywood with high hopes of a brilliant screen career. The women were living together at the Lido Apartments. Virginia was a blackmailer who had picked up many young women before Sylvia and had trained them all in the fine art of making gentlemen pay through the nose. Sylvia had not yet found any screen roles, but she had discovered a few days earlier that she had managed to get herself pregnant, and had no clue as to whether the daddy had been Tom, Dick, or Harry.

Later, during the trial, Virginia would

Actors in a scandal: Virginia Lopez, and Sylvia ▲▲

tell the court that when she and Sylvia returned to d'Este Drive with Carpenter they were introduced to Eugene Frenke, husband of Anna Sten. (Sten, known in Hollywood as "Goldwyn's Folly," was a Russian actress brought to this country by Samuel Goldwyn in the early Thirties in an attempt to create a star of his own to rival Garbo and Dietrich. Her films bombed at the box office. Goldwyn terminated her contract.) Frenke was the producer of such unmemorable epics as *Miss Robin Crusoe* and *The Lady in the Iron Mask.* Atwill had made his acquaintance when he co-starred with Sten in her first film for Goldwyn, *Nana.* He admired the actress, and although she was playing a whore in the movie they appeared in together, he found her a bit of a Puritan in real life. Her husband, however, was often invited alone to Atwill's house. Virginia would testify that on her next visit, she and Atwill peeped through a window to spy on Sylvia and Frenke, who were disporting themselves with gay abandon on a chaise longue. They were nude, she said, but obviously not sunbathing.

She returned a few days later with Sylvia and a ravishing hairdresser, Laverne Lolito, for Lionel Atwill's 1940 Christmas Party. The year that was concluding had throbbed with distant, yet insistent war drums, and America was about to enter a new decade, tinged with fear and uncertainty. Yet, vicariously and paradoxically, this *angst* brought a ripple of excitement to the plains and hills of Hollywood. It is an unpleasant truth that for many people war is an aphrodisiac. America was under the spell of Mars. Anything could happen, the senses were alerted to primeval dangers, the sky could fall. Even in sun-sedated California, the populace suddenly felt threatened. Japs—or even Martians—courtesy of Orson Welles' "War of the Worlds" radio caper—were out there somewhere.

There were no Japs or Martians at the party, but a most unlikely Father Christmas was there to greet the guests at the door. The hacienda on d'Este Drive was bedecked with an outsize Santa's sleigh on its tile roof. The Mad Doctor had definitely decided that it was the season to be jolly. Garbed in full Santa guise, Atwill was in fine spirits, his expressive eyes twinkled, his Harlow-white beard tickled. Thanks to a complaisant studio costume department, the red plush velvet St. Nicholas suit was trimmed with real ermine. Atwill had planned the evening in the spirit of the ancient pre-Christian Yule, a fertile feast to appease Jack Frost and celebrate the winter solstice with proper ebullience. He had agendaed things down to the last detail: after dinner, coffee, and brandy, the orgy would begin at a certain signal. The starting gun was to be a chord on the grand piano, struck by Alec Templeton

▲ Eugene Frenke

(the blind pianist who could be counted on to see no evil), who would break into the strains of "The Blue Danube." More than a quarter of a century before Strauss' lilting melody became glued to the slowly revolving images of Kubrick's space station in *2001*, that same tune was the accompaniment for Lionel Atwill's carefully choreographed *ballet d'hiver*.

As the Straussian strains issued from the Steinway, Santa's beard was shed, like a mask in *Ivan the Terrible*. Zip!—off came Santa's pillow belly as the guests' tuxes were shed and Adrian evening gowns, Sulka shorts, and Antoinette lingerie were peeled off. House rules requested that jewelry be left on— diamond bracelets decorated a few Hollywood backs with some pretty mean scratches that evening! The Lionel Atwill floor show was worthy of one of the censored scenes from Von Stroheim's *Merry Widow*. It was an evening that no one present would ever forget— although several would have good cause to regret it.

The Pacific Palisades Christmas Party became the subject of a court case resulting from a complaint that originated, not in California, but in Smalltown—read Hibbing, Minnesota— USA. The day Sylvia first turned up at d'Este Drive she was already pregnant. A few weeks later, early in 1941, she was more manifestly pregnant, and without the money to "take care of herself." She wrote to her parents back home, requesting a large sum of money; her father, the masseur, got suspicious and went to the local police, who contacted the Hollywood police. They picked up Sylvia at the Lido Apartments and took her to Juvenile Hall. Virginia immediately phoned Atwill, Frenke, and Carpenter to inform them that Sylvia was in the hands of the law, and all hell would break loose if she talked. Although no one could have accused Atwill of being responsible for Sylvia's condition, he was ever the gentleman, and told his friends that he was for giving the women any money they required. Frenke was fearful lest unfavorable publicity regarding him injure his wife's career—although Anna Sten's days of stardom were well over by then.

The partygoers' confabulations were of little avail—the judicial wheels had already been set in motion. From then on, it was more or less everyone for him/herself. A breathless Virginia told the grand jury that Atwill had rolled out his 16mm projector during the Christmas party, and that during the orgy on the tigerskin rug two films were shown: *The Plumber and the Girl* and *The Daisy Chain*. Atwill denied that he had ever touched Virginia or Sylvia or shown any "blue" movies. "In fact," he said, under oath, "I don't own any such pictures. The only films I have ever shown my guests are travelogues and short subjects dealing with home life in many lands." He added that his rug was bearskin, not tiger. Carpenter confirmed that the parties *chez* Atwill had been "clean and orderly." Virginia did not make a favorable impression on the jury. Instead, they were favorably impressed by Atwill's dignified demeanor and his personal and professional reputation. The jury decided it was all a tempest in a teapot: Atwill was cleared. *Virginia* was arrested on a technical rape charge, for corrupting her underage protégée. She was sentenced to a year in prison, but was soon out on probation. Sylvia was packed off to Minnesota, where she had her baby and was never heard from again.

Atwill breathed a sigh of relief, thinking he was out of the woods. A year later, he was back in again, deeper than ever!

Carpenter fell on hard times and was

Lionel Atwill's stag movies ▶

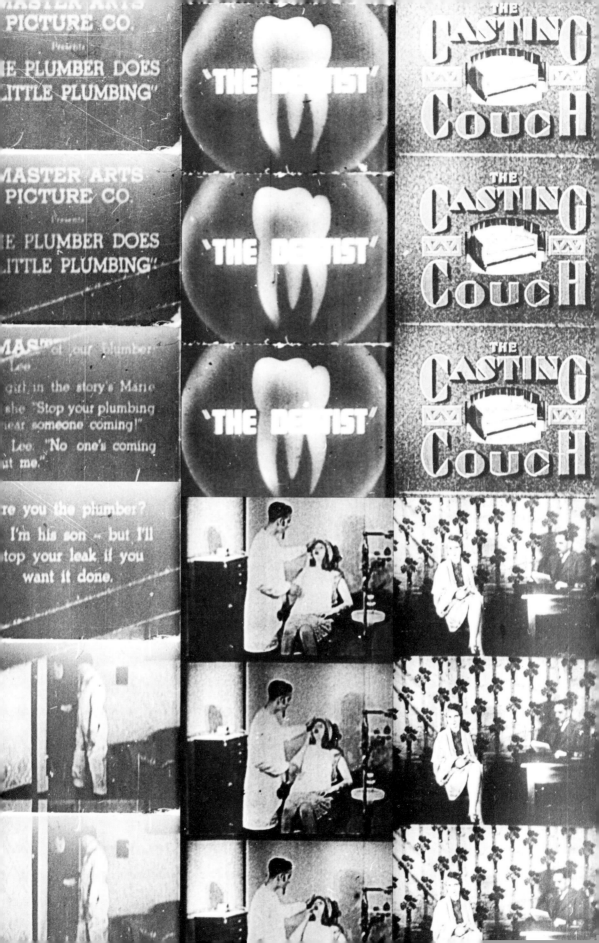

eventually sent to a road camp, sentenced there for paying debts with bouncy checks. At the camp, he became vindictive, and decided that it was he who had saved Atwill—but that no one had helped him when he needed help in order to stay out of jail. He wrote the grand jury and said he was now ready to tell the true story about the Christmas party. Carpenter furnished the D.A. with a complete list of those present and corroborated the story that Virginia had told the year before, in addition to supplying spicy details about the orgies and the films.

Atwill was recalled, and on his lawyer's advice, stood on his right to refuse to testify for fear of incriminating himself. The statute of limitations had expired on the old charge of contributing to Sylvia's delinquency. He could, however, still be charged with perjury. Atwill, scared as stiff as a victim of Lionel Atwill's in a

horror film, went to Isaac Pacht, a judge and attorney well known in movie circles, who strongly advised him to tell the truth. When he faced the jury again, he suddenly remembered that he did have a few blue films in his possession at one time. They had been rented to entertain a friend who was a Royal Canadian Mounted Policeman. The Mountie had been a house guest; the films had been shown at a stag party for him, Atwill admitted, but he had never seen them himself. If someone had ever shown them at his house, he had been unaware of it—he must have been out playing tennis. He denied any improper conduct at his home, and added that he was the victim of an attempted shakedown. The 1942 jury was not convinced—it returned a bill of indictment charging him with having perjured himself to the 1941 jury.

On August 12, Atwill was named in a second perjury indictment, accused of having lied two years in a row. The trial was set for September. When it came around, the actor admitted that he had "lied like a gentleman to spare the reputation of friends," and was permitted by the judge to change his plea from not guilty to guilty on a portion of his perjury indictment: he admitted having shown the two porno films to his friends. Upon this admission of perjury, the prosecution dropped the charges concerning the orgies on the tiger- (or bear-) skin rug. Although he could have been sentenced from one to fourteen years on the perjury charge, the actor applied for probation and was released. The district attorney, when agreeing to drop the orgy charge, had to admit that if the case did go to court as scheduled, the prosecution witnesses would consist solely of persons with criminal records—Carpenter and Virginia Lopez.

On October 15, 1942, Atwill was given a five-year probationary sentence. He

Lionel Atwill in court: too-familiar territory ▲

was obliged to pay weekly visits to the thumb-screw boys at the Hollywood Vice Squad, and comply with a rule imposing check-ins with an L.A. probation officer who could have been Bull Montana's stand-in. Most troublesome of all was the unwritten law of the Hays Office and the studios that employment in the movie industry would be refused to persons on probation. After seven jobless months, Atwill applied for the termination of his sentence.

Judge McKay, who had sentenced Atwill, heard the case and decided: "Whereas this court does not condone any violation of the law, it still takes into consideration all the circumstances of the case. The person who caused this complaint to be made against Atwill was not actuated by a sincere desire to bring about justice, and I am convinced that the ends of justice have been met at this time." He completely exonerated Atwill of all charges, saying, "You are now in the position, Mr. Atwill, where you can truthfully say you have not been convicted of a felony." Tears brimming from his eyes, Atwill thanked the judge and rushed from the courtroom in a blaze of flashbulbs.

Louise was finally granted a divorce in June 1943, and although quite wealthy in her own right, she received a considerable property settlement. While in Washington, during her husband's well-publicized adventures in court, she had received a ton of hate mail from a potential lynch mob that included several Gold Star mothers, who suggested that a woman capable of leaving MacArthur, to take up with a Hollywood sex fiend, had a patriotic duty to commit hara-kiri. Louise declined, and hinted to friends in Washington that if she made public all she knew about the General and about Atwill "it would shake some circles harder than the earthquake in Alaska." Breeding prevailed, and publicly at least, Louise held her upper-class tongue.

Atwill no longer felt at home in Hollywood. The town, plunked down in a sunny dustbowl populated largely by Okies and assorted Midwestern nomads, was and remains in many ways a moral Kansas. He was exonerated in the eyes of the law, but in the eyes of Tinseltown he was a mad doctor *non grata.*

He left for New York in search of work on Broadway. There were no offers. When he returned to Hollywood, although not officially boycotted, he was never again offered a major role by a major studio. Universal did deign to throw him small parts in two features and in a few serials. And then, Lionel Atwill, who had acted in some of the finest and most prestigious films made in Hollywood during the Thirties, who had been directed by some of the greatest directors—Frank Borzage, Michael Curtiz, Rouben Mamoulian, Tod Browning, James Whale, Henry Hathaway, Allan Dwan, and Josef von Sternberg—who had worked with a galaxy of stars—Irene Dunne, Marlene Dietrich, Myrna Loy, Claude Rains, Lionel Barrymore, Spencer Tracy, Rosalind Russell, Errol Flynn, Olivia de Havilland, Dolores Del Rio, and Margaret Sullavan—now found himself an employee of the most poverty-stricken of all the Poverty Row Studios— Producers Releasing Corporation. There, he was directed by Steve Sekely and Terry Morse, alongside such performers as Marcia Mae Jones, Douglas Fowley, and Sharon Douglas. At PRC, where the studio head was the indomitable ex-accountant Leon Fromkess, Atwill was reduced to "quickie" features that were shot in five days. Even one re-take was considered an extravagance. While working on *Lost City of the Jungle,* a serial, he suddenly died of pneumonia, and his re:naining scenes were completed by a double.

☆ STUMPFINGER ☆

William Tatem Tilden III, better known as Big Bill Tilden, was the primo tennis player *assoluto* of the first quarter of the twentieth century. Hollywood beckoned. Tilden came a-running, brought his backhand and starred in several wholesome silent movies of the Aw-Shucks Virgin Boy school of Americana. In the Thirties, he regularly appeared in Universal's Sports Reels shorts and was a commentator for British Lion films.

Though a whiz on the court, Big Bill was so painfully, pathologically shy (weirded out by Mother) that he never stripped in the locker room or shower. He usually did not shower after a fast-and-furious game. His B.O. was legendary: the rank goats leaping from Tilden's armpits were enough to make women faint at a distance of fifty feet. If he had any best friends, they didn't tell him.

His Ma, Selina, was bent on feminizing him. She called him "June" until he was eighteen. He grew up, unarousable by men or women. Boys were Bill's devotion and his undoing.

Tilden pretended to pursue some of Hollywood's most famous female stars. All the time, he kept himself surrounded on the courts by a bevy of fresh-faced ball boys, prepubescent Ganymedes in clinging white seersucker shorts. One astute observer at Wimbledon remarked: "Looks like Tilden's got himself a *harem*

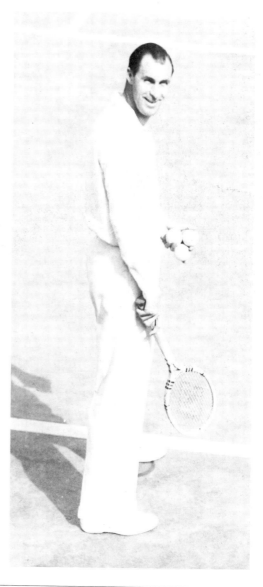

◀ Court ace: Big Bill Tilden scores Tennis, anyone? ▲ Bill Tilden and Junior Coghlan in *Gallagher* ▶

105

of ball boys." The observer in question was Vladimir Nabokov—years later, Bill turned up as Ned Litam—"Ma Tilden" backwards, as Lolita's tennis teacher in Nabokov's classical novel of heterosexual child dalliance.

Tilden was the toast of celebrity courts in Hollywood in the Twenties: he played with Valentino, Louise Brooks, Ramon Novarro, Clara Bow, and Chaplin.

At age twenty-nine, an infected fingernail led to an operation during which the tip of the middle finger of his serving hand was amputated. It did not affect his game, but it provided him with a new nickname: "Stinky" became "Stumpfinger."

As often happens with amputees, the missing part—Tilden's stumpy middle finger—became eroticized.

Big Bill's sex life was in his fingers— his Mama's hysterical hangups had made him impotent. When after years of

Bill and Ben Alexander: partners on the court and on the screen ▲   Sports heroes: Tilden and Dempsey ▶

furtive boy-love, the law's thick fingers finally closed on him—on November 23, 1946—the accusation by the Beverly Hills police was for "fondling." What the officers had glimpsed through the window of Tilden's parked car was a hand job administered to a willing kid. Big Bill later testified: "I met one lad on the court who showed unusual promise. Somehow we drifted into a foolishly schoolboyish relationship. Coming home from *Lassie Come Home* at the Wiltern we indulged in horseplay. . . ."

The lad who showed promise was the son of a noted producer at 20th Century-Fox. When the fuzz delivered Junior to the family manse in Beverly Hills and informed Daddy that he had been caught with his pants down in Big Bill's car, Daddy beat the bejesus out of him in his trophy-bedecked den. (Years later, in a scene right out of *King's Row*, Junior took his revenge when he slapped his father's corpse in a Forest Lawn slumber room.)

For his "horseplay" with Junior, Tilden served eight months in a so-called "honor farm" where he became "June" again—serving meals to fellow prisoners and washing up.

He was released to the fuzz-haunted streets of Beverly Hills. One day the beady eyes of the law peering through Zeiss binoculars espied him loitering by a school that was letting out. They waited while Tilden made his chicken pass. The molested minor of Camden Drive identified Big Bill by his stumpfinger. "That was the Beast with Five Fingers that was playing with my privates!"

This time Tilden's punishment was the road camp. After his first arrest, the champ who had consorted with four U.S. presidents, who had partnered Chaplin, Errol Flynn and Spencer Tracy, and who had coached on the courts of Tallulah Bankhead, Katharine Hepburn and Garbo, found that his acquaintances no longer knew him. After his second arrest, no friends at all remained. He was penniless—his money had been eaten up by endless legal fees. His last remaining bucks disappeared in a disastrous investment in a 1940s stage revival of *Dracula* in which he played the lead—a role with which he identified.

On June 5, 1953, he died of a heart attack and was found in his modest apartment on a seedy side street, lying on his bed fully clothed with a few bucks in his pocket. Big Bill died of a broken heart, abandoned by the high and the mighty. His body was removed to Philadelphia where he was buried at his mother's feet.

◄ Teacher and pupil: too much solicitude

▲ Tilden: at Mother's feet

☆ WITCH JOAN ☆

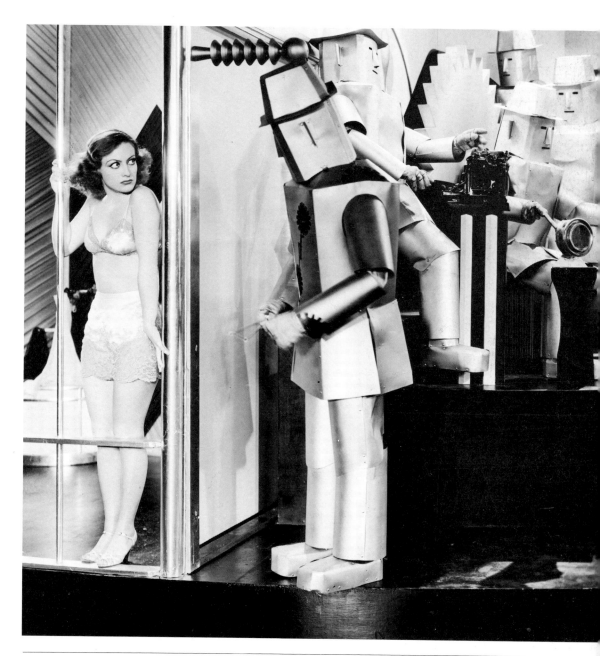

◀ Joan Crawford, Miss Halloween of 1925   ▲ Propositioned by a robot

Joan: made up as a mulatto ▲   Semi-nude "art model" ▶   Nude ▶▶   "Bosom Buddies" ▶▶▶

◀ Mommie Dearest's Mommie   ▲ Joan's adopted kids: Christopher, the pampered "twins," and Christina

From the desk of

JOAN CRAWFORD

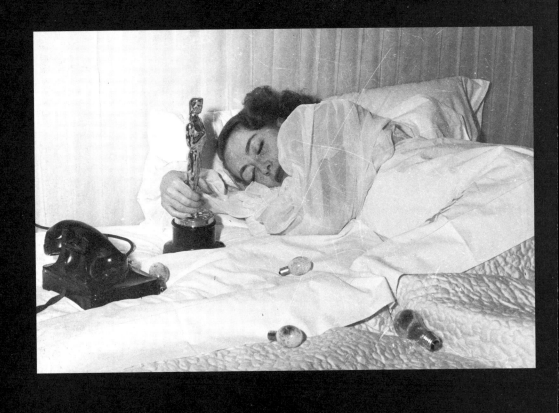

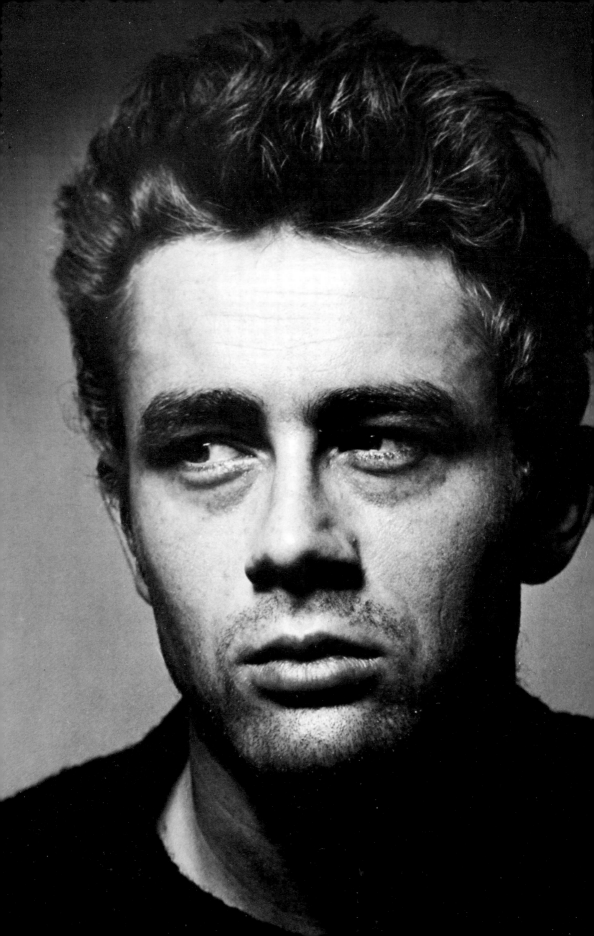

☆ THE TROUBLE WITH JIMMY ☆

During production of *Rebel Without a Cause*, James Dean was host to a thriving colony of crabs. He acquired the critters from a binge of sleeping around. Natalie Wood, Sal Mineo and Nick Adams had all observed their grungy co-star indulging in off-camera crotch-polishing; they thought he was imitating the scratch-'n-itch mannerisms of his slobbish hero, Marlon Brando. Director Nicholas Ray, amazed at his star's unconversance in such manners, dragged Dean off to a Burbank drugstore and treated him to a bottle of pungent crabocide.

Dean had taken to hanging out at the Club, an East Hollywood leather bar. The predatory night prowler, who dug anonymous sex, had recently discovered the magic world of S and M. He had gotten into beating, boots, belts, and bondage scenes. Regulars at the Club tagged him with a singular moniker: the Human Ashtray. When stoned, he would bare his chest and beg for his masters to stub out their butts on it. After his fatal car crash, the coroner made note of the "constellation of keratoid scars" on Jimmy's torso.

Dean had avoided service in Korea by leveling with his draft board—he informed the Fairmount Selective Service Unit that he was gay. When Hedda Hopper asked him how he had managed to stay out of the Army, he

The COMPOSER

replied: "I kissed the medic."

Shortly after arriving in Hollywood, Dean had adopted the route taken by many other broke, aspiring actors—he moved in with an older man. His host was TV director Rogers Brackett, who lived on posh Sunset Plaza Drive. The fan magazines spoke of their father-son

◄ James Dean: a dark side　　　　　　　　▲ High school doodles

relationship. If so, it was touched by incest.

During the period just before his death, Dean should have been sitting on top of the world. *East of Eden* had been released and was a hit. Dean was twenty-four. *Rebel Without a Cause* and the ambitious *Giant* had been completed; neither was yet released, but it was evident from the preview of *Rebel* that the movie would be big. A great career lay ahead.

Or did it? Dean was withdrawn, compulsively promiscuous, but friendless, suspicious, moody, uncooperative, boorish and rude. He could, on occasion, be charming; on most occasions he was annoyingly nuts.

He betrayed a psychopathic personality, with fits of despondency that alternated with fits of wild jubilation. A classic manic-depressive. Mr. Nice Guy he wasn't—but his tormented screen persona hit a nerve with men, women, the young and the not-so-young.

Although his stage and screen experience was limited, he nonetheless felt himself competent to order camera and script changes. He blew his top when his suggestions were not taken. Directors humored him; behind his back they cursed him. His childish bids for attention were the talk of Hollywood. He turned up at dress affairs in sweatshirt and jeans; at a dinner party with Elia Kazan, Tony Perkins and Karl Malden,

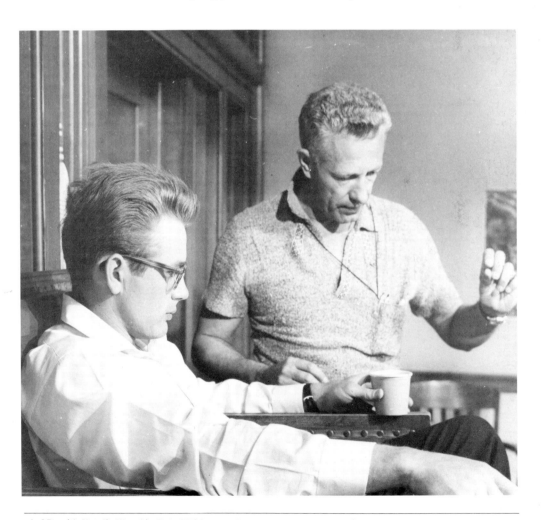

◀ J.D. with Natalie Wood in *Rebel Without a Cause*　　　▲ J.D. and Nick Ray: fatherly advice

Marlon Brando gives the finger to fan Jimmy

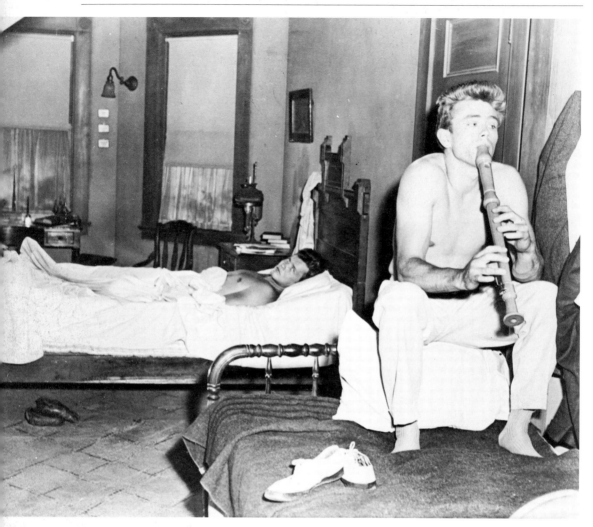

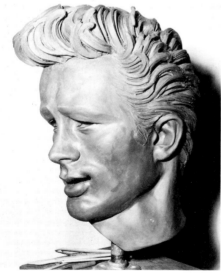

when the steaks arrived, Dean picked his up and threw it out the window. He spat at the portraits of Bogart, Cagney and Muni that adorned the walls of Warners' reception hall. At Chasen's his requests for service were accompanied by table-banging and silver-clanging.

He hid money in his mattress, slept on the floor at the homes of acquaintances, forgot rehearsals, and stayed out all night balling on the eve of studio calls. Toward the end, he was slow to learn his lines. He fluffed dialogue and fumed on the set. He was a confirmed pot-head. Writers who obtained interviews with him (few did) came away in

Dean memorial head ▲   ▲ Bedroom idyll in *East of Eden*

consternation. The actor had babbled irrelevancies or sat still and mute, staring at his visitors without batting an eye.

On the eve of his death, he had attended a gay party at Malibu, which had ended in a screaming match with an ex-lover, a man who accused him of dating women just for the sake of publicity. On September 30, 1955, he was doing a reckless 85 miles an hour in his silver Porsche on Highway 41 at Chalome, near Paso Robles. He was speeding, en route to a sports car race at Salinas, when he smashed into another vehicle. He was mangled, DOA at Paso Robles Hospital.

At first, public grief was modest.

Warners was grieved for financial reasons—*Rebel* and *Giant* had not been released and films starring recently deceased actors generally had bad track records. Then, without any studio hype, a legend grew. It was only several months after his death that the cult began to grow to vast proportions. The release of *Rebel* set off the greatest wave of posthumous worship in Hollywood history; it exceeded that for Valentino. Some fans committed suicide. Although Dean's career had been but a brief comet, many of his fans refused to accept his death. Thousands of letters poured in at the studio each day; most were from teenagers. Today, thirty years after his death, the fan mail

▲ Leave-taking in the Porsche: before and after ▶

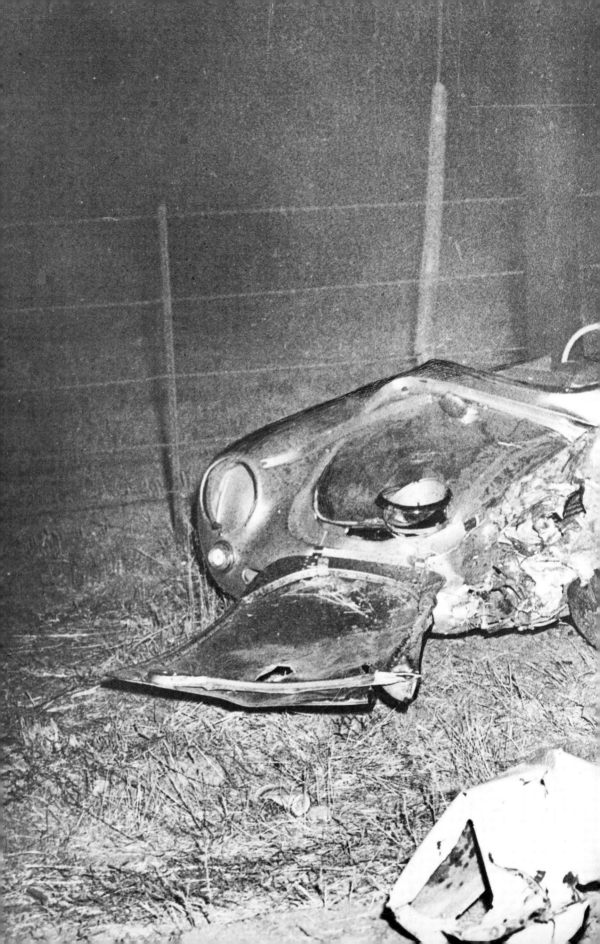

for Jimmy still keeps arriving.

Kids across the country identified with the troubled youngster, the man-boy anti-hero played by Dean in *Rebel.* Warners found that it had a hot cold property on its hands. As the cult spread, mementos of the actor—plastic models of his head, bits of his wrecked car, parts of his motorcycle—were auctioned at top prices.

It is quite likely that, even if he'd not been killed, Dean would not have made another movie after *Giant.* He was coming apart at the seams, on a self-destructive course, well before he was totaled with his car.

His tombstone in Fairmount, Indiana, bears only his name and the stark dates: "1931–1955." A brief epitaph might have been: "Pretty much of a tramp." And yet, today, if Richard Gere, or Matt Dillon—or any of the other members of the boring regiment of James Dean clonettes spewed out by Francis Ford Coppola in *The Outsiders*—were to suffer Dean's fate, would cults arise, fans commit suicide, would mash notes arrive thirty years after their demise? Doubtful—Jimmy may have had crabs, but he also had durable charisma.

Dean: over and out ▲

☆ ODD COUPLES ☆

Hollywood is a funny place where rivals who hate each other's guts are forced to soul-kiss each other under slow-broil lights while a crowd of unsympathetic onlookers observes them with singular intensity. Though it happened at one of Hollywood's offshore outposts, the situation is summed up nicely by an incident on the set of *Bolero,* when Bo Derek, after a week of soul-kissing scenes with an Italian, discovered that her handsome partner's lip had blossomed with an open sore of active herpes. Little Bo freaked. The poor guy was fired and replaced; it took some sweet-talking from hubby John to coerce her to continue with another hunk.

The Herpes Kiss! So ends our romance with Hollywood.

Yet Hollywood has been the scene of some *great* couples. True Love. True Romance, Take 1: Carole Lombard and Russ Columbo. Take 2: Carole Lombard and Clark Gable. Take 3: Carole and War Bonds. Fade to Black. Mitch Leisen and

◀ Symphonic pair: Greta and Leopold   ▲ Afloat in domestic bliss: the Karloffs at home

141

Billy Daniels. The gay Hollywood couple, seemingly *Semper Fidelis,* until Billy's one indiscretion was discovered by Mitchell, who complained cuttingly. Billy snuffed himself.

Hollywood's *intense* quickie affairs are more common. Who's to say that *fabulous* one-night stands are less than a "lifetime of fidelity"? So let me set forth for your contemplation Tinseltown's most *unlikely* couples, and I'm not talking about holding hands.

Are you ready for Tallulah? Her ambidextrous, AC-DC nature is fairly well known. A female Don Juan, to her, conquest was all—which led her to tackle the challenge of Sister Aimee Semple McPherson, as if to say, "You,

too, can be had."

Patsy Kelly, on the other hand, was just a steady pal, comfy as an old shoe.

The challenge: well, did you know Tallulah was also a *chubby chaser?* Are you ready to picture La Bankhead making it with Female Inkspot Hattie McDaniel?

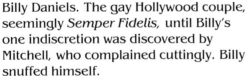

Two loves of Tallulah: Hattie McDaniel and Patsy Kelly▲   Marlene Dietrich and Claudette Colbert ▶

Taloo loved to disappear from the Hollywood honkie crowd now and then and head for Darktown over on West Adams in L.A., where Hattie, "through wit' de' menfolk" after her painful divorce, found comfort on the bosom of another Southern lady. Southern soul spoke to Southern soul, and that's why those ladies were no tramps.

Are you ready for Clara Bow, Brooklyn's red-hot redhead, having mad, passionate sex with *Bela Lugosi?* Yes, Clara, often the aggressor, picked Bela up after she saw him on stage at the Biltmore in the 1928 touring company of *Dracula.* Three years before it all began again for Bela on the old Universal lot. Three years before mental breakdown took Clara away from the too-much-of-everything Tinseltown scene to twenty years of insomnia in Nevada. Afterward, Clara would speak

Opposites attract: Clara Bow and Bela Lugosi ▲   ▲ Clark Gable and second wife: a liking for older women

Gable and Oliver: Edna May got lucky ▲

Fun pair: Cary Grant and Randy Scott ▶

◄ Cary and Randy: at home, at the pool, harmonizing, and out at the fights ▲

fondly of Bela. Ships that cross in the night.

Will Rogers and Shirley Temple. Will's secret *obsession!* Hit between the eyes by bold little Shirley, the Oklahoma Cowboy found no philosophy to heal his shattered heart. *Unrequited love!* It drove the randy old rope-twirler to devise a way to bore a hole into Shirley's dressing room at T. C.-Fox, in an agony evocative of *Death in Venice.* Did Shirley know? Listen, Graham Greene was right in a way when he accused her in 1934 of being a fifty-year-old dwarf. She knew. She knew a *lot.* And she loved Will. Like an uncle.

William Randolph Hearst and Marion Davies. Now surely there are no surprises regarding this long-exposed-to-public-scrutiny, illicit, adulterous affair. Yet picture it: Willie and Marion meeting cute at the Follies: she just barely sweet sixteen, he big, proto-Warbucks rich and powerful, pushing sixty. And they hit it off immediately and made a *perfect pair!* It hadn't been written yet, but the Follies orchestra should have been playing "September Song."

Hearst had a double reason to be furious with Herman Mankiewicz, his erstwhile houseguest at San Simeon who told tales out of school. Marion never walked out on Hearst, as Susan Alexander walked out on old fusspot Charlie Kane. Marion remained *faithful* and *devoted* and *in love* with William Randolph until death and his estranged sons took his body away.

And there was a further reason why William Randolph Hearst was *really* so livid with Mankiewicz and his proxy,

Charlie Chaplin and Marion Davies: affair under Hearst's nose ▲

radio interloper, upstart, "Boy Wonder" Orson Welles. Hearst's secret, pet, love name for his "little girl" lover's pussy-poo, his shared fun-tag for the (clinically) Douras genitalia and its perky "love bump"—Marion Davies' clitoris—was the adorable, and quite graphic, *Rosebud.* Marion, of course, drank (the only character trait she shared with the fictional Susan Alexander) and someone—was it Louise Brooks?—shared the giggled confidence; well, as secrets will, one whisper led from mouth to ear to the steel-trap mind of Herman Mankiewicz—and he made a mental note: *Marion Davies = Rosebud.*

We all know where *Rosebud* ended up—on the dying lips of Charles Foster Kane. To the crusty old "role-model" for this fictional RKO photoplay (originally titled simply *American*), the slightly sagging totem pole W. R. Hearst, it was

▲ The hands have it: Conrad Veidt and friend

151

Engraved by JOHN HELD JR

rotten enough that Marion's clitoris was mentioned throughout the *Kane* picture—everybody is always harking back to *Rosebud,* niggling away at the word like a kid with a loose tooth—but for Hearst it was even worse that old man Kane died with *Rosebud* on his lips!

Much worse, that *cinematic cunnilingus,* than the final sight of *Rosebud* frying and blistering on the flaming sled in Xanadu's furnace!

But riled almost beyond all human endurance, Old Dragon Fafnir Hearst proved that he was a *gentleman.* He wasn't a Texan. No guns were called for; Orson and Herman squeaked through, their triumph not a material one. *Citizen Kane:* the movies' magnificent put-on.

Edgar and Charlie: what's a few splinters between friends? ▲   Closer than close: Bobby and Billy Mauch ▶

☆ CLOSELY WATCHED BLONDES ☆

The famous fear merchant had settled down in an expansive wing chair comfy to his bulk. At this point in his career, he looked like E. T.'s grandfather. His head was pressed close to the eyepiece of a tripoded, powerful telescope that poked out from a window into the soft Laurel Canyon night.

A mile away, the bedroom was brightly lit. No curtains, torn or otherwise, blocked the view. The blinds were up. The future Lady Bountiful of Monaco was about to perform the single greatest act of charity of her charmed life.

Slowly, thoughtfully, as if returning from a night on the town, Grace Kelly disrobed. Her hat came first, then the gloves. The straps of her evening gown slipped down from white shoulders, allowing the sensuous *crêpe de Chine* to glide to the floor. There was a bra to unsnap. The last to fall were her French lace panties.

Across the shadowed canyon, "Cocky" (the obese one's nickname when he had been a schoolboy back in England) rose to the occasion.

Scopophilia—the gratification of sexual desire through gazing—is the cleanest of kinks. The scopophiliac is safe from flesh contact, germs, and from the squeeze plays that might court rejection. Linked as she was to him only by polished optical lenses across the abyss, the lovely ice-blond ex-model from Philadelphia had consented to indulge Peeping Al's whim *just this once*. It would be over in a mere five minutes when she snapped off the lights.

Years later, when she had eluded his control and captured one of the few remaining crowns in Europe, a petulant Hitchcock was sometimes to be heard grumbling about the co-ruler of the wee land of roulette twirlers and his ex-actress wife, whom he then referred to as

▲ Grace Kelly: a class act

"Princess Disgrace."

Lose one, find one: the agreement between Alfred Hitchcock and his subsequent ice-blond leading lady, "Tippi" Hedren, put this former fashion model under bondage-contract for seven years, shackled her first name in quotes, and put the seal on the strained, obsessive relationship that produced *The Birds* and *Marnie*, two of the director's more perverse thrillers.

While shooting *The Birds*, "Tippi" agreed to the dictates of the Master of Suspense: she was to be tied down, while live birds, bound to her body, pecked at her parts. One little pecker nearly blinded the lady; she suffered a nervous collapse.

Hitchcock's misogyny, his enjoyment of brutalizing beautiful women on screen, had reached a fever pitch a few years earlier, when, in 1959, Audrey Hepburn had refused to work in *No Bail for the Judge*, a movie he had been preparing especially for her. It was to feature a graphic and nasty rape scene.

Too graphic for Audrey, who had recently emoted quite religiously in *The Nun's Story* to much acclaim. She begged off, pleading pregnancy—just as Vera Miles had two years earlier in backing out of *Vertigo*. *No Bail for the Judge* became an abandoned project—at a cool loss of two hundred grand—and in its place, Hitchcock made *Psycho*, with its rape-like shower killing. His later movies seemed to lay the blame on women for stirring uncontrollable passions in men.

Despite Hitch's chaste devotion to his wife Alma—the woman, he used to jest, who saved him from "going queer"—he developed a powerful romantic and sexual obsession for Hedren.

She was the right blonde (but at the wrong time) in the director's souring love life, and paid dearly for piquing his passions. It had been planned that during the climactic avian attack in *The Birds*, mechanical trick chirpers would be used. When they did not appear lifelike enough, the director insisted on

◄ Young Grace Kelly: bathing beauty   ▲ Hitch: now voyeur

the use of real ones. For an entire week, "Tippi" was pelted with frenzied live crows and sea gulls. She was bound to the floor by concealed elastic bands; the nervous beaked creatures who had been attached to her dress by nylon threads were then encouraged to peck at her person. One bird did its best to claw out her left eye; the incident left a deep gash on the lower lid. The actress gave in to hysteria. She finally broke down completely, causing a full week's halt in production.

With their next film, Hitchcock became even more possessive and domineering. While *The Birds* had been shooting, he had plied Hedren with martinis during rehearsals. During the making of *Marnie*, beyond scopophilia, he was plying himself. This odd "Beauty and the Beast" courtship lasted for some time. During it, Hitch sent a peculiar gift to Melanie, Hedren's five-year-old daughter: a custom-made portrait doll of her mother, dressed and coiffed as the character she portrayed in *The Birds*—and enclosed in a small pine coffin.

Later, he took advantage of a makeup

session (which included tests for "wounds") to order a life mask made of "Tippi," which he then kept jealously guarded in a red velvet box. One day he would send her effusive and passionate letters; the next day she would receive cool, business-like memos from him.

Although she informed him of her intention to remarry—she was going to wed her agent after completion of the film—he remained undaunted. He gushed that she was everything he'd ever dreamt about. If only Alma went to sleep and did not wake up . . .

The screenplay of *Marnie* can be seen as a symbolic exposure of the director's futile pursuit of his star: in it, a frigid kleptomaniac resists her husband's advances on their honeymoon and then attempts suicide after he rapes her.

During its filming, Hitch pursued his old lech's dream—he must have sensed that wheelchair and pacemaker were lurking in the wings for him. The movie became a senior citizen's *cri de coeur*. One day, halfway through the film, he propositioned "Tippi" in her trailer. The essence of the scene was Victorian melodrama—the villain threatened to ruin her if she would not comply. She would not. From that moment on, he refused to address her directly on the set. He would inform his assistants to "Tell that girl to . . ."

His physical and moral decline was marked after *Marnie*. Severely depressed, he inserted into *Frenzy* the most brutal and terrifying rape scene he had ever put on film.

References to bondage abound in Hitchcock's films. Yet it was on his audience that he performed the ultimate S and M exercise. He held them spellbound in darkness—through cunning, through genius, through skill. Bound to their seats, the fear master tormented them to his heart's content. And, unlike Grace and "Tippi," they kept coming back for more.

Tippi and tormentor ▲

Tippi Hedren: Hitchcock's ideal ▶

☆ BABYLON BOOZERS ☆

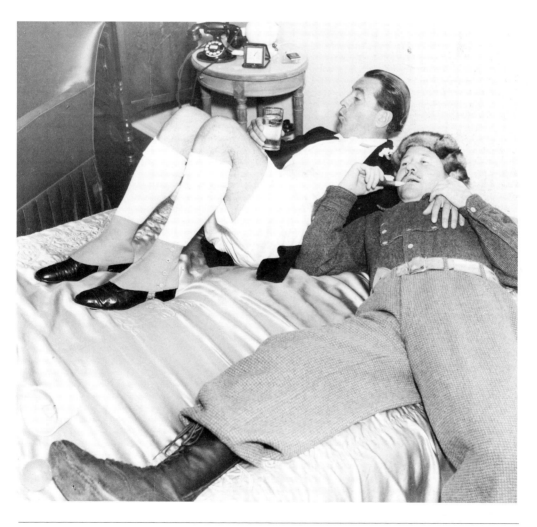

◀ Warren William: one more for the road   ▲ Richard Barthelmess and Jack Oakie flake out at party

D. W. Griffith ▲   George Bancroft ▲   W. C. Fields with terminal case of gin blossoms ▶

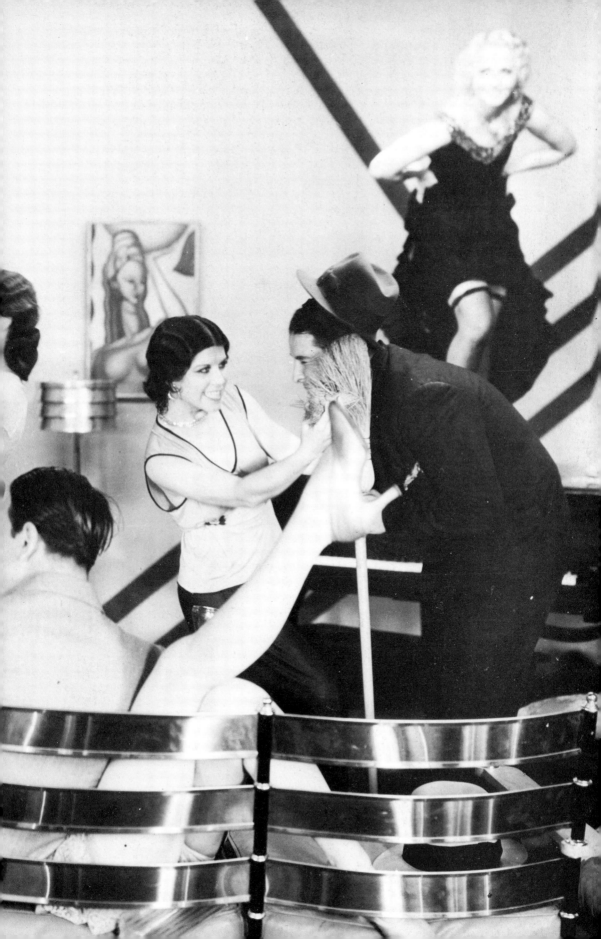

◀ Mae West and anti-boozer Billy Sunday—anything for a laugh   ▲ John Barrymore fails a breath test

▲ Lillian Roth: drunken brawl with hubby and recovering in hospital ▶

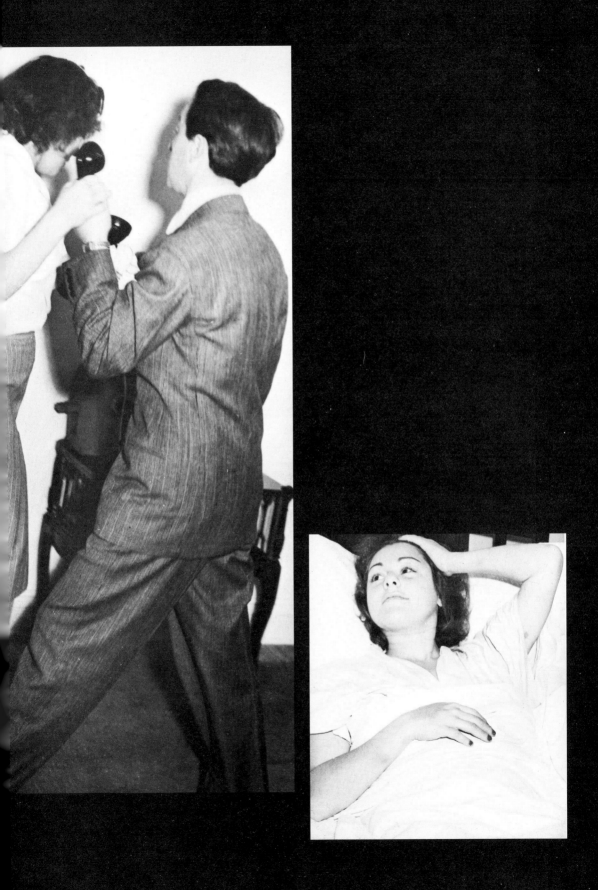

Mary Pickford: serious imbiber ▲   Errol Flynn: high jinks with teenage "horsie" ▶

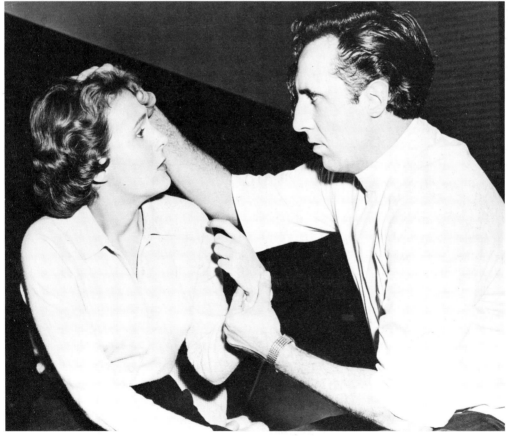

◀ Dan Dailey laces Broderick Crawford   ▲ Thirsty thespians: Bruce Cabot, Dan Duryea, Timothy Carey

◀ Bruised knuckles: Robert Walker arrested   ▲ Dixie Lee Crosby: Bing drove her to drink

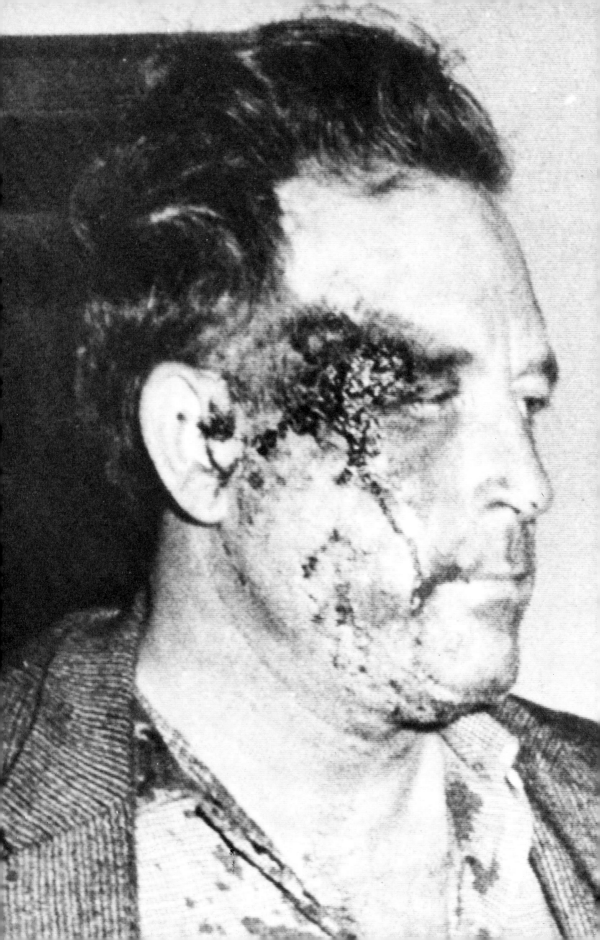

▲ Cass Daley: died in a drunken fall

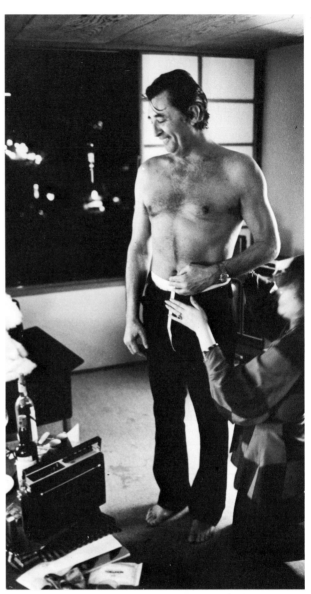

▲ Bob Mitchum: checked out of the Betty Ford clinic

◀ Lawrence Tierney: after a boozy battle   The battle continues: Shelley Winters and Tony Franciosa ▶

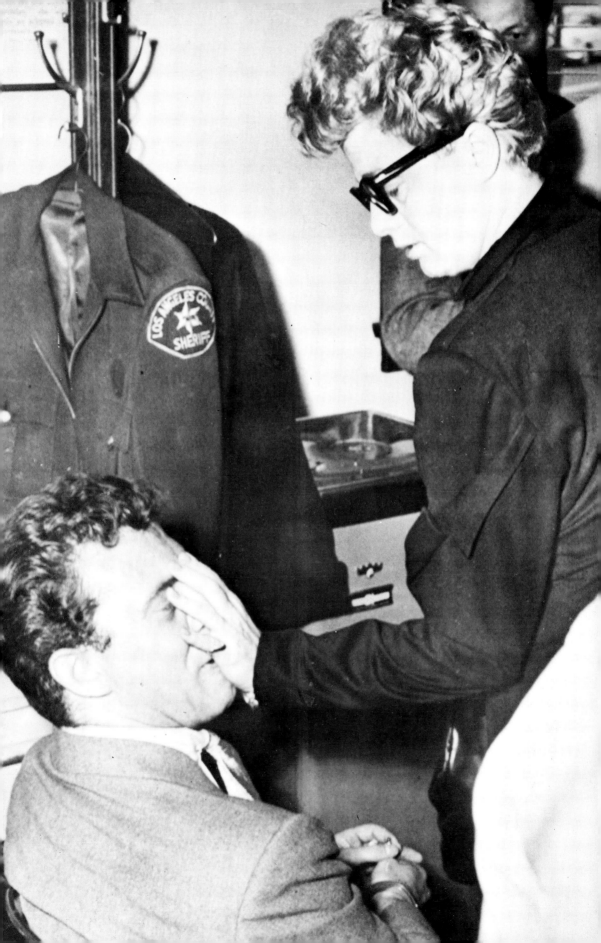

▲ Boozers all: Louella Parsons, Truman Capote, Richard Burton ▶

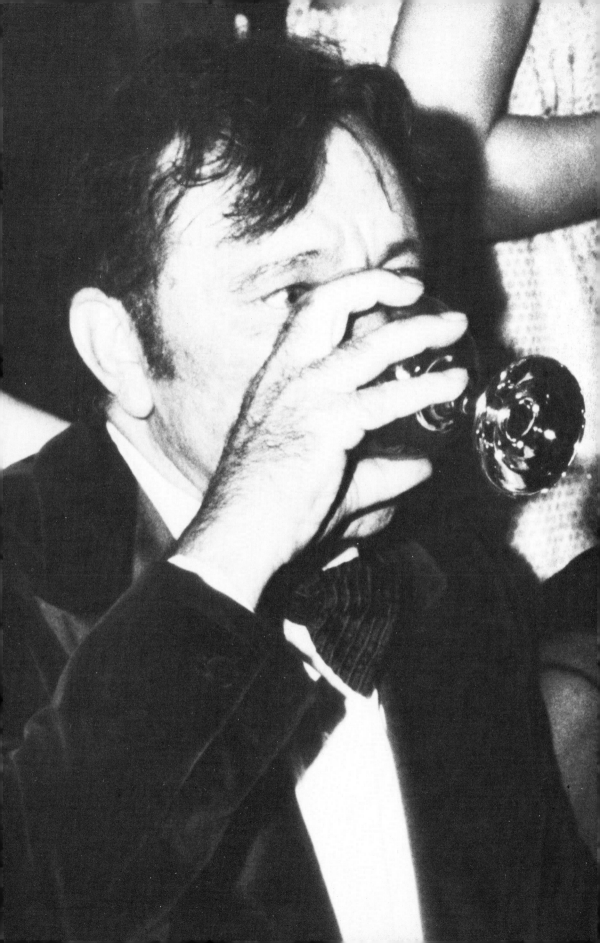

☆ LOST BOY ☆

Ted Tetzlaff's *The Window* (1949) was Bobby Driscoll's best movie, made when the irresistible kid star was twelve years old. Driscoll plays Tommy Woodry, a boy from a working class New York family. When seen today, this gripping suspense thriller about the paranoia adults inspire in children takes on a somber, bitterly ironic resonance. At one point, Tommy's mother (Barbara Hale) forbids him to go out of their modest Lower East Side tenement apartment. He replies: "There's no place for me to go." After a brilliant and promising early career (a movie star at six, an Oscar-winner at eleven, thirty films to his credit—most of them made with the top stars of Hollywood), by the age of seventeen, Driscoll had become a junkie has-been, arrested many times on various charges. In 1968, his corpse was discovered in an abandoned tenement on New York's Lower East Side—the locale of his most impressive film. At the time of the grisly discovery, the body was not identified, and the Oscar-winner who had earned $60,000 a year was buried in a pauper's grave.

Bobby Driscoll was born in Cedar Rapids, Iowa, in 1937. When he was six, his family moved to California. A barber cutting the child's hair was adamant—this cute kid should be in pictures! A visit to MGM for an audition proved the barber knew his beans—Bobby was given a part in *Lost Angel,* starring Margaret O'Brien, the cutesy-pie kiddie sensation of the day. (O'Brien was also destined never to graduate to adult roles, but her life was spared the tragedy that beset Bobby's.)

A little ace at memorizing lines, Bobby was also a spontaneous, natural actor. He was soon being shuttled from studio to studio. He appeared alongside Anne Baxter in Lloyd Bacon's *Sunday Dinner for a Soldier* at Fox, then with Veronica Lake and Lillian Gish in *Miss Susie Slagle's* and with Alan Ladd in *OSS*, both at Paramount. When he worked in *So Goes My Love* at Universal, he made a great impression on the film's veteran leads. Myrna Loy remarked: "He has so much charm, if Don Ameche and I aren't on our toes all the time, the audience will be looking at the youngster and ignoring us." Ameche said: "He's got a great talent. I've worked with a lot of child players in my time, but none of them bore the promise that seems inherent in young Driscoll."

His boyish appeal is also much in evidence in *From This Day Forward,* with Joan Fontaine; *The Happy Time,* with Charles Boyer; *The Scarlet Coat,* with Cornel Wilde and George Sanders, and *When I Grow Up,* with Robert Preston. In this last one, Bobby manages to run away from home—

◄ Bobby Driscoll: Disney's favorite money-spinner

something he'd threatened to do in several other movies.

In 1946, when he signed up for Walt Disney's *Song of the South,* Bobby became Disney's first flesh and blood contract player. In it, he portrays little Johnny, who lives on his grandmother's plantation—his companion is the great Hattie McDaniel. As the tale unfolds, Uncle Remus (James Baskett) tells Johnny stories to keep him from running away from home. Their moral, as summed up by Remus for the child, is: "You can't run away from trouble—there ain't no place that far." (Too bad the real life Driscoll didn't listen to Uncle Remus!) This beautiful and delightful movie was a major money-spinner for Disney when released—it made further piles when reissued in 1956 and 1972. It should come back every year.

Studio personnel have been quoted to the effect that Bobby's charm worked wonders on "Grumpy" old Disney— some animators stated that the boss seemed to have fallen in love with the boy. There may be truth in this—if so, it was a love which deepened with the successive hefty box office returns of the films Driscoll made for Uncle Walt—all five of them were big bucks hits. In *Melody Time* (1948) Bobby asks Roy Rogers why the coyotes howl—the cowboy then unfolds the rousing tale of Pecos Bill, a boy raised by coytoes. In *So Dear to My Heart,* released the same year, Bobby was joined by veterans Beulah Bondi, Harry Carey and Burl Ives. In reviewing this film, *Time*'s critic wrote: "Bobby Driscoll is a rarity among child actors; when relaxed, he is an attractive kid, and when called upon to act, he is not at all repellent."

The non-repellent kid received a special Academy Award "as the outstanding juvenile actor of 1949" for his work in *So Dear to My Heart* and *The Window.*

In Disney's 1950 *Treasure Island,* filmed in England, Bobby gave one of his most accomplished performances— it was superior in every way to that of Jackie Cooper in the same role of Jim Hawkins in MGM's 1934 version of the story. Disney's enthusiasm was returned—Driscoll seemed genuinely fond of Uncle Walt. He took direction better than any child performer within memory—everyone at the studio sang his praises. In 1953 his voice was used for that of Peter Pan, and his acted performance in the title role was filmed, then rotoscoped for the animated *Peter Pan.*

When the Peter Pan from Iowa started growing up in real life—became an adolescent and developed acne—the adorable kid star turned into a surly and belligerent teenager. He was offered few roles—Bobby appeared once as a teenager in a guest spot on the Loretta Young TV Show.

He was nineteen when he married Marilyn Brush in 1956. They had three children, but the marriage ended with a

Bobby's beginnings: good trouper ▲

painful separation. 1956 was also the year his life and career turned into a mudslide. Bobby and a buddy were booked on felony narcotics charges. Dressed in torn jeans and a dirty sweater, he was arrested at his Pacific Palisades home. He was still a very handsome young man. His mother later stated: "Drugs changed him. He didn't bathe, his teeth got loose. He had an extremely high I.Q., but the narcotics affected his brain. We didn't know what it was. He was nineteen before we knew."

After a three-year absence, he returned to the screen in 1958, in a B-programmer—Bernard Girard's *The Party Crashers.* By a curious coincidence, his co-star was the lobotomized Frances Farmer, making *her* benumbed comeback after sixteen years away from the movies. *The Party Crashers* was to prove the last film for both of these tragic figures.

Bobby's triumph: *The Window* ▲   ▲ Bobby in *The Party Crashers*

In 1959, when sheriff's officers noted needle marks on his arms and found Bobby in possession of a "narcotics outfit," he was arrested for heroin use and jailed as an addict.

In 1960, he was booked on a charge of assault with a deadly weapon. Driscoll said he had been washing a friend's car when some hecklers annoyed him. He appears to have pistol whipped one of the bunch. Driscoll claimed that the man "had bumped into the gun."

In early 1961, he was arrested for robbing an animal clinic; later that year he was arrested for forging a stolen check, and on various narcotics charges; he was sent to serve a six-month term at the Narcotics Rehabilitation Center of the Chino State Penitentiary. The accused addict told the courtroom: "I had everything . . . was earning more than $50,000 a year, working steadily with good parts. Then I started putting all my spare time in my arm. I was seventeen when I first experimented with the stuff . . . mostly heroin, because I had the money to pay for it.

Now, no one will hire me because of my arrests. I'm looking forward to the coming months at Chino."

After his release, Bobby dropped out of sight. He drifted around and eventually landed in New York, on the Lower East Side, which was then a hippie/junkie drug heaven/haven. By then he was a wired speed freak, cadging money from acquaintances. On March 30, 1968, two children playing in a deserted tenement near Avenue A discovered the corpse of a young man, surrounded by religious objects and other litter. No I.D. was on the body, but tracks were on the arms, Methedrine in the bloodstream. The unidentified stiff was fingerprinted, then buried on Hart Island, off the Bronx, New York's potter's field.

Nineteen months later, Disney executives received phone calls from Bobby's mother—his dad was dying and calling for his son. She had gone to the F.B.I. for assistance—to no avail. Peter Pan was still missing. Through the efforts of the Disney people and a Los Angeles county law agency, it was discovered through a fingerprint check that it had been Bobby's corpse which had been found in New York the previous year and buried in a pauper's grave. The discovery was made two weeks after Daddy Driscoll died.

Three years later, Disney revived *Song of the South.* It made more money than ever before. Bobby was not there to witness the great appreciation of his film work by a whole new generation of fans and the glad tidings the revival brought to Disney's accountants. When asked how she felt about the revival of *Song of the South,* Mrs. Driscoll replied: "It will be painful to see him on the screen, but it will be nice, all the same. He was such a fine boy. Please tell people that no woman ever had a finer, more generous son."

Bye, Bye Bobby.

Adolescent Bobby: not in demand ▲   Driscoll on the Lower East Side: near the end ▶

☆ ATTILA THE NUN ☆

"The chocolate-covered black widow" does not evoke the image of one of Hollywood's most beautiful faces, but it is just one of the unlovely epithets which have been used over the years to describe Loretta Young. Intimates have called her "Gretch, the Wretch" (she was born Gretchen Young, in 1913, in Salt Lake City), "The Steel Butterfly," "Hollywood's beautiful hack," "The Manipulator," and "a willow with an iron backbone." Her latter-day assumption of the robe of moral rectitude has resulted in her being dubbed "Saint Loretta" and "Attila the Nun." On one occasion, at a party *chez* Joan Crawford, producer Ross Hunter was about to sink his butt into a comfortable chair. Crawford grabbed him just in time—"Not there, Loretta Young just sat there. It has the mark of the cross in the seat." At a Hollywood roast, Jack Hellman was presented with a bowl of water "upon which Loretta Young had once walked."

And yet—there had been many a slip 'twixt the bowl and the lip. . . .

When her mother moved to Hollywood with the children, Loretta was schooled at the Ramona Convent. (She later was to play the title role in *Ramona* and a nun in *Come to the Stable.*) As a child, she was seen in a quantity of bit roles, among them that of an Arab urchin in Valentino's *The Son of the Sheik.* Her first important part was opposite Lon Chaney in his 1928 *Laugh Clown Laugh.* She shot up to stardom during the early sound period, but for most of her films her wardrobe got better reviews than its wearer. Bosley Crowther, the *New York Times* critic, reviewing *And Now, Tomorrow,* wrote the definitive statement on Young, the thespian: "Whatever it was that this actress never had, she still hasn't got it." Her face (full lips, prominent cheekbones) was her fortune—she knew how to use it for maximum effect on camera and how to upstage everyone else on the set. Her body was no big deal—on various occasions her breasts, buttocks, calves and thighs were padded for the benefit of the lens.

In 1930, at seventeen, she eloped with actor Grant Withers, shortly after the pair appeared together in *The Second Floor Mystery.* Withers was not a Catholic; they were not married by a priest. She was refused communion for a year; in the eyes of the Church, the marriage never happened. It was annulled in 1931. Withers' career fizzled out; he later killed himself.

For one who has viewed the latter-day Loretta in her appearances at the Academy Award ceremonies, smiling wanly as she tosses off barbs at the "dirtiness" of current movies, or who has seen her primly flouncing about as a Mother Superior of glamour in her TV

◀ Latter-day Loretta

shows, it is difficult to believe that this immaculately preserved, demurely posturing lady was once one of Hollywood's "wild" girls. She was, in fact, the *Call of the Wild* girl. The year was 1935.

"The Manipulator" had been cast opposite Clark Gable, in William Wellman's screen version of Jack London's saga of a man, a woman and a dog, set in the frozen Klondike. Loretta played the woman.

The Gable-Young chemistry was heady—on and off screen. Loretta's daintiness was a perfect foil for Gable's good-natured macho persona. It was common knowledge that the star with huge ears was estranged from his wife Ria; the fans were titillated by reports from Louella Parsons, Hollywood's oafish gossip-monger-in-residence, that romance had nested in the hearts of one of the cinema's most beautiful women and the town's best known sex symbol.

In his autobiography, director Wellman recalls that the romance was so intense it interfered with his production schedule: "We had trouble on *Call of the Wild*, big trouble. Gable wasn't tending to business, not the business of making pictures. He was paying a lot of attention to monkey business." As time went by, it was rumored that the affair would culminate in church—that Gable would divorce Ria and wed Miss Young.

That did not happen, but puzzling items soon appeared in *The Hollywood Reporter* and *Variety*. It was announced that Fox would retire Miss Young from the screen for a full year "for reasons of health." In a *Photoplay* article, Dorothy Manners denied rumors that Loretta Young was "in retirement to have a secret child." (In 1935, public knowledge of a baby born out of wedlock would have been ruinous for a star's career.)

After a full year's absence, Young

Clark and Loretta in *Call of the Wild:* the real thing ▲

resumed her film career. Then, on May 11, 1937, the romance with Gable again became a subject for speculation when Loretta managed to adopt a certain little girl, despite California rulings prohibiting the adoption of a child by a single person. She claimed she had fallen in love with the child when she first noticed her while decorating a Christmas tree in a San Diego orphanage. At the time of her adoption little Judy was twenty-three months old—she was born a few months after production on *Call of the Wild* ended, during the period of Loretta's "retirement."

When the film's director was queried, Wellman replied: "All I know is that Loretta and Clark were very friendly during the picture, and it was very cold up there. When the film was finished, she disappeared for a while and later showed up with a daughter with the biggest ears I ever saw except on an elephant." (A few years after the adoption, Loretta saw to it that little Judy received cosmetic surgery which flattened her auricular protuberances.)

When Loretta wed advertising executive Thomas Lewis in 1940, the girl legally became Judy Lewis. The year before Young's second marriage, the star had returned to the headlines because of a tenebrous financial affair. Her 1939 boyfriend, William Buckner, was indicted for defrauding wealthy Hollywoodites with the sale of worthless Philippine railway bonds. He was sentenced to a prison term.

The marriage to Lewis seemed successful. Loretta increasingly displayed the outward signs of Catholic

▲ Daughter Judy Lewis: amazing resemblance

piety. Fonts of holy water were installed beside each doorway in her home. Lewis' favorite hobby was taking Madonna-like photos of his wife, reverently posed as if she were the Blessed Virgin. As fate had it, when she and Clark Gable were again cast as screen lovers (in *Key to the City*, 1950), she was rushed to the hospital from the studio during production—it was later revealed that she had had a miscarriage.

Throughout her career, Young's holier-than-thou airs were a source of annoyance to her peers in the acting community. It was noted that during production of *The Devil's in Love* she refused to kiss Victor Jory: she was a star, he wasn't. Chastened language was the order of the day for those appearing on "The Loretta Young Show" (her gussied-up sudser TV series, aired from 1953–61). She installed a "swear box"

Saint Loretta ▲

on the set. Anyone heard using profanity during production was fined and obliged to contribute to St. Anne's Maternity Hospital for unmarried mothers in Los Angeles. When a famed Broadway star swore mildly, Loretta informed him that she was fining him fifty cents. He pulled out a bill and thrust it at her, saying: "Here's ten bucks. Now fuck off, Loretta!"

As president of Citizens for Decent Literature (during Reagan's term as California's governor) she lectured throughout the state, reviling pornography and explicit sexual literature. In several small towns, local porn shops were firebombed by vigilantes the night after her appearances. In 1966, syndicated Catholic papers ran Loretta Young's advice column to the lovelorn—prudent advice, tidbits of Victoriana.

In 1970, she filed suit to obtain a restraining order against 20th Century-Fox to compel the studio to remove a clip from *Call of the Wild* which had been included in *Myra Breckenridge*. Miss Young objected to the use of a scene from one of her movies in a film "depicting unnatural sex practices." Three years later, her own son, Christopher Lewis, was arrested because of his alleged sex practices—on charges of "lewd conduct with two thirteen-year-old boys." Chris Lewis pleaded "no contest," to child molestation, which meant he was considered guilty of that charge. Lewis, who was then twenty-nine, was described as a filmmaker with Lyric Productions. One "lyric" production made by him was *Genesis's Children*, a so-called kiddie porn movie. It had been seized in the laboratory. (Some who saw it called it an "artistic toddler nudist film"—for others it was an "inch-worm festival.") A scoutmaster, a camp counselor and the heir to a Texas oil fortune numbered among the defendants. The press dubbed them a

"chicken ring."

Detective Lloyd Martin of the vice division characterized the defendants as "not homosexuals at all, but sick child molesters who bring discredit on the gay community." Martin said the boys, who ranged in age from five to seventeen, were induced by "flattery, money, and such treats as horseback riding trips, to perform sexual acts on camera with each other and also with the men."

In the opinion of James Grodin, Los Angeles Deputy District Attorney, Lewis should have served jail time; he got off with five years probation and a fine of $500. His mother will not discuss the case; the holy water fonts in her house are always filled.

In 1976, it was announced that Loretta Young had been cast as Mother Cabrini in a biography of the first American to attain sainthood; the film was to be directed by Martin Scorsese. Scorsese declared that he viewed Mother Cabrini as "an unsaintly saint who hustled in the streets and clawed her way through society." Casting "Attila the Nun" in the role was a fascinating idea. The movie, unfortunately, was never made. Saint Loretta's comeback never came.

▲ Loretta in *Kismet:* a woman's fate

☆THE MAGIC OF SELF-MURDER☆

For the movie audience, the suicide of a star was the ultimate scandal. While not condoning adultery, loose-living, multiple marriages, alcoholism and drug addiction, the public could still, in such cases, prove forgiving—if the star's image had projected enough warmth and sympathy. But for a star—or even a familiar featured player or character actor—to commit self-murder was unthinkable. They had money and fame, everything *we* wanted—and it still wasn't enough. They must have been sick.

And sick they often were. Along with the occasional suicide de passion, the long list of Tinseltown's self-murderers includes those who had lost or were losing their health as well as those who were scared shitless of losing their youth, their appeal. (The still-ravishingly beautiful Pier Angeli killed herself at thirty-nine, because "being forty would be the end of everything.") Illness or a physical debility that would show up on camera was the greatest of all curses. Suicide often seemed preferable to a slow recovery for those who had been brain-washed and brain-damaged by their own beauty and glamour, and for whom the loss of the public, of fan mail, of "image" was the loss of self.

The film industry's suicides were, in the majority, actors and actresses. Few aging editors, wrinkled sound men, arthritic script girls, senescent makeup artists, or grips unlucky-in-love reached for sleeping pills or revolvers. Pills were the vehicle of choice for stars—male and female—desiring a quick trip to that great projection room in the sky. Most of those who used guns were men. The drowned were men. Suicide by carbon monoxide poisoning seems to have been an exclusively masculine affair as well.

SELF-MURDER BY CARBON MONOXIDE POISONING

Character actor TYLER BROOKE got into his car on March 2, 1943, turned on the gas and died. His most notable roles had been in Howard Hawks' *Fazil,* in Cecil B. De Mille's *Dynamite* (in which he played The Life of the Party) and in Rouben Mamoulian's *Love Me Tonight* (as The Composer).

SPENCER CHARTERS, the popular comic actor, who often played judges, got in his car on January 25, 1943, gobbled some sleeping pills, turned on the gas and died. During a thirty-six-year stage career, he had appeared in 479 plays and was in dozens of George M. Cohan comedies. He created the role of Jerome Underwood in Florenz Ziegfeld's Broadway musical hit *Whoopee* and was brought to Hollywood to repeat the role with Eddie Cantor in Sam Goldwyn's

two-color Technicolor screen version of *Whoopee*, choreographed by Busby Berkeley. Charters appeared in over two hundred films. He can be seen in *The Front Page, Palmy Days, Wonder Bar, The Raven, Mr. Deeds Goes to Town* (as Mal), *The Hurricane* (as The Judge), *Young Mr. Lincoln* (as Judge Bell), *Drums Along the Mohawk* (as Fisk, the Innkeeper), and *The Hunchback of Notre Dame*, among others. In one of his best films, Roland West's *The Bat Whispers*, Charters appears alongside Chester Morris, another candidate for suicide. Both Charters and Tyler Brooke appear in Henry King's *In Old Chicago*—which

makes this disaster movie a double-carbon-monoxide-suicide film.

JACK DOUGHERTY was a handsome featured player in action pictures and Westerns during the Twenties *(Chain Lightning, The Burning Trail, Arizona Express)*, but was perhaps even better known as the husband of actress Virginia Brown Faire and then of the beautiful alcoholic star Barbara La Marr, who died from a drug overdose. Dougherty attempted suicide in 1933 and bungled it. If at first you don't succeed . . . On May 16, 1938, he got in his car, turned on the gas, and died.

Tyler Brooke (with cane): life of the party ▲   Spencer Charters strangles Una Merkel ▶

196

AUTOCIDE

CHARLES BUTTERWORTH was one of the more fluttery—and likable—comedians to grace American screen during the Golden Thirties. Butterworth was usually cast as a timid and scatterbrained bachelor of means who hardly ever got the girl. He was born in Indiana in 1896, studied law at Notre Dame and for a brief period was a practicing journalist. Acting was his ultimate goal, however, and after several years in Broadway musicals and comedies, he made his film debut in Hollywood in 1930. He appeared with Boris Karloff and John Barrymore in Michael Curtiz's *The Mad Genius;* in Rouben Mamoulian's masterpiece, *Love Me Tonight,* he is Jeannette MacDonald's mooncalf suitor, the Count de Savignac. His other films include: *The Cat and the Fiddle, Magnificent Obsession, The Boys from Syracuse, Second Chorus* and *This Is the Army.* In *Every Day's a Holiday,* Butterworth buys the Brooklyn Bridge from con woman Mae West. This West vehicle was a *three* suicide movie—it also featured Herman Bing and West's lover, Johnny Indrisano, both of whom eventually put an end to their days.

Butterworth's death was officially listed as an accident, but he did, in point of fact, kill himself. Dusty Negulesco,

wife of director Jean Negulesco, a close friend of both Butterworth and his bosom buddy, humorist Robert Benchley, recalls that the actor was inconsolable after Benchley's death. A few months after Benchley's death, he went out and killed himself in his car on June 14, 1946.

DEATH BY DROWNING

JOHN BOWERS was a handsome leading man in many silent movies; he is largely forgotten today. Norman Maine is a household word for movie fans—who can forget Judy Garland affirming, "This is *Mrs.* Norman Maine!" Yet Norman Maine was John Bowers, or rather, the life and tragic death of John Bowers were the source of all three movie versions of *A Star Is Born.*

Bowers was born John Bowersox, in Indiana, and entered films in 1916. He married Marguerite De La Motte, a petite brunette star who had studied dance with Pavlova and who came to prominence in several roles opposite Douglas Fairbanks. Bowers and De La Motte appeared together in several films *(Richard the Lion-Hearted, Pals in Paradise,* and *Ragtime).* Bowers was one of several actors tested for the title role in *Ben Hur.* He didn't get the job, and with the coming of sound his career took a nosedive. De La Motte divorced him. He appeared in three early talkies—in supporting roles of little importance—and then could find no movie work at all.

He lost all his savings when he backed a flying school that flopped. He became an alcoholic, and one day told a friend he was going to kill himself by "getting in a boat and sailing away into the sunset." (His favorite hobby was yachting.) And he did just that. At age thirty-six, the ex-leading man rented a sailboat on November 15, 1936. A few

Charles
BUTTERWORTH

BELIEVE IT OR NOT, BUT IF BUTTERWORTH DECIDED TO QUIT THE MOVIES TODAY HE COULD GET A JOB ON ANY LARGE NEWS-PAPER---- BEFORE CHARLIE ENTERED PICTURES HE WAS A WELL KNOWN WRITER ON A NEW YORK NEWSPAPER!

Copyright © King Features

been preparing a film whose lead, though not unattractive, would be "just one of the crowd," not a typical Hollywood face. When he espied Murray, he saw what he wanted. He approached him, introduced himself, gave him his card, and asked the actor to call him the following day. Murray never called. Vidor had him traced through the studio—it turned out that Murray hadn't believed that the director of *The Big Parade* was a director, or had a job for him. He was tested, and when the test was shown to

days later, his body was washed onto the beach at Malibu.

The first version of *A Star Is Born*, with Janet Gaynor as Vicki Lester and Fredric March as Norman Maine, was made shortly after the suicide of Bowers, with the event fresh in everyone's mind—especially that of Dorothy Parker, who wrote the screenplay. The film is, of course, a rising star–falling star story of a small town girl who achieves fame and Oscardom in Hollywood. Her ex-star husband walks into the Pacific.

In 1936 the corpse of a shabbily dressed, unshaven bum was found floating in the Hudson River. It was JAMES MURRAY, the star of King Vidor's *The Crowd*, one of the greatest American films ever made. Murray was born in the Bronx and studied at Yale, where he appeared in a short student film. He went to Hollywood in search of a movie career. He had landed mostly extra parts and bit roles until the day, in front of the MGM casting office, when he caught the eye of King Vidor. Vidor had

John Bowers: sailing into the sunset ▲   ▲ James Murray: the river called

Irving Thalberg, the producer agreed with Vidor that this Hollywood extra was one of the best natural actors he had ever seen.

As they traveled by train to New York, where *The Crowd* was to be shot, Murray pointed out to Vidor the different railway stations where he had shoveled coal or washed dishes—or from where he had ridden the rods under boxcars, in order to get to Hollywood.

The Crowd opened at the Capitol Theater in New York, where Murray had once worked as an usher. It received excellent reviews and became an instant classic—it was the last great silent movie made by MGM. (It unintentionally created quite a stir by being the first American film to show a bathroom that contained a toilet.)

Murray then starred opposite Joan Crawford in *Rose-Marie* as Jim, the mysterious soldier of fortune. Unfortunately, he had become a chronic alcoholic, undependable on the set, and although he was given jobs in other films, his career quickly suffered a decline.

In 1933 Vidor was casting *Our Daily Bread,* and thought of Murray for the lead. No one in Hollywood knew the actor's whereabouts. One day, the director was accosted by a panhandler on Vine Street who asked for money for a meal. It was Jimmy Murray. Vidor gave him ten dollars and invited him to the Brown Derby for dinner. Murray insisted that they sit at the bar. Over a drink, Vidor asked him if he could pull himself together if he were given the lead in *Our Daily Bread.* Murray said he thought he could. When Vidor added that he would have to go on the wagon, Murray retorted, "Just because I stop you on the street and try to borrow a buck, you think you can tell me what to do. As far as I'm concerned, you know what you can do with your lousy part!" He wiped his mouth on his sleeve and walked out.

Vidor never saw him again.

There is a scene in *The Crowd* in which John Sims (Murray), having hit bottom, is about to commit suicide and is kept from it by his little son, who playfully tugs at his sleeve, urging him to keep moving. Unfortunately, in real life, Murray had no one to tug at his sleeve.

JAMES WHALE killed himself on May 29, 1957. From 1930 to 1936, this great director made a dozen of the most entertaining and sophisticated movies ever produced in the studios of Hollywood.

Whale's suicide note was discovered by a maid, who gave it to his business manager. When *he* died, it was given to David Lewis, who had been Whale's companion for many years. Whale was homosexual, and had a close circle of devoted and brilliant friends of both sexes. But beyond that circle, this difficult, witty, demanding, and bitchy craftsman was not well liked in Hollywood. The suicide note was kept secret for some time, and until its existence became known, there were persistent rumors of foul play concerning the director's death in his swimming pool.

Whale was born in England in 1896. He began acting during World War I while in a German prisoner-of-war camp. He did not like war; he hated being a prisoner of the Germans, but he made the best of it. In the post-war years he worked in the London theater as actor, set designer, and stage director. *Journey's End,* a play about life in the trenches, was staged by Whale in London and on Broadway and was a great hit in both cities. Whale was brought to Hollywood in 1930 to do a movie version of it. He settled in Hollywood and made a long series of literate and enjoyable movies in different genres, most of them for Universal.

He is best known for a quartet of great horror and fantasy films: *Frankenstein* (it was Whale who selected Boris Karloff for the role of the monster), *The Bride of Frankenstein, The Old Dark House,* and *The Invisible Man.* All bear Whale's personal trademark: campy black humor, stylish and mobile camera work, and razor-sharp editing. His other films from the Thirties give strong proof of the director's taste, imagination, and rapport with actors: *Remember Last Night?,* a delightful comedy-melodrama; *By Candlelight; Waterloo Bridge; The Kiss Before the Mirror; The Great Garrick; One More River,* a superbly acted courtroom drama; and his elegant and beautifully detailed *Show Boat* with Irene Dunne, Helen Morgan, and Paul Robeson. Whale's is by far the best of the three screen versions of Jerome Kern's musical. It was Universal's big film for 1936, and was popular with the press and audiences (it became one of that year's top moneymakers). But trouble was brewing for the director of these masterpieces.

Under the aegis of moguls Carl Laemmle and Carl Laemmle, Jr., Whale had enjoyed creative independence at Universal. His films did well, he was permitted to cast and direct them in his fashion, and then supervise the final cut. In 1935 Laemmle was forced to sell the studio and Junior was obliged to resign as Universal's production chief. One of Junior's biggest triumphs had been *All Quiet on the Western Front* (1930), based on the famous Erich Maria Remarque anti-war novel. It won Oscars for Best Film and Best Direction (Lewis Milestone) and greatly enhanced Universal's prestige. It is still considered one of the greatest of all films about World War I. In 1936 Whale was assigned the direction of another Remarque World War I novel, set in

Germany, *The Road Back.*

While the film was in production, the German consul in Los Angeles wrote the twenty principal actors working on the film, the production staff, and Universal executives, threatening a German boycott of all the future films of everyone involved; their work would be banned in Germany unless the film was cancelled. It was completed as planned. *Life* magazine previewed it, selected it

James Whale: the first and last time he used his pool ▲

as Movie of the Week, and gave it a rave review. Meanwhile, the Nazi Ministry of Propaganda increased pressure on Universal: all of the studio's films, past and present, would be banned in Germany if *The Road Back* was released without drastic changes—everything considered offensive to The Master Race must be cut.

Charles R. Rogers and J. Cheever Cowdin, who had acquired the studio from the Laemmle family, surrendered to the Nazis without a fight. In this Hollywood scandal—infinitely more shocking than the drug addictions or kinky dalliances of the stars—of 1937, Adolf Hitler was able to dictate to an American movie studio (founded by Jews) what it should make. The film was withdrawn and emasculated, whole sequences were butchered. A total of twenty-one cuts were made, and the cut sequences were replaced by foolish comic scenes with low comic Andy Devine. It was remade with a new director, Ted Sloman, and a new editor, and finally got the Nazi seal of approval. Whale, who loathed war, and loathed the Nazis even more, was appalled. *The Road Back*—originally one of his finest films—was ruined. Only the butchered version has survived.

The embittered director then worked at MGM and Columbia, where he was assigned weak scripts that he was not permitted to improve. He was rarely tactful with producers and soon lost interest in making movies over which he had no creative control. His later films bear little trace of his directorial genius—he could not whip up much interest in second-rate stories like *They Dare Not Love* or *Green Hell* (which starred George Sanders, another eventual suicide).

Although Whale had invested well in land and stocks and was secure financially, his life began to fall to pieces. Shortly after his arrival in Hollywood he had met David Lewis, a handsome young actor who later became Irving Thalberg's personal assistant at MGM. Whale bought a house at 788 Amalfi Drive, Pacific Palisades (between Beverly Hills and Malibu), and Lewis moved in with him.

Lewis enjoyed a successful career at MGM, where he was executive producer of Garbo's *Camille* and other major films. After Thalberg's death, he worked for a while at Warner Bros., where he was associate producer of *King's Row* (which gave Ronald Reagan his best role: "Where is the rest of me?") and Bette Davis' *All This and Heaven Too.* His last big movie was *Raintree County.*

By the early Fifties his relationship with Whale had gone *phfft.* Whale spent a year in Europe, where he met a young Frenchman named Pierre Foegel whom he hired as chauffeur-companion. He returned to Hollywood and announced that he would be installing Foegel in the house he shared with Lewis. Lewis moved out, his departure accompanied by some bitter squabbling. Foegel moved in, and Whale soon set him up in a filling station business.

Around this time, Whale had a swimming pool built. Although he could not swim, the pool was mainly for parties at which the director enjoyed the sight of young men in bathing trunks. Whale kept a diary of his gay sex fantasies and read them to his guests at poolside parties. Not all of them were amused.

Professionally, he was a forgotten man. For lack of film work, Whale occupied his time with painting. His main interest in life seemed to have become fine cigars—when his house caught fire once, he walked into the blazing building, ignored his paintings, and rescued a box of his precious Havanas.

Whale's health began to fail in 1956. He suffered several strokes, was hospitalized and stupidly and unnecessarily given shock treatments. He was released in early 1957. He could no longer paint, drive, or even read a book. Existence seemed purposeless. By the end of May, he had made his final decision. The director of *Frankenstein* found that life had become too monstrous to be lived any longer—in spite of his wealth and brilliant friends. He put on his favorite suit and sat down in his studio to pen a note:

TO ALL I LOVE,

Do not grieve for me—my nerves are all shot and for the last year I have been in agony day and night—except when I sleep with sleeping pills . . . I have had a wonderful life but it is over and my nerves get worse and I am afraid they will have to take me away . . . The future is just old age and pain . . . My last wish is to be cremated so nobody will grieve over my grave—no one is to blame.

Jimmy

He put the note in an envelope and left it on the blotter in his studio. He walked out to the pool and threw himself in the shallow end, striking his head against the bottom.

This was the first and last time James Whale used his swimming pool.

THE GAS GIRLS

BARBARA BATES, a model born in Denver in 1925, made her movie debut in *Salome, Where She Danced,* an absurd camp cult classic film. (In it, she appears with Albert Dekker, another candidate for suicide.) She sought an "image" and was advised to become a blonde. When signed by Warner Bros. in 1947, producer William Orr told her, "You're not the blonde type. Be yourself." Herself, blonde or brunette, proved to be a very disturbed girl.

She worked at Warners for two years; one of her best roles there was in *June*

Bride with Bette Davis. She got the leading female role opposite Danny Kaye in *The Inspector General,* but much of her footage was cut at the insistence of Sylvia Fine—Mrs. Kaye. She was unhappy at Warners and had personal problems. She made the first of a series of suicide attempts, but L.A. is a company town, and the studio managed to keep reports of them out of the papers. At Fox she worked in *Cheaper by the Dozen* and appeared in an important scene at the end of *All About Eve,* as Phoebe, the ambitious girl who ingratiates herself with Anne Baxter. (Phoebe is obviously a budding Eve.) Her role in this memorable film was small, but it remains her best-remembered part. (*Eve* was "SSS"—a triple suicide movie. George Sanders and Marilyn Monroe were also in the cast.)

▲ Barbara Bates: she turned on the gas

Bates then appeared in *All Ashore*, directed by Richard Quine. (This was "SS"—suicide Ray McDonald appears in it with her.) Director Quine noted, "She was easy to work with, but with moods of depression." In 1953 she appeared as Jerry Lewis' girlfriend in *The Caddy*, and in 1954, at MGM, in *Rhapsody* as a music student with Elizabeth Taylor. Personal problems began to affect her work: she was taken off two big movies after shooting had begun. Her last film was *Apache Territory* (1958) for Columbia. She looked tired; the glow had disappeared. Her elderly English husband, Mr. Coan, died of cancer. Bates became a dental assistant. She severed all ties with Tinseltown and returned to Denver, got a job in a hospital, and married a childhood sweetheart. Shortly afterward, on March 18, 1969, she turned on the gas.

Bella Darvi: gas in Monte Carlo ▲

In June 1951 Fox mogul Darryl Zanuck and his wife Virginia were in Paris. They spotted actor friend Alex D'Arcy sitting at a sidewalk café on the Champs-Elysées. (D'Arcy was a specialist in gigolo roles.) He was with a sexy girl who immediately interested Zanuck. Of all Hollywood's "piggy" moguls, Zanuck was the biggest casting couch hog. The girl was Bayla Wegier, born in Poland. At twelve, the Nazis had put her in a concentration camp. In 1950 she married Alban Cavalade, a rich businessman, and frequented the gambling tables of the Riviera with him. They soon divorced.

The day following the meeting with the Zanucks, Bayla sent flowers to *Mrs.* Zanuck. Shortly afterward, Mr. Zanuck started "shtooping" the Polish girl. She told him she had to sell her clothing in order to pay off her gambling debts. Zanuck gave her $2,000 to reimburse the casinos and invited her to Hollywood. She turned up in Tinseltown in November 1952 and moved into the Zanucks' Santa Monica beach house. The daughter of the house, Susan Zanuck, and the Polish import hated each other at first sight.

Zanuck gave Bayla a screen test and changed her name to BELLA DARVI— from Darryl and Virginia. (The Zanucks and Darvi are said to have formed a *ménage à trois* during this period. Mrs. Zanuck had had a bit of a movie career of her own earlier in life: as Virginia Fox she appeared opposite Buster Keaton in several shorts made by the great comic in the early Twenties.)

Fox's publicity department started issuing its standard barrels of mendacious tripe on the new actress— all of which was scooped up by the papers. Hearst's *New York Journal-American* informed its readers that "A newly-arrived French doll by the name of Bella Darvi, who has the voice of Marlene Dietrich, the eyes of Simone Simon and the allure of Corinne Calvet, is hitting Hollywood with the impact of TNT. She's got zip, zoom and zowie and in parlez-vous she's ravissante, chi-chi and très élégante."

Zanuck put the "French doll" in a submarine, casting her as a French scientist's daughter holed up with a bunch of horny sailors on a secret mission in Arctic waters in Sam Fuller's *Hell and High Water.* He then cast her as Nefer, the courtesan, in the CinemaScope version of Mika Waltari's best-seller, *The Egyptian.* Marlon Brando was to play the male lead. A few readings were scheduled with the actors before shooting started. The night after the actors had gone through their first reading with director Michael Curtiz, Zanuck got a phone call from Brando's agent. Brando had already left for New York; he had decided not to do the movie. "He can't stand Bella Darvi," the agent told Zanuck.

Zanuck was bitten by what the French call *le démon du midi*—in plain English: middle-age macho menopause madness. He started behaving like a lovesick schoolboy. At an Oriental costume party at Ciro's to welcome back Terry Moore, who had been entertaining "the boys" in Korea, he got drunk, dropped his suspenders, and started doing acrobatics on the dinner table. He wanted to prove he was still a young stud. The photographers had a field day. Virginia dragged him home. The next day Zanuck called his friend Henry Luce in New York requesting that all pictures of his party antics be killed. *Life* nonetheless printed a full-page picture of the mogul doing his besotted trapeze act. Susan told Virginia that pig daddy's behavior was due to his infatuation with Darvi. Virginia threw Bella out of the house.

The public threw her off the screen. Moviegoers did not respond to her, in spite of the studio's hoopla. There were no Bella Darvi fan clubs. Her "zip, zoom

and zowie" had somehow disappeared on the way from Fox's P.R. department to the movie theaters. The critics spoke of her as "Unconvincing," "charmless," "giving no sign of magnetism," "contributing very little to the movie . . ." *The Egyptian* was judged a "pretentious risible parody."

Bella returned to France. Zanuck followed. It was the beginning of the end of his career (although he would hit the jackpot once again with *The Longest Day*). He had been head of production at Fox for twenty years. But times were changing; the old Hollywood was about to hit the skids. Instead of remaining there to consolidate his position, Zanuck was off in Europe chasing pussy. In 1956 he resigned as production head at Fox. He was going to make independent films—in which roles could be written for his mistresses.

Darvi was soon back in action at the gambling tables of Monte Carlo, and lost a fortune. Zanuck was short of cash. He was obliged to borrow money from Howard Hughes to pay off Bella's debts. His romance with Darvi finally ended with much bitterness. He consoled himself with Juliette Greco, and then with Irina Demick and Geneviève Gilles.

Darvi attempted suicide in Monaco in August 1962, at Roquebrune in April 1966, and in June 1968 in her Monte Carlo hotel—and botched each attempt. She was then put in a clinic on the Riviera. Her face was blotchy, splotchy, and puffy—she did not look "chi-chi and très élégante." Monaco's Hotel de Paris had kept her clothing—in lieu of an unpaid hotel bill. Zanuck paid the bill. She went right back to the gambling tables and found a new gent to pay her debts—temporarily.

She was soon friendless, broke, and again deep in debt. Zanuck would no longer bail her out. Her number finally came up on September 10, 1971. She opened the gas taps of the cooking stove in her modest Monte Carlo apartment. A week later, her stinking decomposed corpse was discovered.

In 1931 the public saw a pert teenage ingenue, CLAIRE MAYNARD, in two Fox films: Henry King's *Over the Hill,* a tear-jerker about mother love, with Mae Marsh and James Dunn, and *Good Sport,* in which Miss Maynard could be seen alongside John Boles, Minna Gombell, and Hedda Hopper. The petite blonde had been born in Brooklyn and, while modeling in a dress shop, had caught the eye of a Fox talent scout. Fox did not renew her contract, and after a few years of stage work, she felt herself over the hill and was not a good sport about it. She turned on the gas in July 1941.

A 26-GUN SALUTE TO HOLLYWOOD SUICIDES

Tall, lithe, and handsome, ROSS ALEXANDER was born in Brooklyn in 1907. He appeared on Broadway in *Let Us Be Gay,* was signed by Paramount and brought to Hollywood in 1932. Most of the rest of his career was spent at Warner Bros., where his major films were Frank Borzage's *Flirtation Walk* (as Oskie), Max Reinhardt's *A Midsummer Night's Dream* (as Demetrius), and Michael Curtiz's *Captain Blood* (as Jeremy Pitt) with Errol Flynn. Actress Aleta Freel, his first wife, had little success with her career; she killed herself with a rifle in 1935. He then married screen actress Anne Nagel, who had appeared with him in several films. On January 2, 1937, the twenty-nine-year-old actor, who was deeply in debt,

Ross Alexander: replaced by Reagan ▲

worked on *The Conqueror,* a "cursed" film about Genghis Khan (it starred his close friend, John Wayne), which was shot on location in Nevada near the site of an atomic bomb test. Its director, Dick Powell, and two of its stars, Wayne, and Agnes Moorehead, died of lung cancer; the female lead, Susan Hayward, died from a brain tumor. While working on *From Russia With Love,* Armendariz learned that he had lymph cancer. On June 18, 1963, after he was admitted to the UCLA Medical Center, he shot himself in the hospital with a gun he had smuggled in. Mrs. Armendariz said her husband generally carried a gun with him.

entered the barn on his ranch and shot himself in the head. Later that year, Ronald Reagan began his career at Warner Bros. It has been said that Reagan was signed by the studio as a replacement for Alexander and that Reagan's voice and manner somewhat resembled that of the dead actor. (They both had radio announcer's voices.) The difference was that Alexander had charm and talent.

Although PEDRO ARMENDARIZ was considered a Mexican actor, his mother, Della Hastings, was American. When she died, he went to live with her relatives in San Antonio, then studied engineering at California Polytech. After becoming Mexico's top male star, he appeared in over forty American movies. His virile presence was an asset to several John Ford pictures—*The Fugitive, Fort Apache,* and *Three Godfathers.* He appeared in John Huston's *We Were Strangers* and as The Sultan in Michael Curtiz's *Francis of Assisi.* In 1952 he was awarded a Mexican Oscar. In 1955 he

DONALD "RED" BARRY saw the light of day as Donald Barry d'Acosta in 1912 in Houston. He was a football star in high school, then acquired some stage experience and made his movie debut in a clumsy 1936 RKO cheapie, *Night Waitress.* His career really got going in 1940, when he appeared in the title role of *The Adventures of Red Ryder,* a serial, and became a popular star of Republic Westerns. The 1942 *Motion Picture Herald* Fame Poll voted him one of the top ten money-making Western stars.

He was featured in *Sinners in Paradise* (directed by James Whale, who also killed himself) and in several films of Howard Hawks—*The Crowd Roars, Only Angels Have Wings* and *Rio Lobo.* During the Red scare hysterics of the McCarthy period, producers asked him to change his name. When he refused, stories were planted in the fan magazines, explaining that Barry was not nicknamed "Red" because of his politics, but because of his flaming red hair, which was as bright as that of Susan Hayward—with whom he can be seen in *I'll Cry Tomorrow.* Barry directed and starred in *Jesse James' Women* in 1953. He can also be seen in *Orca* and *SOS Tidal Wave.*

Pedro Armendariz: hospital shot ▲

He married actress Peggy Steward. On July 17, 1980, after an argument with his wife, Barry shot and killed himself.

Screenwriter, producer, and director PAUL BERN wrote scripts for Lubitsch (*The Marriage Circle*) and Von Sternberg, before he became Irving Thalberg's top assistant at MGM, where he supervised the production of many of Garbo's films. When he married Jean Harlow in 1932, he was twice her age. This talented man seems to have had a potency problem. A bare two months after their wedding, he shot himself in the head with a .38 pistol in his wife's bedroom. The suicide note apologized to Harlow for the events of the previous night—apparently Bern had attempted to penetrate the platinum blond star with a dildo.

HERMAN BING was one of the most lovable and amusing character comics in the history of the cinema. He was born in Frankfurt; his father, Max Bing, was a well-known operatic baritone. Herman appeared in vaudeville and

circuses in Germany. In 1926, he arrived in Hollywood in the entourage of the great German director F. W. Murnau, who had been invited to this country by Fox. Murnau knew little English; Bing translated for him. He worked as a writer and assistant director for Murnau and also served as the director's major domo and scapegoat.

When Murnau was killed in an auto accident near Santa Barbara, Bing and some colleagues were following close behind in Bing's car. (Murnau was on his way to New York for the world premiere of *Tabu*. He had been told by an astrologer not to go by car; he was warned that if he did there would be a catastrophic accident. He changed his plans and decided to go by boat from San Francisco, which would get to New York via the Panama Canal. The fatal accident occurred on the way to the boat.)

Fox production chief Winfield Sheehan offered Bing an acting job after Murnau's death. He rolled his "r"s at great length and endeared himself to audiences by deliciously mutilating the English language in comic fashion. He was called "the tongue-twisting dialectician." His voice was once compared to the sound of a schnauzer talking in its sleep.

Bing appeared in dozens of films, including *Dinner at Eight, The Bowery, Twentieth Century, The Black Cat, Footlight Parade* (as James Cagney's orchestrator it is a joy to hear him recite, in Bingian fashion, the names of all the songs he can think of with "puzzy cat" in the title), *The Music Goes Round, The Great Ziegfeld, Maytime, Every Day's a Holiday* (with Mae West), and *The Great Waltz*.

During the Thirties, he often appeared in stage shows at Loew's Theatres—especially at New York's Loew's State, where he was a great favorite with audiences.

◀ Don "Red" Barry: saved the last bullet for himself   ▲ Paul Bern: disappointed Harlow

---

CLYDE BRUCKMAN was one of the key figures in the history of American screen comedy. His first movie job was writing scripts for comedian Monty Banks. In 1921 he went to work for Buster Keaton, who always regarded him as his most talented gagman. Keaton and Bruckman remained lifelong friends. For Keaton, Bruckman wrote *The Three Ages, Our Hospitality, Sherlock Jr., The Navigator, Seven Chances,* and *The Cameraman* among others. Keaton's best film, *The General,* was both written and co-directed by Bruckman. His scripts for Harold Lloyd included *The Freshman, Professor Beware, The Cat's Paw, Welcome Danger, Feet First,* and *Movie Crazy.* He easily adapted his work to the rhythm and character of whichever comedian he was working for, and always brought out the best qualities in each performer. (*Movie Crazy,* for instance, is Lloyd's best sound film and one of the finest movies ever made about Hollywood. It also includes some remarkably kinky romantic situations.)

Bruckman directed a few of Laurel and Hardy's best movies: *Putting Pants on Philip,* which involves some outrageous homosexual gags, *The Battle of the Century,* with the best custard pie sequence ever made, *Leave 'Em Laughing,* and *The Call of the Cuckoo.* He later directed two memorable W. C. Fields pictures: *The Fatal Glass of Beer* and *The Man on the Flying Trapeze.*

As the Thirties progressed, Bruckman's alcoholism lost him jobs on major movies. He worked on B pictures, wrote scripts for the "Blondie" series and for some of the shorts Keaton made at Columbia. When he sold Universal a few gags he had originally written for Lloyd's films and they were used in a 1945 Joan Davis quickie, *She Gets Her Man,* Harold Lloyd (who was a multi-millionaire) sued Universal and was awarded several million dollars in damages. This incident made it difficult

In the Forties, he found it difficult to get work. His daughter said, "Dad plodded from studio to studio seeking work, but his type of comedy was no longer in demand. He didn't need the money. He just couldn't stand not working. He had to act and when he couldn't get any parts he became unhappy and nervous."

His daughter and son-in-law were sitting down to breakfast in their Los Angeles home on January 10, 1948, when they heard a shot. Bing was staying with them. They rushed to his bedroom and found the dear man on the floor with a bullet wound in his heart and an old-fashioned revolver in his hand. A suicide note to his daughter was succinct: "Dear Ellen, Such insomnia. I had to commit suicide. Your Daddy." His last film had been *Where Do We Go From Here?*

Herman Bing: cure for insomnia ▲

for Bruckman to find work. He did some uninspired scripts for The Three Stooges and for Keaton's TV show. He soon became a familiar sight around Hollywood—stumbling about with a pint bottle sticking out of his pocket.

In 1955 he borrowed Keaton's pistol "for a little target practice." He left a note to his wife saying he was going out because he didn't want to mess up her nice living room, adding, "I have no money to pay for a funeral." He went into a phone booth on Santa Monica Boulevard and blew his brains out.

Speaking of the Twenties, Bruckman once said, "I often wish that I were back there with Buster and the gang, in *that* Hollywood. But I don't have the lamp to rub. It was one of a kind."

WILFRED BUCKLAND was Hollywood's first great art director and was called "the founder of Hollywood cinema art." Until he arrived in Hollywood, Cecil B. De Mille had never used anyone specifically delegated to design sets. De Mille's mother recommended Buckland, who had been responsible for the scenic beauty of David Belasco's stage productions. For years, he worked eighteen hours a day, seven days a week, often involved in bitter disputes with De Mille.

Several important innovations should be credited to him, among them the use of klieg lights. He originated interior lighting in the American film industry. Until then, directors relied on natural sunshine. Buckland's use of arc lamps produced dramatic lighting for the first time on the screen. He did the sets for De Mille's The Cheat, Joan the Woman (with Geraldine Farrar), and Male and Female (with Swanson). The bathrooms for De Mille heroines, which were conceived as "shrines" to feminine beauty, were designed by Buckland. De Mille generally treated him abominably; for years the miserly director paid his art

director only $75 a week. After many bitter disputes, Buckland parted company with De Mille in the mid-Twenties. His greatest single achievement was the larger-than-life décor for the Douglas Fairbanks Robin Hood (1922).

In later years, he did some work for MGM, and, even when past eighty, went to the studio every day looking for work. The old man by then looked a bit like Teddy Roosevelt. In Europe, a figure like Buckland would have been loaded with honors for his contribution to the art of the film. In Hollywood, in his later years, he was neglected and jobless. The Depression had left him penniless.

His only child, Wilfred Buckland, Jr. (known as Bill), had gone to Princeton and mixed with high society. After the family fortune vanished with the Depression and his mother, the lovely actress Vida Buckland, died of cancer, Bill had a breakdown. The only thing he knew anything about was tennis (for a while he had sought a living as a tennis instructor). He was homosexual and plagued by guilt because of his father's fierce disapproval. He became an alcoholic. When found sobbing on Hollywood Boulevard in an alcoholic stupor, he was taken to Camarillo, the state institute for the insane, where he was given shock treatment—which did him more harm than good. When he was released, his old friend, Jesse Lasky, Jr., got him a "go-fer" job on the set of De Mille's Northwest Mounted Police. When the picture was finished, Bill found himself unemployed and hit the bottle again.

It was clear to old Wilfred that his son would never go on the wagon permanently—and would never be "normal." He realized that he did not have much longer to live, and that when he died there would be no one to take care of his gay alcoholic son. On July 18, 1946, while Bill was sleeping, his father shot him in the head with a .32 caliber Mauser automatic, then shot himself. He left a suicide note which said: "I am taking Billy with me."

Buckland had always been a great marksman. The shooting range in his cellar was one of his favorite haunts. He enjoyed teaching young men how to use a pistol. A 1917 *Picture Play* article on Buckland concluded with: "His hobby is shooting, and on the walls of his home [are] handguns of every make and description, from the time guns were invented. He has the long gun of the Arab and the short blunderbuss. In spite of a heavy work load at the studio— every week he must find some time to shoot."

Actor JAMES CARDWELL shot himself to death in Hollywood on February 4, 1954. He was thirty-three, and had appeared in *The Sullivans, Tokyo Joe, He Walked by Night, Canyon Passage,* and as Sergeant Hoskins in Lewis Milestone's *A Walk in the Sun.*

ARTHUR EDMUND CAREW was born in Armenia, came to this country as a

child, and appeared on the stage for eight years. He entered movies in 1919 in films with Constance Talmadge, but, in spite of his rugged good looks, because of his intense and somewhat spooky manner, soon became associated with horror films and melodramas in which he was most villainous. He can be seen in *The Palace of Darkened Windows, The Phantom of the Opera* (as The Persian), *The Ghost Breaker, The Claw, The Cat and the Canary, Dr. X,* and *The Mystery of the Wax Museum.* His last film was *Charlie Chan's Secret* (1936). He also appeared in Garbo's first American movie, *The Torrent,* and in *The Gay Diplomat.*

Carew reached the pinnacle of his career in *Trilby* (1923), in which he starred as Svengali. It was a hit with the public and critics alike. *The New York Times* headlined its review A SATURNINE SVENGALI, and went on to note: "But charming as Andrée Lafayette is as Trilby, it is Arthur Edmund Carew's revelation of Svengali that dominates this production. His makeup is as true as steel. He has the long fingers, the sharp, aquiline nose, the hollow, cadaverous cheeks, the black matted beard and unkempt hair of the Svengali of the book. His dark eyes are scintillating and gruesome." Shortly after making *Charlie Chan's Secret,* Carew suffered a paralytic stroke and ended his life with a gun on April 23, 1937.

LESTER CUNEO's first film was *Graustark,* with Francis X. Bushman. He appeared in *The Haunted Pajamas,* then met Francelia Billington when they were both working in a Tom Mix movie. They were married and appeared together in a few movies. Cuneo was a handsome piece of silent screen beefcake; he often played a villain, but was generally more attractive than the hero. His marriage went kaput. On November 1, 1925, a

Arthur Edmund Carew: scintillating Svengali ▲

few days after his wife sued for divorce, he went to the home they had shared, had a noisy quarrel with her, then shot himself. Hunky Lester—dead at thirty-seven.

KARL DANE, born in Copenhagen in 1886, was a tall, gawky, funny-looking gent who arrived in Hollywood during World War I and was cast in two anti-German propaganda films, *My Four Years in Germany* and *To Hell with the Kaiser.* His film career didn't amount to much until 1925, when he hit the big time in the role of Slim, the fearless steeplejack riveter who is recruited into the Army and is killed in no-man's-land in King Vidor's *The Big Parade.* The movie was a huge hit; it ran for two years at the Astor theater on Broadway,

and did a great deal to establish MGM as a major studio. Director Vidor remarked, *"The Big Parade* advanced Karl Dane way up the ladder of fame."

It was a slippery ladder. Dane appeared with Tom Mix, with Marion Davies, and played a shifty Arab in *The Son of the Sheik* with Valentino. Toward the end of the silent era he appeared in a series of popular comic shorts with George K. Arthur. His last important movie was George Hill's *The Big House* (1930).

Unfortunately, Dane could not get rid of his impenetrable Danish accent. He made a serial on Poverty Row, but the ex-MGM star ended up running a hot dog stand near the main entrance to the studio. On April 14, 1934, he took out a batch of his old press clippings, his rave

Karl Dane: incurable accent ▲

reviews, his MGM contracts, and spread them out on a table in his tacky furnished room. He stretched out on the clippings and put a bullet through his head.

BOB DUNCAN, born in Kansas in 1904, was a minor-league cowboy star of Monogram and PRC poverty row Westerns during the Forties (*Tumbleweed Trail, Rainbow over the Rockies, Song of the Sierra*) who got the draw on himself—dead with his own gun, March 13, 1967.

Handsome blond Texan TOM FORMAN broke into films with Lasky and then acted in and directed Paramount movies. He played opposite Gloria Swanson in De Mille's *For Better or Worse* (1919) and directed Lon Chaney in *Shadows* (1922). He was recuperating from a nervous breakdown at the home of his parents in Venice, California, when he put a gun to his heart and pulled the trigger on November 7, 1926. Dead at thirty-four; his last screen appearance had been opposite Viola Dana in *Kosher Kitty Kelly.*

CLAUDE GILLINGWATER was born in Missouri in 1870. Apprenticed to a lawyer uncle, he ran away from home to join a wandering repertory company that

Claude Gillingwater: enough is enough ▲

was passing through town. He worked on the New York stage, then made his film debut in 1921 opposite Mary Pickford in *Little Lord Fauntleroy.* The actor was six foot three inches, and therefore a perfect visual foil for Pickford in this movie, in which she was a twenty-four-year-old woman playing a ten-year-old girl. His great height made her seem more diminutive and convincingly little girl-boyish. He bulked large later next to Shirley Temple in *Poor Little Rich Girl* (most people looked smaller next to Gillingwater).

He worked with William Haines in Vidor's *Three Wise Fools;* one of his last silent movies was *Ham and Eggs at the Front.* His talkies include *Dumbbells in Ermine, Daddy Long Legs* (with Janet Gaynor), Capra's *Broadway Bill, A Tale of Two Cities* (as Jarvis Lorry), and John Ford's *The Prisoner of Shark Island.*

In 1936, while acting in a scene with Jack Oakie in *Florida Special* at Paramount, he fell from a platform, injured his back, and found it difficult to perform from then on. His wife died; depression took hold. On November 1, 1939, he blew his brains out in his North Bedford Drive home in Beverly Hills. His suicide note read: "To the Police, I am ending my life because, in my advanced age, in my physical condition, there is no chance of ever being well again and I will not permit myself to become a helpless lingering invalid."

JONATHAN HALE was born in Canada in 1891. He worked briefly as a diplomat before entering films in 1934. He was one of the busiest character actors in Hollywood, appearing in nearly three hundred movies during his twenty-two-year career. He was often seen as a churlish businessman, and is best remembered for his performances as Mr. Dithers, Dagwood's boss, in the popular "Blondie" series made by Columbia. He was something of a series

"specialist," appearing in Charlie Chan, Saint, Maisie, Hardy Family, and Dr. Gillespie movies. In Fritz Lang's *You Only Live Once* Hale was the district attorney; he was Debege in Lang's *Hangmen Also Die.* He played Mr. Anthony (Robert Walker's father) in Hitchcock's *Strangers on a Train,* and appeared with Paul Kelly in *Duffy of San Quentin.* After his retirement, Hale went to live in the Motion Picture Country House at Woodland Halls, California. He shot himself in his cottage on March 2, 1966; the pistol was found next to his body. Attendants said he had been depressed for some time.

BOBBY HARRON was born into a poor Irish family in Greenwich Village. The adolescent Bobby needed a part-time job; one of the brothers at his parochial

▲ Bobby Harron: the morgue instead of the movies

215

school sent him to the Biograph Studio on Fourteenth Street. He was hired by Wallace McCutcheon (another eventual suicide), who gave him a job in the cutting room at $5 a week. He was befriended by D. W. Griffith, and was cast opposite Mary Pickford, Lillian Gish, and then Mae Marsh, in *Judith of Bethulia.* He played four roles in *The Birth of a Nation.* His best performance was that of The Boy in the modern-day sequence of *Intolerance.* His brother Charles was killed in a car crash in 1916. His sister Theresa died during an epidemic of Spanish flu. On September 1, 1920, he was staying at the Hotel Seymour in New York, having come east for the premiere of Griffith's *Way Down East.* By then it was clear that Richard Barthelmess had become Griffith's preferred male star. Barthelmess had scored a great success the previous year opposite Gish in *Broken Blossoms.* Harron went to the morgue instead of to the movies. He was found dead in his room at the Seymour, a revolver at his side, a bullet in his right lung.

JOSE ALEX HAVIER can be seen as Yankee Salazar in Tay Garnett's 1943 MGM production, *Bataan.* He went *Back to Bataan* with John Wayne in 1945 in the RKO movie of the same name. Again with Wayne, he appeared as Benny in *They Were Expendable,* John Ford's saga of PT boats in action. Havier shot himself December 18, 1945. His last film was released in 1946, after his death. It was called *Nobody Lives Forever.*

GEORGE HILL entered films at Biograph and worked as a stagehand, screenwriter, and cameraman. He saw action at Gallipoli during World War I. He was tall, dark and handsome.

He started directing in 1921, and made *Tell It to the Marines,* one of Lon Chaney's better movies. He directed the superb night warfare scenes of Vidor's *The Big Parade,* but his masterpiece was *The Big House* (1930), the first important talking picture about criminals. In 1934, Thalberg sent a film crew to China headed by Hill, who had been selected to direct *The Good Earth.* He brought back a lot of good footage of Chinese cities and countryside and two live Chinese water buffalo. One fine morning in 1934, a few days before shooting was scheduled to begin on *The Good Earth,* George Hill blew his head off with a hunting rifle.

When D. W. Griffith arrived at the Biograph Studio on New York's Fourteenth Street, the house director was "Old Man" McCutcheon, who had directed some of the very first peep-show movies. The Old Man bought a script from Griffith and hired him as an actor. The Old Man, however, worked at a slow pace, turning out only one movie a week. When Griffith was given a chance at directing, he worked quickly and was soon making all of Biograph's films. The rest is history.

At the time of Griffith's arrival at the studio, the Old Man's son, WALLACE MCCUTCHEON, JR., was working there at a variety of jobs. He left Biograph late in 1908. During World War I, although he was an American, he enlisted in the English Army; his valor earned him a promotion to the rank of major. He was wounded, shell-shocked, and had to have a silver plate put in his skull.

After the war, he returned to New York, married Pearl White and acted opposite her in the 1919 serial *The Black Secret,* and in a 1920 feature, *The Thief.* They were later divorced, and shortly afterward, McCutcheon was admitted to a private sanitarium. On January 27, 1928, he killed himself with a bullet to the head. A revolver was found in his hand; his pockets were full of clippings about Pearl White.

Three guns—three actors: NELSON MCDOWELL (Maurice Tourneur's *The Last of the Mohicans, Scaramouche* with Ramon Novarro, *College Swing* with Bob Hope), JOHN MITCHELL (*Mr. Skeffington* with Bette Davis), and BERT MOORHOUSE *(Sunset Boulevard, The Big Hangover)* shot and killed themselves on November 3, 1947, January 19, 1951, and January 26, 1954, respectively.

Superman Kills Himself!—no, not a new episode. This was for real. In 1959 GEORGE REEVES did what no one else had ever managed to do—he killed The Man of Steel.

Reeves (real name George Bessolo) was born in Iowa in 1914 and trained for an acting career at the Pasadena Playhouse. He first turned up on the screen as Brent Tarleton in *Gone With the Wind,* then appeared in *Torrid Zone, Argentine Nights* (with the Andrews Sisters), Walsh's *Strawberry Blonde, Blood and Sand* (as Captain Pierre Lauren), *Jungle Jim,* De Mille's *Samson and Delilah* (as the Wounded Messenger), Lang's *Rancho Notorious,* and *Superman and the Mole Men.* His muscular six-foot-two-inch frame and prowess in judo were important assets in helping him land the job of TV Superman. The series was not only popular here, it became one of the top programs in Japan, and Reeves received a letter from Emperor Hirohito telling him how much he enjoyed the show. Reeves later became discouraged over the slump in his career after he stopped making the Superman series.

There were a few curious aspects to his death. He shot himself through the head with a 9mm Luger on June 16, 1959, and was found naked on the bed in his Benedict Canyon home. A few seconds before the shot was heard, his fiancée, New York socialite Lenore

Lemmon, predicted to visitors in the house that Reeves was going to kill himself. Miss Lemmon had been downstairs when, about 1:00 A.M. some friends rang the bell. Reeves came

▲ George Reeves: killed by Superman

down, irate at being disturbed at that late hour, and threatened to throw them out. When he went upstairs, Miss Lemmon remarked, "Now he's opening the drawer to get the gun." A shot rang out. "See, I told you, he's shot himself." Two months before his death, Reeves had gone to the L.A. District Attorney's office to report that he was being harassed by an anonymous phone caller, whom he believed to be Mrs. Toni Mannix, the wife of Eddie Mannix, the vice-president of Loew's Inc., and former general manager of MGM. Yet Reeves left the bulk of his estate to Mrs. Mannix.

His fiancée blamed Superman for Reeves' death. She said Superman had so dominated the actor's life—he had become so identified with the role—that it was impossible for him to get other movie parts.

Leo Slezak, born in Czechoslovakia, was one of the greatest operatic tenors of the century. For more than twenty-five

years he was a mainstay of the Vienna Opera, the idol of the Viennese. He often sang Wagnerian roles at the Met. He was also a movie star and appeared in many pictures made in Austria and Germany (*Rendezvous in Wien, Die Blonde Carmen*).

Leo's son, WALTER SLEZAK, was born in Vienna in 1902, and was a medical student when he was discovered by director Michael Curtiz. He appeared in Curtiz's epic Biblical movie, *Sodom und Gomorra/ Queen of Sin and the Spectacle of Sodom and Gomorrah,* made in 1922. His most memorable early performance was the title role in *Mikaël/Chained/The Story of the Third Sex.* This masterpiece, directed by the great Danish director Carl Dreyer in Berlin in 1914, was the first important film ever made on the subject of homosexuality. It concerns the love of a middle-aged painter (played by the Danish movie director Benjamin Christensen) for his young male model (Slezak).

When he appeared in *Mikaël,* Slezak was slim, youthful, and epicene. During the next few years, he gained a great deal of weight and could no longer be cast as a romantic lead. He found himself thrust into character parts. He came to this country and appeared often in Broadway shows, making his American movie debut in 1942. His role in *Fanny* on Broadway earned him both a Tony and a New York Critics Award in 1955. In 1957, he appeared in *The Gypsy Baron* at the Met.

He can be seen alongside Ronald Reagan in *Bedtime for Bonzo* and appeared with another eventual suicide, Barbara Bates, in the Danny Kaye vehicle, *The Inspector General.* One of his most impressive performances was as Judy Garland's fiancé, Don Pedro Vargas, in Vincente Minnelli's *The Pirate.* (*The Pirate* is "SSS"—a three suicide movie. In addition to Slezak, its credits

include costume supervision by Irene and instrumental arrangements by Conrad Salinger—both of these talented artists killed themselves.)

During World War II, Adolf Hitler, movie fan par excellence, saw Walter as the U-Boat captain in Hitchcock's *Lifeboat* and in Jean Renoir's anti-Nazi propaganda film, *This Land Is Mine.* Der Führer did not like what he saw—he fined Leo Slezak 100,000 marks. The father was made to pay for "the sins" of the son.

Walter Slezak's last movie role was in *The Mysterious House of Dr. C.* (1976), in which he played Dr. Coppelius. He was afflicted by a heart ailment, which depressed him considerably. In 1983 he shot and killed himself with a .38 in his home in Manhasset, Long Island.

Stuntwoman MARY WIGGINS, who in the course of her career had survived many a dangerous scene, died instantly when she shot herself in her North Hollywood home on December 10, 1945.

GIG YOUNG was born in Minnesota (real name: Byron Barr). His father was a cook in a reformatory. Young Byron worked as a used car salesman, then got his acting start at the Pasadena Playhouse, where he was spotted by a talent scout from Warner Bros. His first good role was that of an artist named Gig Young in *The Gay Sisters*, with Barbara Stanwyck. The preview audience liked him; the studio suggested he take the name of the character.

After making *Old Acquaintance* (with Bette Davis), he enlisted in the Coast Guard and served three years. His second wife, Sophie Rubinstein, a drama coach at Warners, died of cancer soon after their marriage. Young was an alcoholic. In *Come Fill the Cup* (1951)

he played an alcoholic who is saved from suicide by Jimmy Cagney. Young married Elizabeth Montgomery in 1956; they were divorced in 1963. He won a Best Supporting Actor Oscar for his performance as the dance marathon pitchman in the 1969 movie *They Shoot Horses, Don't They?*

Young suffered from skin cancer. Although not life-threatening, he eventually moved to New York because the strong California sun aggravated the condition. While shooting a movie in Hong Kong he met Kim Schmidt, who worked in an art gallery there. He was sixty-four—she was thirty-one. They married, and three weeks after the wedding, in his posh duplex in the Osborne apartments opposite Carnegie Hall on Fifty-seventh Street, Young killed his new wife and himself. He was found holding a .38 revolver. The actor and his wife had each been killed by a single gunshot to the head. They were carefully dressed, and there was no sign of a struggle. This led to conjecture of a suicide pact. The police made a bizarre discovery: in addition to the murder weapon, Young's apartment contained three other revolvers and 350 rounds of ammunition.

In 1971 Red Buttons said of Young: "Beneath Gig's light-hearted sophistication is a man who needs an arm around him." Gig Young himself once stated in an interview: "You can't tell about people from their outside. They've spent a lifetime covering up their fears." His last movie—the movie he was making when he met the girl he was to wed and kill—was entitled *The Game of Death.*

DEATH BY HANGING

By a curious coincidence, ALBERT DEKKER, who hanged himself, made his movie debut in *The Great Garrick*, directed by James Whale, who drowned himself. (He later appeared in another Whale movie as the foppish Louis XIII in the kinky *The Man With the Iron Mask.*)

This odd-looking actor was born in Brooklyn, né Albert van Dekker. While in college, he befriended Alfred Lunt, and then appeared on Broadway in Eugene O'Neill's *Marco Millions,* in which Lunt starred as Marco Polo. From 1944 to 1946, Dekker served as Democratic assemblyman of the 57th District in the California legislature.

Dekker looked spooky naturally—and was often cast in spooky roles. The most memorable of all was the title role in *Dr. Cyclops,* directed by Ernest Schoedsack, one of the creators of *King Kong.* In it, Dekker played the mad Dr. Thorkel, who lived someplace up the Amazon and who reduced anyone foolish enough to visit him to the size of a small doll. Dr. Thorkel was bald and goggle-eyed; very nearsighted, he wore huge lenses that distorted his face. When he picked up the other characters, whom he had miniaturized, Dekker looked like a squinty clean-shaven King Kong. He also made history in this flick—he was the first monster in full three-strip Technicolor.

He also appeared in *Suspense, The Killers, Slave Girl, Tarzan's Magic Fountain, Destination Murder, Kiss Me Deadly, East of Eden, Suddenly Last Summer,* and in a great period suspense melodrama, *Experiment Perilous,* with Hedy Lamarr. Opposite Susan Hayward, in *Among the Living,* he played twin brothers, one of whom is a homicidal maniac. In *Seven Sinners,* he got the girl for once, and sailed off into the sunset with Marlene Dietrich—who was wearing a gown designed by Irene (another suicide). His last film was *The Wild Bunch.*

Dekker's sixteen-year-old son, Jan, was found shot to death in 1967 at Hastings-on-Hudson, New York. Authorities listed the death as self-inflicted. On May 5, 1968, Albert Dekker was found dead in his Hollywood apartment. He was discovered bound and handcuffed, hanging from a shower rod in the bathroom. The bathroom was secured from the inside by a chainlock. The corpse was clad in women's dainty silk lingerie, and in his final moments Dekker had written some unprintable things about himself on his body—in flaming red lipstick.

Ziegfeld discovered the Dolly Sisters dancing in vaudeville. He immediately hired them for his 1911 Follies. They were small and dark, identical twins with a somewhat Oriental exotic charm. Originally Hungarians who had grown up on New York's Lower East Side, Jancsi had changed her name to JENNY DOLLY, Roszicka had changed hers to Rosie.

The Great Ziegfeld dressed them in

Albert Dekker: all hung up ▲

skirts made of dozens of white feathers, capped them with diamond headdresses, and set them awhirl dancing in his shows. Diamond Jim Brady fell in love with them; every millionaire in New York was soon at their feet. In 1915, Jenny starred in the movie *Call of the Dance,* made by the Kalem Studios, then co-starred with her sister in Metro's *The Million Dollar Dollies* (1918).

They went to Europe and Jenny became the queen of the roulette tables at Monte Carlo. She lost and won fabulous sums and converted her winnings into the biggest collection of diamonds that had ever been seen on the Riviera on one human being. She was the gay butterfly; Rosie was less frolicsome than her sister. While Jenny was playing roulette, Rosie went back to the old country and spent some time doing charity work with orphans in Hungary.

They then appeared together at the Casino de Paris and conquered Paris. They introduced the Charleston and the Black Bottom to Europe. They bought a chateau in Fontainebleau where they gave wild and elaborate parties. One of Jenny's admirers was the Prince of Wales—later the Duke of Windsor. They were applauded—at close range—by King Christian of Denmark and King Carol of Rumania. They appeared at Paris' Moulin Rouge, where they received star billing with Maurice Chevalier.

Jenny fell in love with a French aviator, Max Constant. It was a mad affair, punctuated by disputes and reconciliations. After a lover's quarrel with Max, she had a fling with Gordon Selfridge, the owner of London's famous department store. He offered her $10,000,000 if she would marry him. She still loved Max—but she loved diamonds even more. She went off with Max Constant for one last weekend fling before her marriage to Selfridge. The

lovers' car got into an accident near Bordeaux and Jenny was nearly killed. She spent months undergoing surgery at the American Hospital in Paris. Selfridge brought in the world's most prominent plastic surgeons in an attempt to restore her beauty. It did not work. She remained broken in spirit and body.

Rosie had married a rich Chicago businessman. She and her husband brought Jenny back to America. After a few years there was talk of a comeback—but the comeback never came. On June 1, 1941, at the age of forty-eight, Jenny Dolly took some drapes, made a noose from them, and hanged herself from a shower rod in her Hollywood apartment.

In 1945 George Jessel (whose girlfriend, Abigail Adams, killed herself with a fatal quantity of Seconal in 1955) produced a biopic called *The Dolly Sisters* for Fox. It starred Betty Grable and June Haver. The production values were lavish but the script hardly did justice to the lives of the fabulous Dollies.

Actor FRANK GABY, who appeared in Universal's *Mr. Dynamite,* hanged himself on February 12, 1945. He was forty-nine.

Mae West had a weakness for boxers. Brawny pugilist JOHN INDRISANO can be seen with great Mae in one of her best vehicles, *Every Day's a Holiday.* Mae's two major lovers during the late Thirties were Indrisano and Chalky Wright, a fighter who became a chauffeur. Indrisano and Mae lived together for some time. She completely dominated him, but enjoyed the workouts he gave her. He got La West to jog, and exercised her like a boxer. Beefy Johnny also appeared in *Two Fisted, Ringside Maisie, In This Corner,* and *Joe Palooka in The Counterpunch*—in all of which his

boxing ability is on display. Some of his other movies were *Lost in a Harem, Lulu Belle, The Lady Gambles* (with Barbara Stanwyck), *The Yellow Cab Man,* and *A House Is Not a Home.* Indrisano hanged himself in his San Fernando Valley home on July 9, 1968.

The Christine Jorgensen Story, director Irving Rapper's penultimate film, was not exactly his finest cinematic hour. (That surely had been *Now Voyager,* Bette Davis' most inspired soap opera. Rapper also directed *The Gay Sisters,* in which suicide-to-be Gig Young, adopted his nom de screen.) But few who saw the 1970 biopic of America's most famous sex change personality will forget it. One of its assets was a blond cutie-pie moppet named TRENT LEHMAN, who played Christine as a boy—George Jorgensen in her pre-Christine days. In one scene, George dons his mother's long white

dress and smears lipstick on his cute little puss. The role led to the casting of Trent as Butch Everett in the ABC television series *Nanny and the Professor,* which ran for two seasons—1970–1971. It was his only real break. He became typecast as Butch, had trouble finding work as a fast-growing adolescent, and for the ten years following *Nanny,* he did not hold any kind of job. He grew tired of knocking on doors. At age ten, he had been earning $1200 a week; at twenty, he could not find a four-buck-an-hour job. After his suicide, his mother said it broke her heart to see how unwanted he felt—he who once had been so popular. The job rejections changed his personality. From the age of thirteen, he became sullen and withdrawn. When Bobbi Lehman discovered that her son was hanging out with kids who were heavy users of drugs and alcohol, she decided it would do them good to get

Trent Lehman: school reunion ▲

out of Hollywood. She resettled the family in their original home, Colorado Springs. Things seemed better for a while. Trent joined the Job Corps. Four years later, in the summer of 1981, he packed up and moved back to Hollywood. He became a cocaine addict. When his mother saw him again, she insisted that he enter therapy. Trent refused.

On a chilly January night in 1982, Trent's old schoolfriend, Joseph Allen, was returning to his home in Arleta, near North Hollywood. It was 1:45. He pulled the car into his driveway, which was just across the street from the Vena Avenue Elementary School, where he and Trent had gone to school. Trent, as a kid, had had many happy times in that schoolyard. As Allen got out of his car, he beheld a bizarre sight in front of the school. At first, he could not believe his eyes. Someone had tied a leather belt around his neck, climbed to the top of the chainlink fence, tied the belt to the top of the fence, pushed himself off . . . and died. As Allen approached, he recognized his old buddy, former child star Trent Lehman, who had come back to his old school to die. A suicide note was in his pocket.

Jazz drummer and actor BEN POLLACK wore several hats. He wrote songs, led a band, and appeared in early talkie shorts—notably *Ben Pollack and His Park Central Orchestra.* The highlights of his film career were Anthony Mann's *The Glenn Miller Story* (1954), with James Stewart and June Allyson, and *The Benny Goodman Story* (1955). Pollack hanged himself on June 7, 1971, in Palm Springs.

JUMPERS

Screen actress LOIS BERNARD jumped to her death on April 25, 1945. The most celebrated Hollywood death leap,

however, was that of a little lady who made only one picture. PEG ENTWISTLE was born Lillian Millicent Entwistle in London. In 1929 she got excellent notices in the Broadway hit show *Tommy* and then appeared in some Theater Guild productions. After coming to Hollywood, she appeared in one more play, *The Mad Hopes,* with Billie Burke. Peg's notices were good, but the show flopped after playing two weeks in Los Angeles to half-empty houses. She finally found a screen job in RKO's murder mystery, *Thirteen Women* (with Myrna Loy). In spite of a good cast, the movie was not a hit, and Peg did not find herself on the way up. Hollywood is a lonely place for those who haven't made it—the handshakes are reserved for those who have. After her film performed badly at the box office, Peg was told by the studio that there was nothing for her "just now." She spent weeks trying to find another movie job, weeks of trying to keep a brave face when she met people who had known

▲ Peg Entwistle: Hollywood sign celebrity

her as a successful Broadway actress.

Well, she found the way up—after her own fashion. On September 18, 1932, she climbed the steep slopes of Mount Lee to the great HOLLYWOODLAND sign, which spelled out in giant letters the name of Mack Sennett's ill-fated real estate venture. There were thirteen letters in that sign, and it had a fatal fascination for Peg, who had ridden near it on horseback nearly every day. She left her coat and purse on the ground and climbed a ladder a workman had left, right to the top of the fifty-foot *H*. No one will ever know how long she gazed down at Hollywood that night; no one will know her bitter thoughts. She could see several of the studios from that height—including RKO, where, for a while, she had held a brief hope that fate would be kind to her. She leaped to her death. Her pitiful suicide note read: "I'm afraid I'm a coward. I'm sorry for everything." She did not know that at the moment of her suicide a note was in the mail to her from the Beverly Hills Community Players. They were offering her a juicy role in their next stage production—that of a girl who commits suicide at the end of the third act.

Screen actress GLADYS FRAZIN (her career was mostly limited to the Twenties) jumped from her New York apartment window on March 9, 1939. She had been married to comedian Monty Banks, who played in films with Fatty Arbuckle and later directed Laurel and Hardy in *Great Guns*. After his divorce from Frazin, Banks married Gracie Fields. Frazin's best film was *Let No Man Put Asunder* (1924), a drama about divorce in which she co-starred with Lou Tellegen—who also committed suicide.

RUSSELL GLEASON was the son of James Gleason, one of the most talented and best-liked character actors in American movies. James Gleason generally played grouchy urban types—cops, robbers, reporters, fight managers—with a heart of gold underneath the bluff *(Meet John Doe, Here Comes Mr. Jordan, Arsenic and Old Lace, The Night of the Hunter, The Last Hurrah)*. He met his wife, actress Lucille Gleason, when they were appearing together in a stock company run by her father. Russell was born while his parents were in stock in Portland, Oregon. When three months old, he was carried on stage and appeared with them in a play. There were hardly any father-mother-son combinations in the movies. The Gleasons were one of them. All three appeared together in *The Higgins Family,* as well as other films. Lucille can be seen as Big Tess, in

▲ The Gleasons

Klondike Annie, with Mae West. She was active in politics, ran for the California Assembly, and was vice-president of the Screen Actors Guild. Russell made his screen debut in *The Shady Lady* (1929), which starred Phyllis Haver as a fugitive from justice. (Miss Haver also killed herself.) Russell's first important role was as the dreamy schoolboy Muller in *All Quiet on the Western Front.* His last film was *The Adventures of Mark Twain* (1944), with Fredric March. In December 1945, he was billeted at New York's Hotel Sutton with other personnel of the Army Signal Corps Photo Center of the Astoria Studio. On Christmas Day, Sergeant Gleason plunged from his fourth-floor room at the Sutton. His body landed with a thud, awakening other soldiers.

IRENE (Irene Gibbons) spent the first sixteen years of her life on her father's Montana ranch. She went to design school, then opened a simple dress shop in Los Angeles near the University of Southern California. One day, by chance, Dolores Del Rio dropped in and was struck by the high quality of Irene's work. The actress bought several frocks and told her friends about the place. Irene became fashionable. In 1936 she married Eliot Gibbons, a screenwriter *(Give Us Wings, Flight at Midnight, Honeymoon Deferred)* and the brother of Cedric Gibbons, the renowned supervising art director at MGM. Irene soon left her simple store to head the "ultra swanky" salon at Bullock's Wilshire in downtown Los Angeles. In 1938 she began designing for the movies, working mostly at Universal.

In 1941, Adrian, the genius chief fashion designer at MGM, declared that he was fed up with the studio. For years, there had been no budget limitations on his extravagant creations for glamourous MGM stars. Lately, however, he had been ordered to dress Garbo more like an ordinary American woman, and the corporation executives had started to limit his budgets. Adrian left MGM to open his own couture salon. Irene left Bullock's to succeed him as executive designer at MGM. Over the years, she created beautiful gowns for Marlene Dietrich, Elizabeth Taylor, Claudette Colbert, Hedy Lamarr, Judy Garland, Lana Turner, and many others, and became famous for her soufflé creations.

Late in her career, she worked on several Doris Day films. The actress and the designer became friends. Day noticed that Irene, who had always been nervous and introverted, was drinking too much. Her husband lived out of state, and she rarely saw him. Irene had loved to shoot and go on hunting trips, but she no longer took pleasure in these activities. She confided in Day that she was in love with Gary Cooper and that he was the only man she had ever loved. Cooper died in 1961. On November 15, 1962, Irene took a room at the Knickerbocker Hotel in Los Angeles, under an assumed name. She cut her wrists. When this did not prove fatal immediately, she jumped to her death from the window of the room on the fourteenth floor. A note found in it said: "I'm sorry. This is the best way. Get someone very good to design and be happy. I love you all. Irene."

Linda Christian never attained much fame as a leading lady, but via the fan magazines became quite well known because of her off-screen romances. Eventually, she married Tyrone Power. He was taken from her to the big projection room in the sky in 1958. In 1964 she played the role of an American movie actress in Francesco Rosi's Italian-Spanish co-production *The Moment of Truth,* a film about the life of a bullfighter. She took a liking to the *toreros* she met during the shooting and

---

◀ Irene: out the window

romanced one of the most famous of all, Luis Dominguin. When the movie was finished, she returned to Rome and her terraced penthouse atop a highrise in Parioli, the poshest neighborhood in the Italian capitol. She was frequently visited by her bullfighter friends there, some of whom even made her presents of the ears of bulls they had slaughtered. MOUSIE, her pet chihuahua, with whom she had been wont to share her bed ever since he was a puppy, became increasingly jealous of her *torero* visitors—on one occasion he tore to tatters one of the bulls' ears destined for Linda's collection. Mousie was thrown out of bed once too often to make room for the bullfighters. The moment of truth came for the jealous chihuahua in June 1964, when the neurotic pooch, who had been receiving less and less attention, finally jumped off the terrace in a fit of suicidal canine despair.

Linda Christian, "star of stage, screen and funerals"—with Mousie ▲

PILLS AND POISONS

Cowboy star ART ACORD was a genuine cowboy. He was half Ute, born in Stillwater, Oklahoma, in 1890. As a young man, after a few years spent cowpunching, he joined Dick Stanley's Wild West Show and then performed with Buffalo Bill's outfit.

Acord started working in movies in 1909 and appeared in De Mille's *The Squaw Man.* Buck Parvin, the character he played in a 1916 series of pictures was based on Acord himself. He was a born rider. He had an incredible private collection of trophies, a veritable museum, which he took with him wherever he went: pearl-handled revolvers, silver spurs, thirty-six silver bridles, hand-carved saddles, and twenty-one pairs of boots.

He served as an infantryman during World War I and won a *croix de guerre* for hand-to-hand fighting. He killed many Germans with his bare hands. He loved fighting on and off screen. When he returned to movies after the war, it was apparent to everyone that Acord and rival cowboy star, Hoot Gibson, loved to beat each other up. Their fights were legendary. Tim McCoy said, "They'd beat the hell out of each other. And then they'd come to the bar and have a drink. They loved it." He was the wildest of all the cowboys, a fantastic sight when he was drunk and angry. Once in a bar, Victor Fleming claimed he was not a real Indian. Acord promptly broke the nose of the future director of *Gone With the Wind.*

He did many serials *(In the Days of Buffalo Bill, The Oregon Trail),* worked for Bison, and by the mid-Twenties was starring in features at Universal. He married Louise Lorraine, his co-star in *Oregon Trail.* Acord was fearless—stocky and short and a hard man to kill. On one occasion, he was hospitalized and given up for dead after shooting a scene in which he went over a cliff on horseback and the horse landed on top of him.

Acord starred opposite Fay Wray in William Wyler's first feature, *Lazy Lightning,* made at Universal in 1926. Wyler said of him, "He was not a great actor, but he had a kind of sincerity. He wasn't handsome, but he looked good on a horse. He was a nice fellow. We got along fine."

Acord was the only major western star who could not make it at all in sound movies. There were voice problems, but vocal training could have remedied them. He was too busy drinking and fighting to worry about his voice and, as a result, he could not get roles in talkies. He served a prison term for rum-running, then worked for a while as a miner in Mexico. He lost all his money, but would not agree to the discipline of vocal training. He thought he might be able to make a comeback if he got some publicity, so he staged a phony kidnapping of himself with the help of some Mexican bandits. The plan fell through. When he tried to commit suicide at the Palacio Hotel in Chihuahua, an American buddy knocked the bottle of poison from his hands. But Art had hidden another bottle of cyanide in his room. He may have been a hard man for others to kill, but he was finally able to do it himself—on January 4, 1931. His body rotted in Chihuahua for a week before his family turned up to claim it.

ABIGAIL ADAMS was married to Lyle Talbot, an actor mostly seen as a mobster in Warner Bros. B movies, and who later appeared on TV on the Burns and Allen show. At twenty-seven, she divorced Talbot. Columbia still considered her a "promising starlet." She didn't want riches—she just wanted to be a star. In 1950 she slashed her wrists and was saved by a hospital intern. She then got engaged to George Jessel, a producer at Fox, widely known as "America's Toastmaster General." Adams remained a starlet and became a barfly. Stardom eluded her, but she did make the back pages in 1955 after a large fatal dose of Seconal and ethynyl. Jessel observed, "She had a rather frustrated life, but of course, you never know why people do these things."

NICK ADAMS was born Nicholas Aloysius Adamshock in Pennsylvania, the son of a Lithuanian coal miner. He joined the Coast Guard, then later came to Hollywood, hoping to meet his idol, James Dean. (They did work on a film together, *Rebel Without a Cause,* in which Adams had a small part.) Adams found work in movies during the Fifties and Sixties, but only achieved some measure of real fame as the star of the TV series "The Rebel." He was

nominated for a Best Supporting Actor Oscar for his work in *Twilight of Honor,* his last good role. He then worked in one of Boris Karloff's least interesting films, *Die Monster Die!,* and in another gooseflesh epic that deserves mention, if only for its name, *Frankenstein Meets the Giant Devil Fish.*

When "The Rebel" was cancelled after two years, Adams found it difficult to obtain anything but small roles. He was very attached to the two children (Allyson and Jeb Stuart) he had had with actress Carol Nugent, his divorced wife. Adams made headlines when he alleged that Carol "had been allowing a male friend to chastise and discipline the children although she was unmarried to said male friend." He went to court and was given custody of the kids. Their mother was given reasonable visitation rights, but "not in the presence of non-related male adults."

Adams' health began to deteriorate and a doctor prescribed paraldehyde, a drug used to treat alcoholics with the D.T.s. On the night of February 7, 1968, a buddy, Erwin Roeder, decided to find out why the actor had stood him up for dinner the previous evening. When Roeder arrived at Adams' lonely hillside house on El Roble Lane in Beverly Hills, he found the actor's car in the garage, but there was no sign of life in the house. Roeder broke in a rear window and discovered "Johnny Yuma" dead in his bedroom, propped against the wall, his eyes open in a blank stare. The Los Angeles coroner, Thomas Noguchi, performed the autopsy and found paraldehyde "in the organs, mixed with sedatives and other drugs—enough to cause instant death."

PIER ANGELI was born in Sardinia in 1932. Her first American movie was *Teresa,* the story of an Italian girl who marries an American soldier. Her wistful face and natural acting made a strong

Nick Adams: drastic cure for D.T.s ▲

230

impression on the public. She remained a leading lady for nearly a decade. Her sister, Marisa Pavan, was then also imported to toil in Tinseltown. Angeli co-starred with Paul Newman twice—in *The Silver Chalice* and *Somebody Up There Likes Me*. But she fell in love with James Dean. Her mamma did not approve and pushed her into a marriage with singer Vic Damone. Marriage to Damone turned out to be a disaster; after Dean's death, she began to go to pieces. In 1971 she wrote to a friend: "I'm so afraid to get old—for me, being 40 is the beginning of old age . . . Love is now behind me, love died in a Porsche."

Angeli never made it to forty. She offed herself with an overdose of barbiturates in her Beverly Hills apartment on September 11, 1971.

Producer Sam Spiegel *(On the Waterfront, The Bridge on the River Kwai, Lawrence of Arabia, Betrayal)* married starlet LYNNE BAGGETT in 1948. In 1954 Mrs. Spiegel made headlines when her car slammed into a station wagon filled with boys returning from a summer camp, injuring four of its occupants and killing a fifth, nine-year-old Joel Wathick. She fled the scene. She was acquitted of

▲ Pier Angeli: life ends before 40

manslaughter, but served a fifty-day sentence for hit-and-run driving. Spiegel and Baggett were divorced in 1955.

The lady appeared in *DOA* (with Edmond O'Brien), in *The Times of Their Lives,* and *The Ghost Steps Out.* She never became a star. By 1959 her career was seriously flagging. She attempted suicide with sleeping pills, and botched it. In a freak accident, two months later, she was trapped for two days in a folding bed. She was undergoing treatment for barbiturate addiction in March 1960, when her nurse found her on her bed, dead from an overdose of sleeping pills.

SCOTTY BECKETT, one of the cutest of all screen kiddie actors, was born in Oakland in 1929. He made his movie debut at the age of three in an Our Gang comedy. He played the young Anthony in *Anthony Adverse,* appeared as the Dauphin in *Marie Antoinette,* and as the young Parris Mitchell in *King's Row.* He was Barbara Stanwyck's son in *My Reputation,* and the teenaged Al Jolson in *The Jolson Story.* The first of his

many bouts with the law occurred in 1948 when he was arrested for drunken driving. In 1954 he was arrested for carrying a concealed weapon. In 1957 he was arrested at the Mexican border for possessing dangerous drugs. In 1960 he was sentenced to a 180-day suspended jail sentence for hitting his stepdaughter with a crutch. He slashed his wrists in 1962, recovered, became a car salesman, and killed himself with sleeping pills in Hollywood on May 10, 1968.

CLARA BLANDICK is a household face, if not a household word; she is known the world over as Judy Garland's kindly Auntie Em in *The Wizard of Oz.* Born in

Scotty Beckett: growing up is no fun ▲   ▲ Clara Blandick: over the rainbow

1881 aboard an American ship in Hong Kong harbor, she entered films in 1929 and appeared in over one hundred movies. She was often a kindly aunt—Jackie Coogan's in *Tom Sawyer* and *Huckleberry Finn*—but she could also play a memorable bitch and is unforgettably nasty as Barbara Stanwyck's mother-in-law in *Shopworn*. She also can be seen in *The Bitter Tea of General Yen, Broadway Bill, Anthony Adverse, Gentleman Jim* and *A Stolen Life*.

On April 15, 1962, she decided she could no longer bear her severe arthritic pains and failing eyesight. The old gal went out and had her hair done, put on her best Sunday frock and spread out stills and memorabilia from her long career around her apartment. She took a large dose of sleeping pills, and to make sure she would not survive, tied a plastic bag around her head. Auntie Em was shortly Over the Rainbow.

CHARLES BOYER, one of the screen's "great lovers," was also a fine and restrained actor. After an international career, he settled in Hollywood in 1935. Some of his more memorable roles were in *The Garden of Allah* (opposite Marlene Dietrich), *History Is Made at Night, Algiers* (as Pépé le Moko), *Love Affair, All This and Heaven Too* (opposite Bette Davis), and in Lubitsch's *Cluny Brown* (with Jennifer Jones). In 1934 he married British actress Pat Paterson. Their son Michael shot himself in 1965 at age twenty-two. Paterson died of cancer in their home in Phoenix. Two days later, on August 29, 1978, Boyer killed himself with an overdose of Seconal.

DOROTHY DANDRIDGE was born in Cleveland in 1923, the daughter of a minister. She and her sister Vivian learned singing from their mother, and at the age of four, little Dorothy began

Charles Boyer: couldn't live without her ▲

ALAN LADD carved a niche for himself as one of the screen's memorable tough guys, in spite of his short height and a generally stone-faced acting style. He entered pictures as an extra and remained a bit player for years, getting nowhere in B quickies at Republic and Monogram; he owed his first big break to the persistence of his second wife, agent Sue Carol, who kept pushing for him. In 1942 she landed him an important role in Paramount's *This Gun for Hire.* It was a good little thriller with Veronica Lake; female fans by the droves fell for Ladd's image of sensitivity combined with ruthlessness. His next appearance at Paramount, again with Lake, in *The Glass Key,* confirmed his popularity. He was co-starred with Loretta Young, Dorothy Lamour, and Deborah Kerr, and by 1947 was one of the country's top ten movie stars. He will probably be best remembered for his work in George Stevens' *Shane* (1953), the climax of his career, in which he scored a huge

her show biz career as half of a song-and-dance act called "The Wonder Children." She made her screen debut in *A Day at the Races* with the Marx Brothers. She was one of the first black performers to attain real stardom in mainstream American motion pictures. This occurred in the Fifties, with two films directed by Otto Preminger: *Carmen Jones* and *Porgy and Bess.* In the latter, Dandridge played Bess, although her voice was dubbed by Adele Addison; in *Carmen Jones,* she was dubbed by Marilyn Horne. In 1963 she went bankrupt after losing all her money in a get-rich-quick oil investment scam. On September 8, 1965, the forty-one-year-old actress was found dead on the bathroom floor of her Sunset Strip, Hollywood apartment. A large quantity of sleeping pills had cured her of amnesia for all eternity.

Dorothy Dandridge: cured her amnesia ▲   ▲ Alan Ladd: like mother, like son

success in the role of a mysterious gunfighter. His career declined after *Shane*—most of the later films were routine actioners. Ladd's drinking problem, which reached serious proportions at this time, was no secret in Hollywood. In 1963, "while searching for a suspected prowler" late at night on his ranch, he shot himself in the chest. A year after this incident, which was in all likelihood a botched suicide attempt, Ladd got it right. On January 29, 1964, at the age of fifty, he did himself in with "a high level of alcohol combined with three medicines and sleeping pills." His mother had committed suicide in 1937.

Shapely blond CAROLE LANDIS rose to stardom in Hal Roach's *One Million B.C.*, in which she played a primitive cavewoman. Her 1948 Fourth-of-July suicide, provoked by unrequited love for Rex Harrison, caused a hullabaloo and a half for Mr. and Mrs. Moviegoer. Rex found Carole's body lying on the bathroom floor of her Pacific Palisades home, her head resting on a jewel box, one hand clutching a crumpled envelope that still contained a sleeping pill. On the vanity table of her bedroom was a suicide note addressed to her mother. At the time, Harrison was married to Lilli Palmer. He had dined with Landis the night of her suicide. Landis was married to Broadway producer W. Horace Schmidlapp. When informed that his wife had been found dead, Mr. W. Horace Schmidlapp said, "Oh, my God!"

MARIE MCDONALD was dubbed "The Body" by Tinseltown press agents, and the name stuck. There was not much to be said about her acting talent. The lady was a former model and showgirl from Kentucky who turned up in such memorable movies as *Pardon My Sarong* and *Getting Gertie's Garter.* She was married seven times, and was quoted as saying, "Husbands are easier to find than good agents." Even good agents could not build her into a true star. In January 1957 she was found in her pajamas on a desert road near Indo, California. She said she had been kidnapped from her house by two men. The affair was clearly a publicity stunt to boost her sagging career. Soon afterward she was arrested on drug charges, then for drunk driving. In 1963, while on tour in Australia, she suffered a nervous breakdown. She was arrested later that year on a charge of forging Percodan prescriptions. In October 1965 she obtained some more Percodan—enough to kill herself with. And she did.

MAGGIE MCNAMARA was born in New York in 1928. A successful fashion model while still in her teens, she twice appeared on the cover of *Life.* After starring in *The Moon is Blue* on Broadway, the diminutive and sensitive

▲ Marie McDonald: no more body

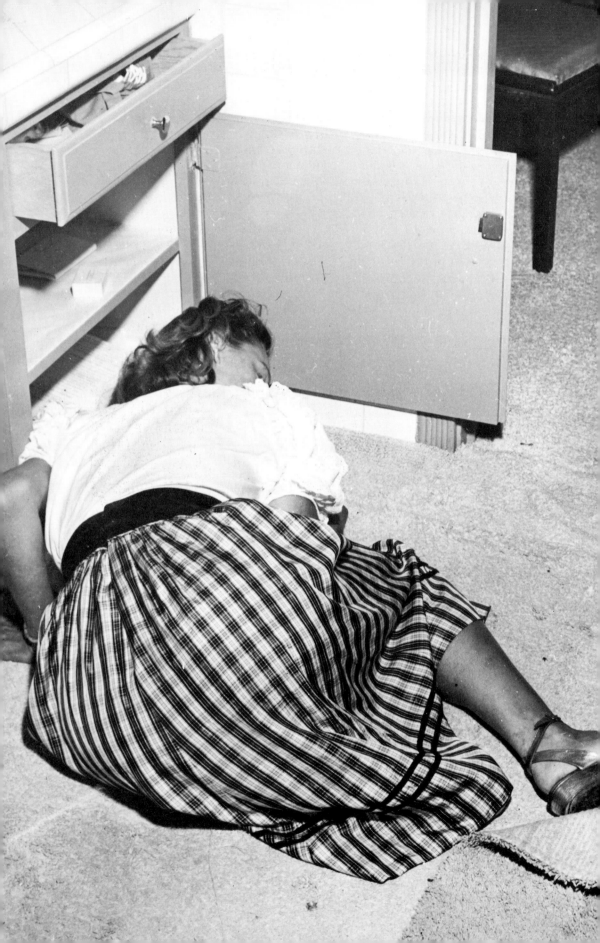

brunette made her movie debut in 1953 in Otto Preminger's controversial screen version of that play in which she was seen as a stubborn virgin fending off the advances of William Holden. The Breen Office refused to pass the movie unless the word "virgin" was eliminated; the Catholics condemned it from the pulpits. Preminger refused to cut the movie and United Artists helped him to break the power of the Breen Office by agreeing to distribute it without a Production Code seal. It was a smash hit. McNamara was nominated for a best actress Academy Award.

She went on to make *Three Coins in the Fountain* (1954) and *Prince of Players* (1955). She then disappeared from the screen, divorced her husband, director David Swift, and suffered a nervous breakdown. She made a brief return to the movies in 1963, when Preminger cast her in a small role in *The Cardinal*. She worked for a while as a typist. In February, 1978, she killed herself with an overdose of sleeping pills. She left a suicide note; the coroner's report mentioned that she had had a history of mental illness.

It is surely fortuitous, but Otto Preminger holds the record for the director with the highest number of suicides among his leading ladies: McNamara, Dorothy Dandridge and Jean Seberg.

Enough ink has been spilled in speculations of murderous foul play in the death of MARILYN MONROE. Theodore J. Curphey, the Chief Medical

◄ Carole Landis: a broken heart   Marilyn Monroe: hers too! ▲   Marilyn's bedroom ►

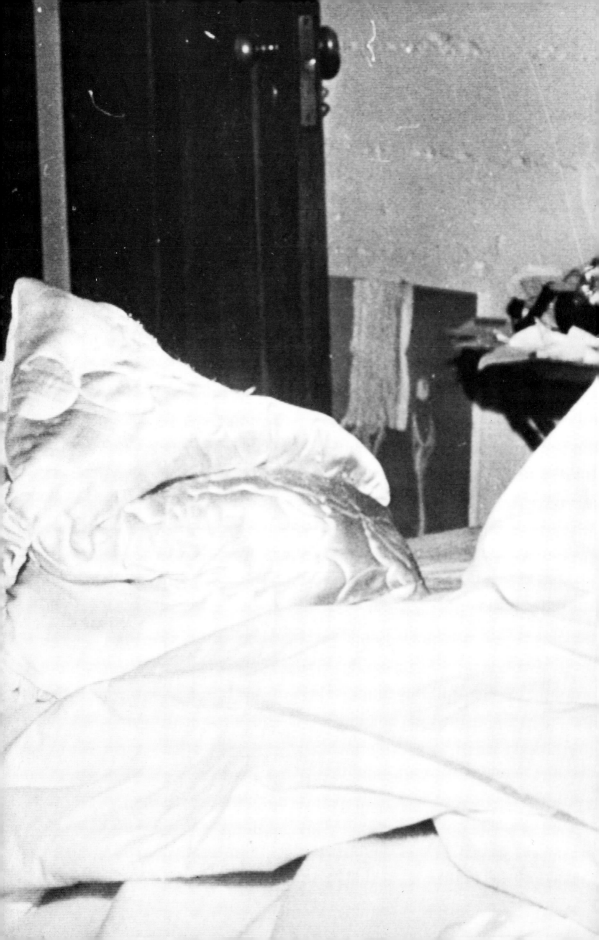

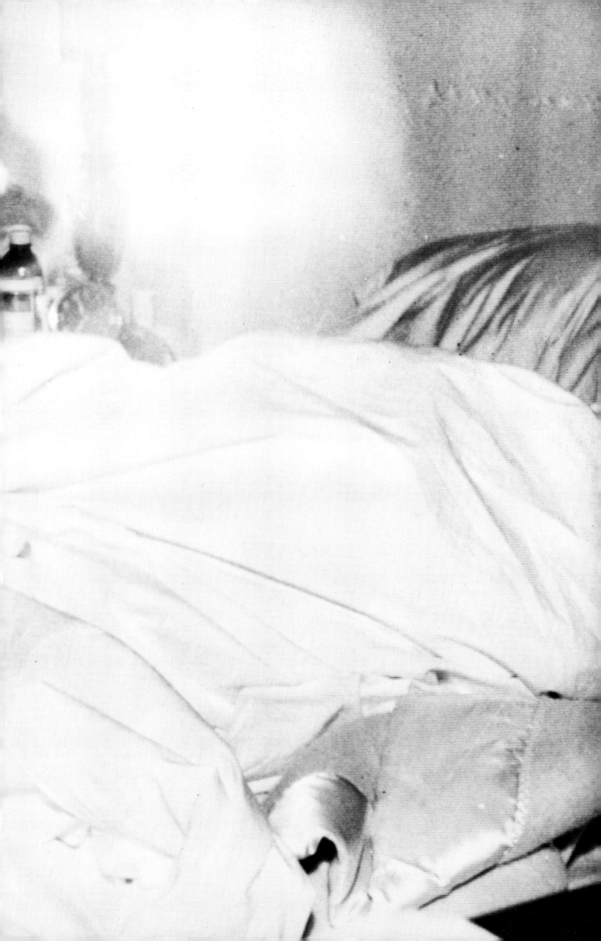

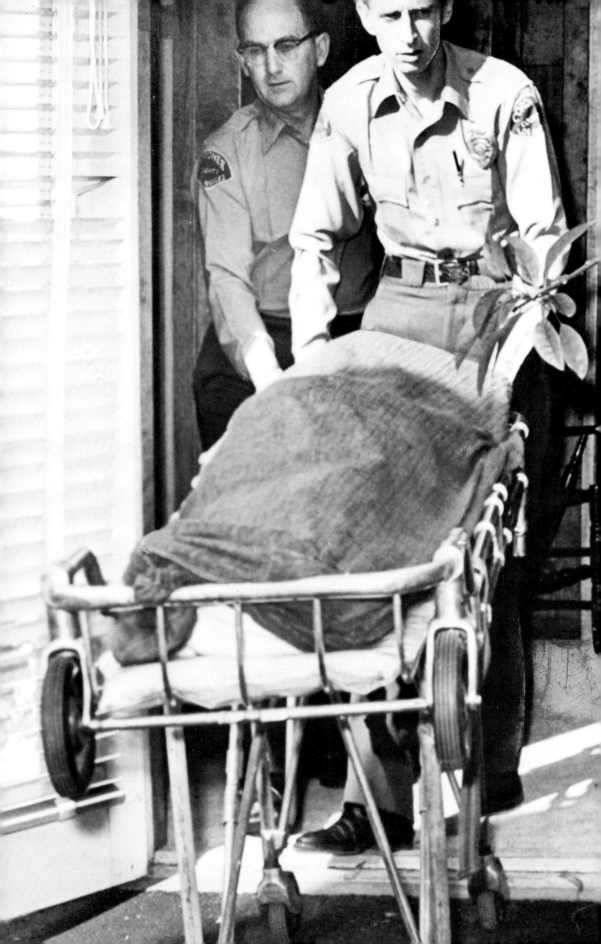

◄ Removing Marilyn Monroe's body   ▲ Sealing her crypt

Examiner in 1962, concluded on the basis of the autopsy performed by pathologist Thomas T. Noguchi, then a young medical examiner, that the star had died from an overdose of Nembutal and chloral hydrate pills. In 1982, twenty years later, in spite of all the intervening fuss, Noguchi still considered Monroe's suicide "very probable." As yet, nothing has been revealed that would seriously refute his conclusion.

Marilyn's poodle, Jewel, is removed by the police ▲

The Monroe furs ▶

CHESTER MORRIS was born in New York in 1901. Both his parents were successful stars of the stage. The De Mille family and the Morris family were old friends; it was Cecil B. De Mille who gave Chester Morris his first screen role—as an extra in *The Road to Yesterday*. It was D. W. Griffith who gave him his first crack at a leading role—Griffith proposed him to director Roland West for the starring part in *Alibi*. It turned out to be a brilliant gangster movie, with Morris nominated for a Best Actor Oscar for his performance as Chick Williams, an amoral crook who marries a cop's daughter. The actor scored again with his forceful performance as a convict in MGM's *The Big House*. Chester Morris rapidly developed into an attractive, charismatic, and thoroughly professional actor who never gave a bad performance, but somehow never managed to become a major star. He proved an effective foil for Jean Harlow in *Red Headed Woman*. In *Blind Alley*, made at Columbia in 1939, he was

superb as an insane escaped killer. He became the mainstay of the popular Boston Blackie series—B quickies in which he appeared from 1941–1949. (He appeared as Blackie in fourteen movies.) His best film of all was Roland West's ingenious thriller *The Bat Whispers* (1930), in which he appeared as a detective and a murderous psychopath. His last film was *The Great White Hope* (1970), which was released shortly after his suicide.

Morris had been touring in a stage production of *The Caine Mutiny*. To an interviewer who had questioned him about his role as Queeg, he replied, "Captain Queeg is a complete paranoiac. He's a strange man, so offbeat. I like that kind of role. Anybody can play nice boys." The actor was suffering from stomach cancer. He was professional enough to continue on the boards as long as he could, but on September 11, 1970, when the end seemed near, Morris killed himself with

Chester Morris: no hope at New Hope ▲　　　　　　　▲ Ona Munson: freedom at last an overdose of barbiturates in the Holiday Inn at New Hope, Pennsylvania, near the Bucks County Playhouse where he was appearing in *Caine*.

ONA MUNSON began her showbiz career as a dancer in vaudeville. After a successful run in *No, No, Nanette* on Broadway, she made her movie debut in 1930. She had a small but good role in Mervyn Leroy's *Five Star Final* (1931) in which she appeared with Edward G. Robinson and Boris Karloff, but most of her films during the rest of the Thirties were routine tripe. Although what seemed to be the big break of her life came with the role of Rhett Butler's pal, the prostitute, Belle Watling, in *Gone With the Wind*, the part did not lead to much else of note. Her only other role of significance in Tinseltown was that of another madame—Madame Gin Sling in Josef von Sternberg's *The Shanghai Gesture*. Lacquered to the hilt, and pulling the strings of the outrageous melodrama while she observed her puppets with a masklike visage, Munson was sensational in this stylish movie— but it was not a hit and all it led to was a few low-budgeted Westerns. On February 11, 1955, she left a suicide note in which she spoke of her desire to "obtain freedom"—and she obtained it with a massive overdose of sleeping pills.

In the mid-Forties, it seemed obvious that GAIL RUSSELL had a great career ahead of her. The beautiful young woman with blue eyes and jet-black hair went straight from Santa Monica High into a contract with Paramount. She scored a success in her first starring film, *The Uninvited*, an effective ghost tale in which she appeared opposite Ray Milland. Things looked even brighter after her fine performances in *The Unseen* and *Night Has a Thousand Eyes*. Russell was, however, severely neurotic

and the pressures of early stardom in Tinseltown abetted her penchant for alcoholism. She was arrested time and again for drunken driving. In 1954 she divorced her humpy hubby, Guy Madison. After a few suicide attempts, her movie career became a mere memory and in August 1961, she was found dead, at age thirty-six, in her West Hollywood apartment. Her corpse was surrounded by empty vodka bottles and empty tubes of barbiturates.

On July 3, 1906, "an event of major importance took place in St. Petersburg, Russia. A child of dazzling beauty and infinite charm was being born," according to GEORGE SANDERS. The child, of course, was George Sanders. The parents of this ever-modest actor were both born in Russia, but of Scottish ancestry. His father was the best balalaika player in town. They fled the Bolshevik Revolution and settled in England. Most of their relatives

▲ Gail Russell: try, try again

245

remaining in Russia were shot.

After leaving school, Sanders got a job with a tobacco company in Argentina and spent much time in the brothels of Buenos Aires. After his return to London, he appeared in several plays, then made his screen debut as a god riding a horse in *The Man Who Could Work Miracles.* He later turned up in Hollywood, obtained a Fox contract, and was soon used to being typecast as a cynical cad. In several films he played Nazi brutes. He was Charles Strickland (the Gauguin character) in *The Moon and Sixpence,* and Lord Henry Wotton in *The Portrait of Dorian Gray.* The critics adored him in *All About Eve,* in which he appeared as Marilyn Monroe's acerbic lover. His performance in it earned him an Oscar as best supporting actor.

He married Zsa Zsa Gabor, then, later, her sister Magda. He had four wives and seven psychiatrists. Most of his later movies were crappy. The only role of interest during the last decade of his life was that of a drag queen in *The Kremlin Letter.* His friend Brian Aherne wrote that Sanders pursued women solely for their money, dropping them instantly if he found they were not rich enough.

On April 25, 1972, he killed himself in Barcelona with five tubes of Nembutal. The suicide note read: "Dear World: I am leaving because I am bored. I am leaving you with your worries in this sweet cesspool."

GIA SCALA was born in Liverpool, England, in 1934, of an Italian father and an Irish mother. She studied drama with Stella Adler in New York and made her film debut in 1955 in Douglas Sirk's *All That Heaven Allows,* supporting Jane Wyman and Rock Hudson. The attractive green-eyed brunette played leading roles in American and English films during the next decade. They include: *The Garment Jungle, The Tunnel of Love*

and *The Guns of Navarone* with Gregory Peck and David Niven.

In 1957 she was taken into police custody in London when a taxi driver found her on Waterloo Bridge. Friends said she planned to throw herself into the Thames after brooding over the death of her mother. In the early 70s, she took to drinking heavily, smoking marijuana immoderately and attempted suicide to escape unhappy memories of her stalled career and her broken marriage with stockbroker Don Burnett.

On February 7, 1971, she ate roach poison and came so close to death she was given last rites by a priest. Later that year, a friend reported that he had not visited her home for some time without finding her drunk, and that she had offered friends knives and asked them to stab her as a favor. She collected quantities of police citations for drunkenness and one for taking a stroll in public in Hollywood clad only in a pair of panties. In May 1971 she was sent by

▲ Gia Scala: so bizarre

a judge to a state hospital for a psychiatric examination after she collapsed in a Ventura courtroom during an appearance on a drunk driving charge. Two months later she was fined $125 and placed on two years probation for disturbing the peace—the conviction stemmed from a brawl with a parking attendant over a bill of fifty cents. Her probation report stated: "Mental health questionable. Her money is being wasted on liquor and it is feared that she may drink herself to death." The probation officer added: "Her nature appears to have been bizarre for quite some time." The judge appointed a conservator to countersign all checks written by Gia Scala. She was then injured when her sports car overturned on a road near Hollywood. On April 30, 1972, she killed herself by absorbing a large amount of drugs washed down with a vast quantity of booze. Her body was discovered by one of the three men staying in her home.

JEAN SEBERG's saga has already inspired a ton of press articles, magazine pieces, books, videobios, and, most recently, a "musical tragedy" called *Jean Seberg* staged by the British National Theater in London. The subject of all this attention was an Iowa college girl when Otto Preminger chose her to star in his *Saint Joan.* The movie bombed; the critics were not kind to the young Iowan. Preminger then stuck her in *Bonjour Tristesse.* Her career might have ended there had it not been for her appearance in Jean-Luc Godard's *Breathless,* the French New Wave movie that provoked a good deal of critical brouhaha. Seberg only made one more American film of any interest—Robert Rossen's *Lilith,* in which she vividly portrayed a catatonic bisexual.

During the Sixties, while visiting her homeland, she became involved in radical politics and befriended leaders of the Black Panther movement. In an attempt to discredit her, the FBI deliberately spread mendacious gossip to the effect that she had been knocked up by a Panther. The Los Angeles office of the FBI asked bureau permission to "publicize the pregnancy of Jean Seberg . . . by advising Hollywood gossip columnists of the situation." J. Edgar Hoover's Washington office replied that "Jean Seberg has been a financial supporter of the Black Panther Party and should be neutralized. The current pregnancy by [blank space] while still married affords an opportunity for such effort." The *Los Angeles Times* obliged the FBI by publishing a blind item by gossipista Joyce Haber that spoke of an international movie star who supported the Black Revolution and who was expecting. "Papa's said to be a prominent Black Panther." Haber's article dropped hints that the lady in question was Seberg.

Seberg's husband at the time, novelist Romain Gary, claimed that the FBI was directly responsible for her death. The baby died at birth. She transported its corpse to her hometown in Iowa, where it was exhibited in a glass coffin so that everyone could see it was white. Gary said, "After that, Jean became psychotic. Every year, on the anniversary of the miscarriage, she tried to kill herself."

She divorced Gary and married twice again, although the novelist remained a close friend. On September 8, 1979, her decomposed body was found wrapped in a blanket in the back seat of her white Renault. It had been there over a week. She had been quite paranoid for some time and believed that her refrigerator had been spying on her. She killed herself with a large portion of barbiturates. Her suicide note read: "I can't live any longer with my nerves."

Jean Seberg and nemesis: J. Edgar Hoover ▶

Red-haired, freckled EVERETT SLOANE, who became one of Hollywood's best and highest salaried character actors, was born in New York and started his career in radio. By an odd coincidence, he was heard for quite some time as a Jewish son—Sammy Goldberg—on the popular "The Goldbergs" series, and then played Hitler in over one hundred different radio shows.

He joined Orson Welles' Mercury Theater in 1938 and came to Hollywood with Welles. He gave an extremely moving performance in his screen debut as Bernstein in *Citizen Kane,* and was equally fine as Kopeikin, the armaments man, in *Journey into Fear.* He was even better as Arthur Bannister, the impotent husband of *The Lady from Shanghai*

(with Rita Hayworth) in Welles' memorable flop. Sloane's last two movie roles were in support of Jerry Lewis. Sloane was going blind and on July 11, 1965, he put the lights out on an impressive career with a handful of sleeping pills in his West Los Angeles home.

INGER STEVENS appeared in thirteen movies and was not very interesting in any of them. She was born in Sweden, the child of a broken home. She came to the States with her father and at sixteen ran away from daddy and made her showbiz debut in a tacky Kansas City burlesque house. She then came to New York and became a chorine at the Latin Quarter. She studied at the Actors' Studio and then attained some

Everett Sloane: lights out ▲

popularity on the TV series "The Farmer's Daughter."

Her movie debut came in 1957 in *Man on Fire.* Her bumpy romance with co-star Bing Crosby briefly made headlines. She married her agent; the marriage lasted four months. She confessed to a friend, "I often feel depressed. I come from a broken home, my marriage was a disaster, and I am constantly lonely." In her penultimate movie, *House of Cards,* she looked like a pale zombie.

She saw in the New Year on January 1, 1959, by swallowing twenty-five sleeping pills and part of a bottle of ammonia, but the suicide attempt failed. On May 1, 1970, she did not take any chances—she gulped down an enormous quantity of barbiturates. She was discovered—still alive—by the girlfriend with whom she shared her

Laurel Canyon home, but died on the way to the hospital.

MARGARET SULLAVAN was one of the most enchanting and magnetic leading ladies in the history of Tinseltown. Her acting was marked by intelligence and honesty. She was also a very fucked-up lady—insecure, temperamental, neurotic. She loathed acting. The family biography written by her daughter, Brooke Hayward, is significantly entitled *Haywire.*

Her best performances were in Frank Borzage's *Three Comrades* (with Robert Taylor and Lionel Atwill) and *The Mortal Storm,* and Lubitsch's enchanting *The Shop Around the Corner.* A co-star in MGM's *Cry Havoc,* a 1943 war epic about Army nurses on Bataan, noted that she

Inger Stevens: D.O.A. ▲

▲ Margaret Sullavan: something went haywire

kept popping pills all during the making of the movie.

In 1956 she walked out of rehearsals of a TV show in which she was starring and into a private sanatorium in Massachusetts. In 1959 she decided to return to the stage and was appearing in a New Haven tryout of *Sweet Love Remembered,* prior to Broadway. On New Year's Day, 1960, during the run of the play, she killed herself with an overdose of sleeping pills in the Taft Hotel, New Haven.

LUPE VELEZ, the "Mexican Spitfire," was one of Hollywood's livest wires. She was born Maria Guadalupe Velez de Villalobos south of the border, educated in a San Antonio convent, and broke into films in 1926. She made a great impression as the tempestuous leading lady in Doug Fairbanks' *The Gaucho.* She livened up D. W. Griffith's *Lady of the Pavements* considerably, all the while enjoying a well-rounded private life: after an affair with John Gilbert, she took up with young buck Gary Cooper.

Lupe Velez with Blackie and Whitie ▲

She married Tarzan the ape man, Johnny Weissmuller, in 1933, and after their divorce, went through a small army of lovers—cowboys, stuntmen, and American gigolos. Her career hit the skids, and in later years she mostly appeared in a series of B comedies with the dreary Leon Errol.

In 1944, deeply in debt and pregnant by her most recent lover, Harald Ramond, Lupe staged her last night on earth with care. She ordered a huge mass of flowers, invited two girlfriends for a Last Supper, and then, at 3:00 A.M., found herself alone in her big fake hacienda on Rodeo Drive. Her bedroom was chock-a-block with gardenias and tuberoses; it glowed with the flicker of several dozen candles. In this shrine to her own death, La Lupe, gowned in silver lamé, pencilled a farewell note to the father of her fetus, opened a bottle

George Westmore: slow death ▲   Mother and sisters grieving at Lupe Velez's funeral ▶

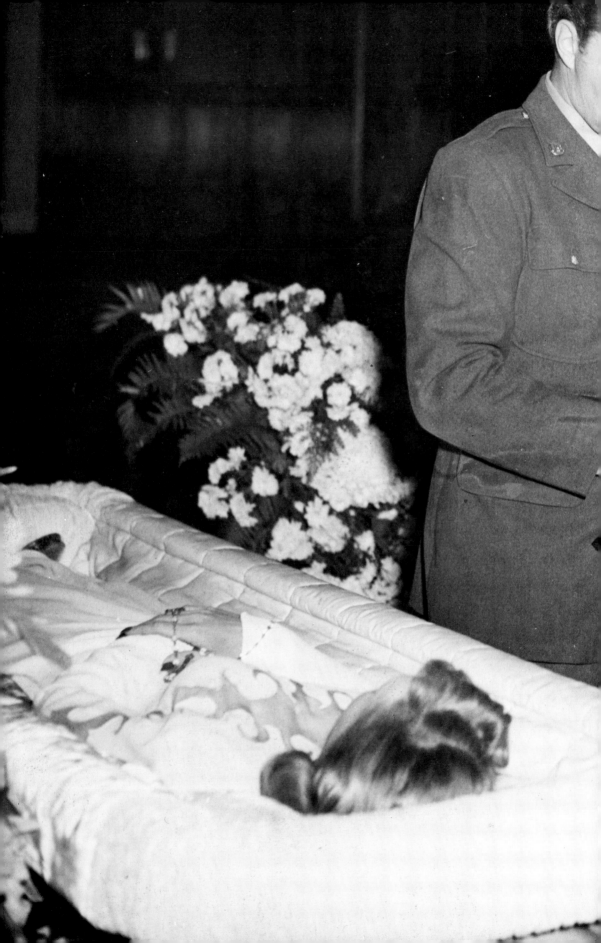

of Seconal, and swallowed seventy-five of the little buggers. She lay down on the bed, hands clasped in prayer, in what she envisioned as a final photo tableau of exquisite beauty. *That* photo was never to be taken. The Seconal did not go down well with her spicy Last Supper. She puked, leaving a trail of vomit from the bed to the bathroom, where she slipped on the tiles and plunged headfirst into the toilet. Juanita, the chambermaid, discovered his mistress's corpse later that morning. The tableau was neither pretty nor vivant.

In 1917, GEORGE WESTMORE founded the first movie makeup department in cinema history. He spawned a lot more—the entire Westmore dynasty, which, over the years, took over the makeup departments of Universal, Warner Bros., RKO, Paramount, and Selznick. Perc Westmore, who presided at Warners for many years, married the beautiful star of *They Won't Forget,* Gloria Dickson (who was later killed in a fire). Bud, handsomest of George's sons, reigned over the powder puffs at Universal and found the time and inclination to wed Martha Raye. La Raye slept with a gun under her pillow on their wedding night, just in case her husband tried to get fresh with her. This was obviously not a marriage destined to last long. It didn't, and Buddy Boy soon found a more satisfactory life of wedded bliss with Rosemary Lane.

Daddy George taught his identical twin sons, Perc and Ern, wigmaking when they were only nine. George and his son Mont did all the makeup on De Mille's *King of Kings,* which was not an easy job, since H. B. Warner, De Mille's Christ of Christs, was an inveterate boozer who turned up each morning smashed and woozy—not exactly in the best shape to have his saintly visage applied. It was Mont Westmore who plucked and reshaped Rudolph Valentino's eyebrows, put Vaseline on his lips to make them shine, and gave Rudy his distinctive slicked-back hairstyle and sideburns cut at an angle.

When *King of Kings* was in the can, old man George opened up a salon on Hollywood Boulevard, convinced he would be the makeup czar of all Tinseltown. It turned out that all the stars preferred Westmore sons to Westmore papa. George went to pieces; he found it unendurable to be his sons' rival. He had expected to be named the head of Paramount's enlarged makeup department in 1926—the job went to his twenty-year-old son, Wally, instead. George then was sure he would be named to head the department at RKO— that job went to son Ern. In 1931 Ern was awarded an Oscar for his makeup work on *Cimarron.* The old wigmaker wigged out permanently: a few weeks after Ern got his Oscar, George Westmore downed a potion of bichloride of mercury and died after four days of agony as the chemical gnawed its way through his guts.

GRANT WITHERS was born in Pueblo, Colorado, in 1904. He came to California in the early 20s as a reporter for the *Los Angeles Record,* then entered films in 1926. He starred in some A pictures but was soon relegated to serials, low-budget action pictures and supporting roles. He often worked for John Ford. His films include *Jungle Jim, Mr. Wong—Detective, Tennessee Johnson, The Fighting Seabees, My Darling Clementine, Fort Apache, Rio Grande* and *The Sun Shines Bright.* His principal claim to fame, however, was his 1930 elopement with the seventeen-year-old Loretta Young, who was then a Wampas Baby Star. It caused a press sensation. The marriage was annulled the following year. John Wayne was best

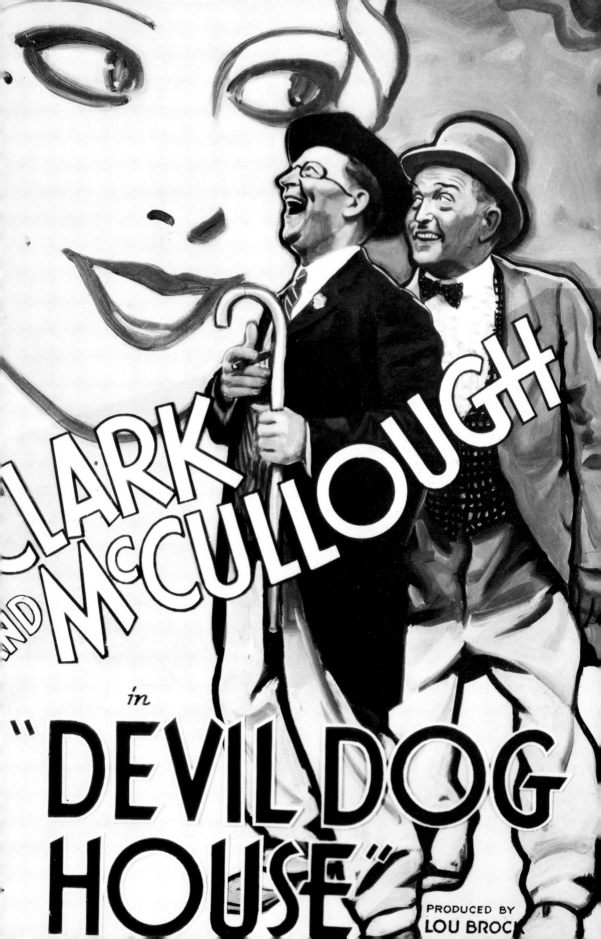

man when Withers married his fifth wife, Cuban dancer Estelita Rodriguez. Toward the end of his life, his activity was largely confined to minor TV roles.

On March 28, 1959, his corpse was found in his North Hollywood bachelor apartment, in bed, wearing eyeglasses and holding the telephone receiver. Withers had killed himself with an overdose of sleeping pills. He left a note which read: "Please forgive me—my family—I was so unhappy. It's better this way. Thanks to all my friends. Sorry I let them down." His landlord said he had been despondent because of financial problems. Loretta Young, informed of her ex-husband's death after she returned home from Good Friday church services, stated: "Oh, I'm so sorry."

THE RAZOR'S EDGE

The popular comedy team of Bobby Clark and PAUL MCCULLOUGH scored on Broadway in the Twenties, first in Irving Berlin's *Music Box Revue,* then in *The Ramblers.* They had been boyhood friends and first appeared together as circus clowns and then in burlesque. Clark's trademark was a pair of "glasses" painted on his face. McCullough sported a droll "toothbrush moustache."

They made a few hilarious one-reel comedies for Fox, shot in New York, which were so successful that the studio brought the team to Hollywood to star in a series of talkie featurettes. Their films of the early Thirties, made at RKO, were filled with outrageous gags. Their most notable films of this period were *In a Pig's Eye, Devil Dog House, Melon-Drama,* and above all, *Odor in the Court,* as zanily nihilistic as anything produced by the Marx Bros.

After a heavy work schedule at RKO in 1935, immediately followed by a stage tour in *George White's Scandals,* McCullough collapsed from nervous exhaustion. He signed himself into a Massachusetts sanatorium. By March 1936 he appeared to have recovered. Clark came to drive him home. On the way, McCullough casually remarked that he needed a shave. The car pulled up to a barber shop. McCullough entered and chatted good-humoredly with the barber. He sat down in the chair, but before he could be lathered, he had left this world. His eye had fallen on the glittering straight-razor the barber had just honed and placed on the sink. The comedian picked it up and slit his throat from ear to ear.

▲ Paul McCullough and Bobby Clark: revenge of the straight man

☆ INDISCREET ☆

◄ De Havilland: Olivia and lace   ▲ Rudy Valentino: camping and boating

Harold Lloyd: star with most illegitimate kids ▲   Daddy dearest: Wallace Beery and adopted daughter ▶

◀ Greta Garbo: sunning   ▲ Carmen Miranda partnered by Cesar Romero: natural air-conditioning

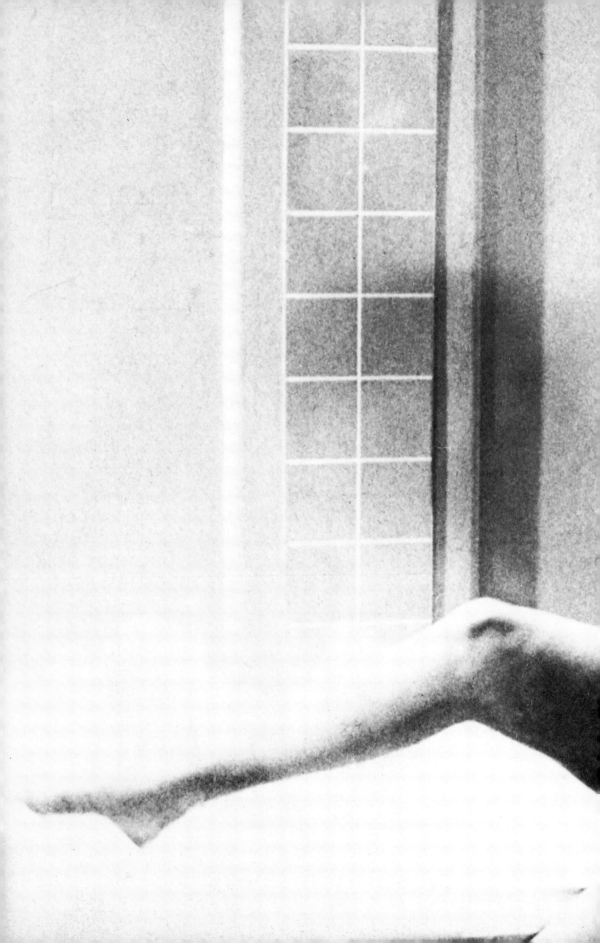

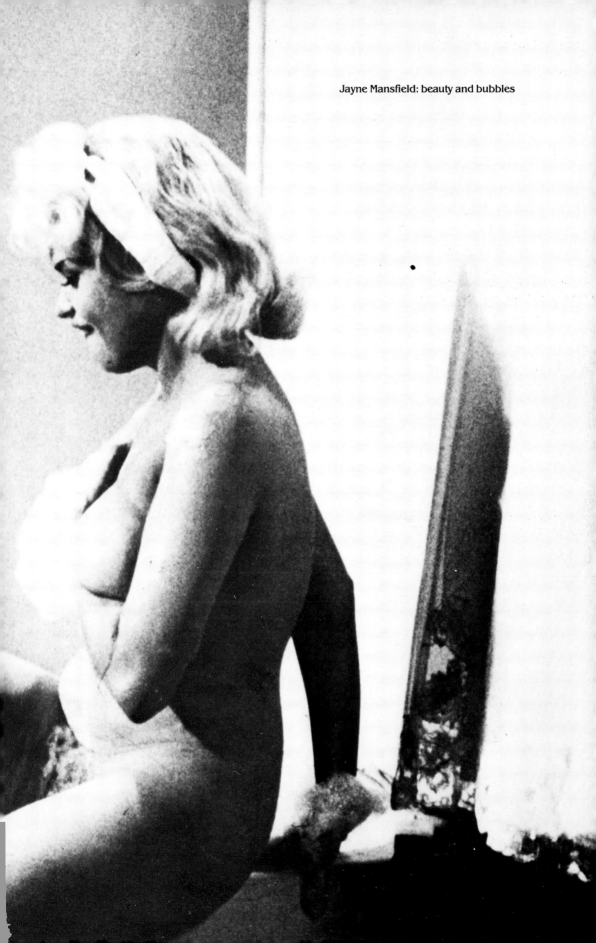

Jayne Mansfield: beauty and bubbles

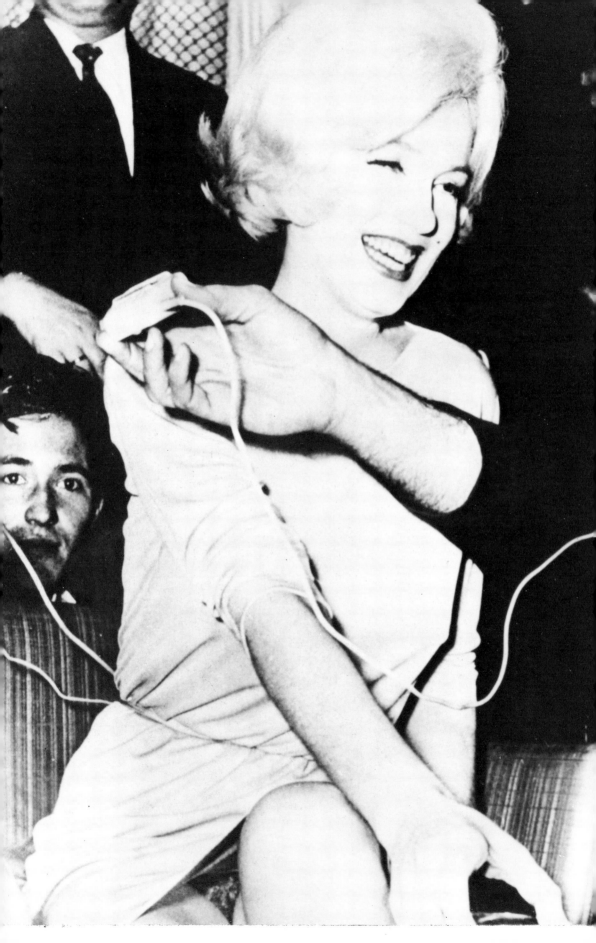

◀ Marilyn Monroe: more natural air-conditioning   ▲ Suppressed photograph of Jean Harlow

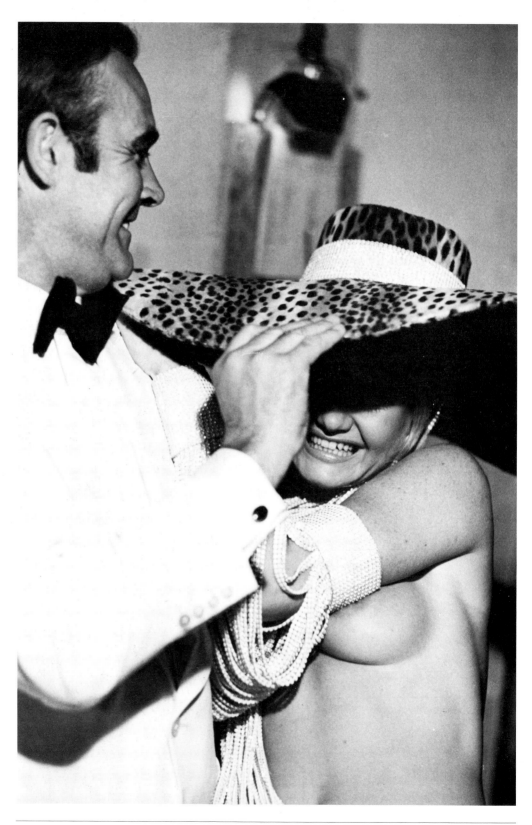

Sean Connery and friend ▲   Zero Mostel sneaks a peek at Shirley Temple's cleavage ▶

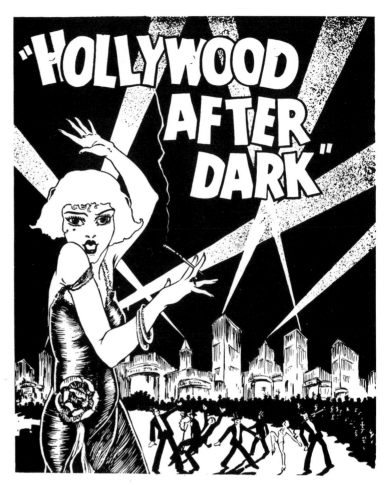

A SCARLET
PAGE FROM
THE BOOK
OF LIFE

Every Mother . . . every father . . . should see this picture. It is a sensational drama of humanity filled with pathos and thrills . . . a story that will satisfy as well as shock a nation.

IT EXPOSES!

Should a child gain sex education by experience?

"SEE HOLLYWOOD AFTER DARK"

STARTLING! SEX-ATIONAL! AMAZING!

A SCARLET PAGE TORN FROM THE BOOK OF LIFE

It's daring . . . it's bold . . . it's frank . . . but so delicately directed that derision is dismayed.

"HOLLYWOOD AFTER DARK"

SEX-ATIONAL

Is Knowledge of Sex a Defense of a Detriment?

The cameras of Hollywood have caught many a thrilling scene, but none to equal the climax in this beautiful story of love and devotion.

IT'S DARING!

"HOLLYWOOD AFTER DARK"

With
NAN PRESTON
DON WILSON
ARNOLD GREY
MARION WARD

Is death preferable to dishonor?
Not a blind-fold test—It's an eye opener.

S—ensational
E—xpose
X—traordinary

Startling in its dareness . . . Fearless in its treatment . . . Frank in its disclosure . . . Amazing in its handling of delicate situations.

A warning to the parents of America that must be heeded if they would stay the present drift to loose virtues by modern youth.

▼ Bruce Cabot: coming clean   ▼ Groucho: as Lydia the Queen of Tattoo

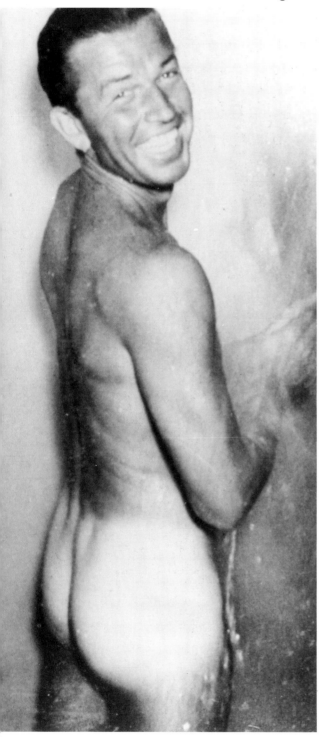

Why is he laughing? He knows I can't print the indiscreet photo of *him*. ▶

☆ HOLLYWOOD HOSPITAL ☆

I'll go nutty in here, shut in with all these nuts!—this was MARILYN MONROE's desperate scribbled letter from the Terminus Station, the Nuthouse. (Her mother had got off at the same station, ending her days at a Loonybin.) For Marilyn it was the Snake Pit. The Warehouse of the Damned.

Marilyn *was* sick, emotionally, but the Menninger Clinic in Kansas City was not the place to dump her. Her plea to Lee Strasberg went unanswered; the great dramatic teacher had no "authority" to spring her from "doctor's care."

Mental illness and Hollywood. Aren't they *all* nuts, did I hear someone say? No, some have managed very well, thank you. "Crazy" Bob Hope bought acres and acres of empty desert around the tiny village of Palm Springs with his first big movie and radio bucks back in the Thirties. Crazy like a fox! Hope and Crosby were rivals for grabbing up cheap acres, back when there *were* cheap acres. Drive through San Fernando Valley, from one end to the other. You have entered what used to be Der Bingle Land; you have cruised through mile after tract-home-boring-smoggy mile of Bob Hope Land. They used to grow walnuts there.

Some haven't managed so well. Some lost their minds. Senile dementia has claimed Love Goddess RITA HAYWORTH. At least we know it's Alzheimer's. Rita now wears diapers and has to be spoon fed. Lucky for Rita she has a devoted daughter.

Senile dementia has claimed BEA LILLIE, who at least is nearer the age we expect things to go wrong. At her last appearance at MOMA, she was led

◀ Rita Hayworth at the airport: first sign of Alzheimer's

▲ Rita watched over by security guards

to the stage of Titus Auditorium, where she proceeded to open her blouse before the fascinated audience of film aficionados, flipping out two pendulous and very weary dugs. (A cloud of MOMA curators quickly settled in around her and led her away, to her high vocal protests. Hell! The star of *On Approval* was having a whacking good time!)

GENE TIERNEY. She had enough reason to break down, poor dear. A retarded child is a heavy number to live with, day after day.

GEORGE ZUCCO. This wonderful character actor, the perfect High Priest of Satanic Atlantis, he of the disturbing glassy eyes, and quick, disconcerting gestures and cat-purr voice, ended his days in the lunatic asylum, after he began believing he was the crazed villains Monogram and PRC kept paying him to play. The High Priest of Mu/Egypt/Atlantis was led away by the fellas in the white coats, dressed to the nines in borrowed Monogram bogeyman finery.

George's faithful wife and daughter moved into the asylum with him, hoping

Gene Tierney has returned to Menninger Clinic for psychiatric care, shattering, at least temporarily, her dream of building a new career in Hollywood.

Gene Tierney: Back in the Shadows

By ERNEST TIDYMAN

Gene Tierney left the Menninger Foundation in Topeka, Kan., last fall after eight months of psychiatric treatment and said.

"I have more peace of mind than I've ever known."

Today, she is once again a patient at the clinic, that peace of mind broken along with her renewed career as an actress.

The announcement was made in Hollywood by her studio, 20th-Century-Fox, where the 38-year-old beauty was to have begun work in 30 days on her first motion picture role since 1954.

The studio was informed that she had returned to the clinic by Miss Tierney's mother, Mrs. Belle Tierney, who lives at the actress' lavish farm home in Westport, Conn.

It was another phase of tragedy for the green-eyed star who has been buffeted by 20 years of personal tragedy, heartbreak, crisis and failure.

There had been the divorce of her parents, the birth of a retarded child after Miss Tierney suffered German measles during the pregnancy, her own divorce from Oleg Cassini and the breakup of romances with Tyrone Power and Aly. Khan.

All of them contributed to the emotional turmoil that sent her to a private sanitarium in Hartford, Conn., four years ago for 18 months of treatment.

She was released briefly, then went to the Menninger Clinic.

Miss Tierney was discharged last September and enthusiastically sought to resume her dormant career with television appearances and a motion picture role.

"My doctors say that my career had absolutely nothing to do with my illness," she said then.

"Perhaps the most important lesson I had to learn was to admit and accept defeat.

"In the other days I felt I had to stand up to any situation and take it. I felt I had to put up with the impossible and try to resolve it.

"I had to learn to say, 'I can't solve that; I give up.'"

She has returned to learn the lesson anew.

◀ Bea Lillie: a vast forgetting   ▲ Gene Tierney: a rough time

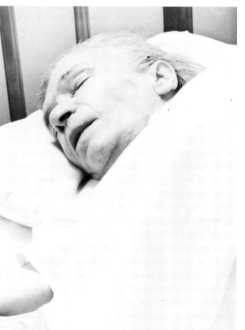

their presence would restore his grasp on reality. Quite the contrary. George Zucco slipped away in the Atlantic fogbanks, finally, one midnight dreary, working himself into a paroxysm of *fear* and *loathing,* screaming he was being stalked by the *Great God Cthulu!*

George Zucco died in the madhouse, from fright. The following midnight, Mrs. Zucco and daughter, unable to live without their meal ticket, unable to face life in Tinseltown without George, joined him in death.

Call him the Easeful Angel. Prince Sirki called.

George Zucco: death in the madhouse ▲   Maria Ouspenskaya and Linda Darnell: both burn victims ▶

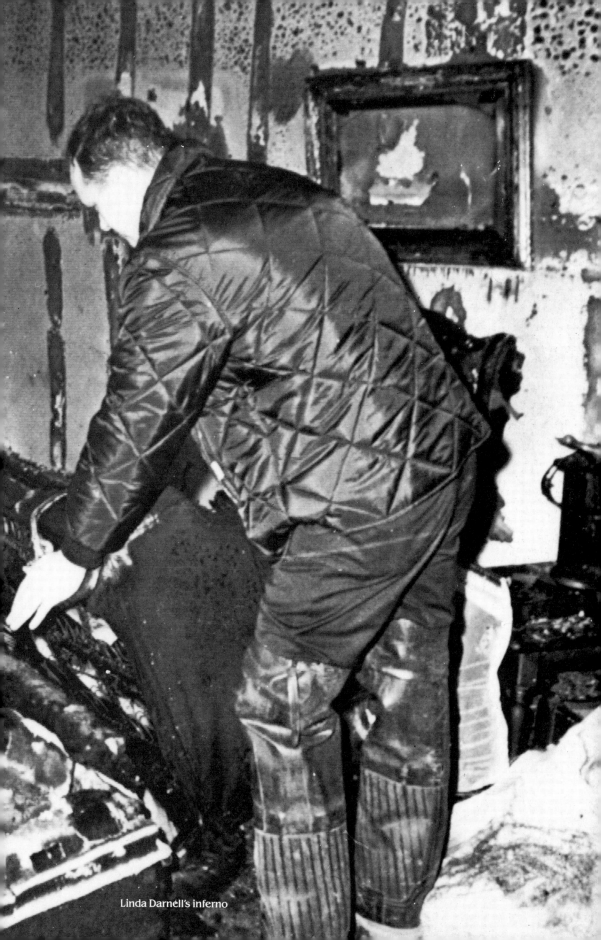
Linda Darnell's inferno

Corinne Griffith: denying who

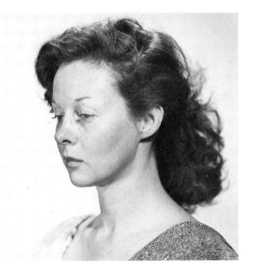

Monty Clift: after the accident ▲   Maria Montez: death by scalding ▲   ▲ Susan Hayward: brain tumor

◀ Marlene Dietrich and her million-dollar cast   ▲ Ellie Powell and William Powell: brave cancer victims

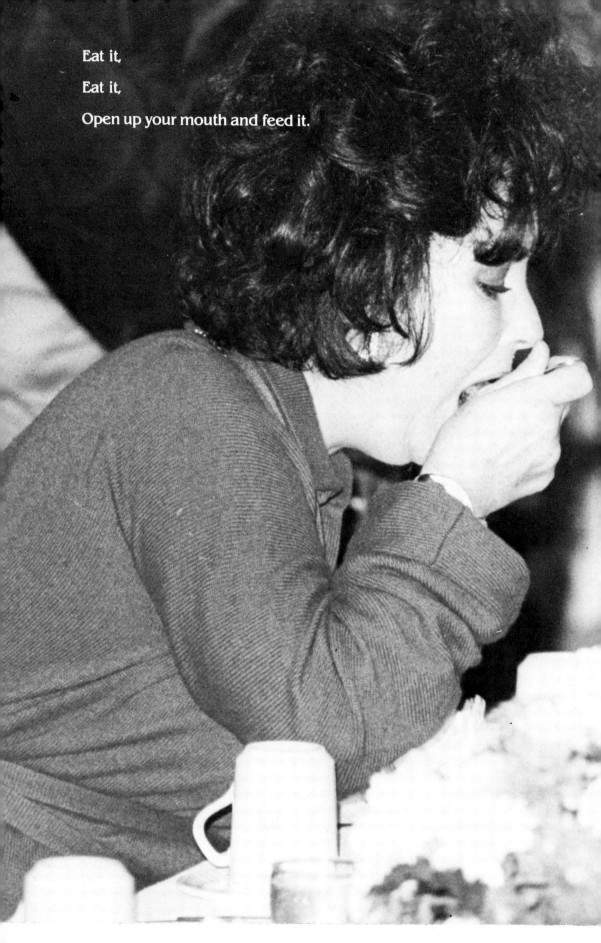

Eat it,

Eat it,

Open up your mouth and feed it.

☆ THE PURPLE ☆
PRINCESS

Wed., Feb. 29, 1984 ☆☆C S.F. EXAMINER   A3

Taking out garbage helped to cure Liz

NEW YORK (UPI) — Actress Elizabeth Taylor said today she was terrified when she entered a rehabilitation center to cure a 25-year dependency on drugs and spent part of the time at the clinic taking out garbage.

"I'm so glad I asked for help," she said on ABC's "Good Morning America. "I was stuttering, stumbling, incoherent. I needed sleeping pills for 25 years. I had learned to rely on them."

Taylor, who celebrated her 52nd birthday Monday, entered the Betty Ford Center at the Eisenhower Medical Center near Palm Springs on Dec. 5 for treatment of an addiction to prescription drugs. She checked out Jan. 20.

Her interview on ABC was the first since her release.

"I'm an addictive kind of person," she said. "It's a disease. I was terrified when I first went there. I had never felt alone in my entire life."

She said she was taking a series of drugs, mainly pain killers, before checking into the clinic. She didn't realize she was an alcoholic, she said, until she entered the clinic.

"There has been a lot of genuine pain in my life. I learned to rely on drugs. I thought I could control it. The clinic was wonderful, very good for me."

She said people in the clinic call themselves "inmates" and that among her duties were taking out the garbage and hosing down the patio.

She said her drug problem is under control and "it is much more fun being lucid. You don't have to worry about forgetting what you said."

◄ The way she was: a *lot* of Liz   ▲ Taylor in 1979   Sideshow Lizzie? ►

☆ HOLLYWOOD DRUGSTORE ☆

The New Wave of Dope in Hollywood got off to a good start when Mrs. Woody Allen—Louise Lasser, remember "Mary Hartman"?—got confused, sat down on the carpeted floor of the posh, twee Rodeo Drive boutique, and began rummaging in her seemingly bottomless purse for something she just *had* to find, strewing woman's tidbits, hygiene and vanity items, and crumpled trash all over the thick rug around her. *Circle of Chaos.*

Persistence pays! Indomitable Louise

Copyright © Walt Disney Productions

found the lump of tinfoil she was looking for—old gum with her favorite flavor, perhaps?—and was proceeding to toke up when the Beverly Hills cops—called by a freaked-out boutique owner, *who should have known better*—arrived and escorted her away. And there you had Mary Hartman in her braids, America's electronic tract-home heroine, on the front pages of papers all over the land, with variations of the headline MARY HARTMAN BUSTED FOR COCAINE.

◀ Lon Chaney: smoking an opium pipe   ▲ Louise Lasser: busted for cocaine

It's a matter of police record, stashed away in the Spanishy Police HQ of our richest town, Beverly Hills. Thus, since it's a *matter of record,* I am permitted to write about it by the legal mavens of my *own* front-office men. (What! Me free to write anything I want? On bathroom walls at Studio 54, maybe!)

Barbara La Marr kept *her* coke in a silver salver on the grand piano. They not only had faces then—they had a touch of taste and style.

Our icons we deserve, for we have made them.

Where's the style in Richard Dreyfuss driving coke-stoned into a palm tree?

Where's the style in Robert Evans' escape-hatch *mea culpa,* a so-called "Warning to Youth" movie he was supposed to make, on the judge's orders, on the perils of fooling around with drugs? Did high-stakes riverboat gambler Evans heed his own little

documentary's drummed-in anti-drug message? Or is it, as gossip has it about *Cotton Club,* a case of hair of the dog?

Now Francis Coppola only has to worry about his addiction to *food,* the Liz Taylor Syndrome. Francis' manic spending sprees, legend in the days of *Apocalypse,* have been smoothed down with daily doses of *lithium*—a drug, to be sure, a deadly poison in the wrong dose, but the mind-doctors and shrink-quacks think they've found the answer to the Big M-D. (Manic-Depressive, anyone?)

Liz Taylor's latest health spa check-in was not so much to knock off some pounds—though after they laughed at her in *Private Lives* the joke went "like trying to squeeze ten pounds of shit in a five-pound bag"—but to try to get a handle on the rainbow coalition of pills she was dropping every night and day. *Pillhead Liz.* Would you believe? And the health spa "clinic" made her sign up for S and M PsychoDrama I, a wacko Hollyweird therapy involving floor-scrubbing à la Joan Crawford (expiating guilt), cleaning, dusting, and yes, *carrying out the garbage!*—and her with that fused disk in her back!

Why even the *Exorcist* girl, the Blair

---

girl, got busted with traces of white powder in her purse (well, it *was* nose powder), and heroine of a certain shoot-out, Jodie Foster, forgot to hide a gram of powder in *her* purse as she passed through Customs at Boston's Logan Airport.

Talk about laid back! Why even fiftyish *Psycho I & II* himself, ever-gaunt, closeted, and neurotic Tony Perkins (the shrink blamed it all on Papa Osgood) got caught in another bit of slapstick airport business, with a supply of sensimilla and three microdots of LSD—now *that's* nostalgia, if not Entertainment: remember LSD?—in *his* purse as he Concorded into London.

The difference between Dope Now, and Dope Then, in the Hollywood scene, is that it's all gone *democratic*. I mean, everyone—the go-fers, the gaffers, the special-effect makers, the guys developing the footage in the labs—is toking away like mad, and it *all shows on the screen*. Mistakes have happened. Stunts have gone wildly wrong. Stunt girls have been paralyzed. Helicopters have dropped deadweight out of the sky, beheading actors, and it *wasn't* in the script, in spite of Hollywood's current wallow in gore-splatter.

O Coke, Where is Thy Sting?

Picture a *big* plate of pure cocaine—I'm talking about big bucks here—piled high in a fucking glittering white pyramid, and then picture the sweaty, coarse, pig-faced comedian—Low Comedy, *very* low—going down in that pile till he came up sputtering for air, a white-faced parody of Pierrot. Then the go-fer girls a-plenty, Playboy centerfolds all, called over by said power-tripping comedian—after all, he *paid* for it, or he was *paid off* with it—to lick it all off his big fat moon face. *Gross Out by John Belushi.* Cocaine Clown. On the Road to Chateau Marmont.

It happened in the bar Chicago Mayor Byrne granted immunity and a 24-hour-

ONE NIGHT OF BLISS FOR A THOUSAND NIGHTS IN HELL!

CAN THEY TAKE IT JUST ONCE AND THEN QUIT?

–just a Few grains of Dope – but it changed their lives!

AUTHENTIC DISCLOSURES ASTOUNDING — FACTS —

a True Biography that leaves Nothing to the Imagination — a sensation in screen Thrills-

•

Women Crave for it, Men will Slay for it, Both will Die for it!

•

SEE "NARCOTIC" Now! as interpreted by Dwain Esper

stay-open-permit, during the long, *long,* location shooting for *The Blues Brothers.* (Now, I ask you, did you find all those car smashups and general lunacy and mayhem all *that funny?* They, the folks that gave you that smash-'em-up movie, thought it was all *very funny*—a *Riot!* at the time. Too bad they can't get all their *audiences* high.) Speaking of duststorms, remember *1941?*

Exploitation movie of the twenties: *Human Wreckage* ▶

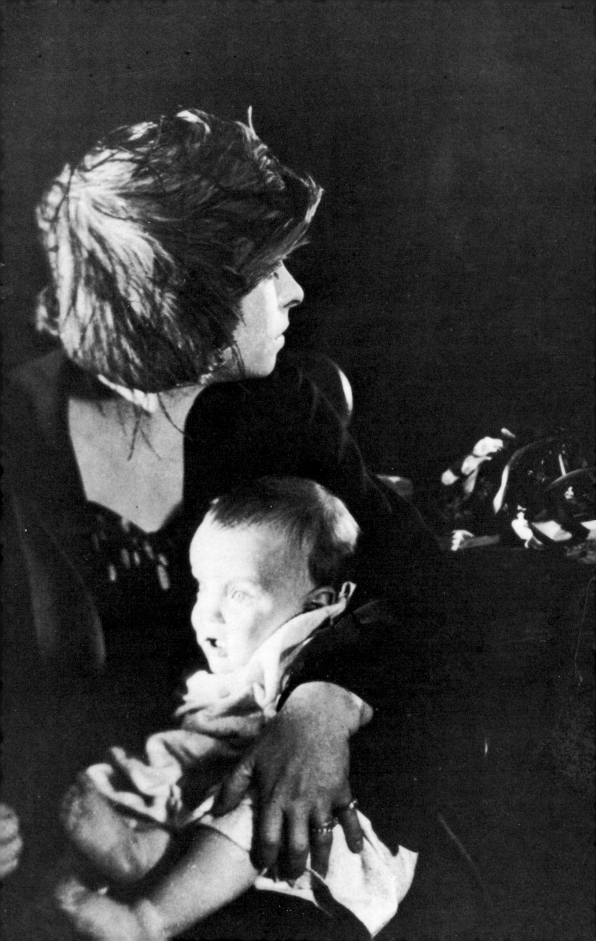

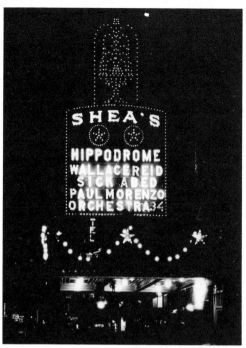

Prophetic title ▲   ▲ Carmen Miranda kept her cocaine in a secret compartment in her platform shoes

Alma Rubens: dead from drugs

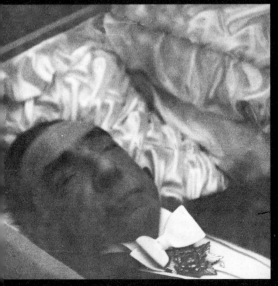

Bela Lugosi: home at last!

Who's surprised that it all had to end, that risk-taking, fool-high recklessness, in triple tragedy, in *Twilight Zone.* Sooner or later, Karma will out: even Tinseltown's "hot" new golden boys eventually collect their dues.

Well, now they've got CokeEnders. and the rest of dazed U.S.A. can always phone 800-C-O-C-A-I-N-E.

The saddest footnote of all was told me by a high-priced Hollywood hooker, who swears she and her big-buck sisters will *never trick again* with certain Coke Head Big Names, no matter *how* much they're offered. Better ways to pass the night than hopelessly labor over a flabby phallus fallen in Terminal Faint! Yes, I'm talking about impotence. (It's hit a lot of *big* names, just like in the last reel of *Scarface II.*) Yet the arrogance of the guys, freebased out of their minds, is that it's up to the *chicks* to *get it up for* them! It's no labor of love, and even prosties draw the line. Coke-cooked limp noodles, thanks, but *no thanks.*

Hail the flaming freebase Richard Pryor Comet, flashing through the Tinseltown night! Scar tissue, anyone?

Nita Naldi: fashionable star ▲   Nita Naldi: fashionable addict, hours before her death ▶

☆ DEATH VALLEY DAYS ☆

Cut off his legs!

—SAM WOOD

Hedda and Louella and everyone in Hollywood considered Jane and Ronnie the cutest and nicest and happiest young married couple in town. Their divorce in 1949 set off shock waves of disbelief. Curiously enough it was the only divorce in history in which two Warner Bros. movies could have been named as co-respondents. In 1948, Reagan had told Hedda Hopper: "If this comes to a divorce, I think I'll name *Johnny Belinda* co-respondent." Wyman's star was rising higher and higher; his was plummetting. She had an Oscar; he didn't. Wyman won her Academy Award for her superb performance as a deaf-mute in Jean Negulesco's 1949 *Johnny Belinda*. Once, when the couple was dining out, the waiter turned to Reagan and asked: "And what will *Mr.* Wyman have?"

The only sensitive and meaty performance of Reagan's entire film career was as amputee Drake McHugh in Sam Wood's 1942 *Kings Row*. It was his all-time favorite movie. He inflicted the picture, time and again, on dinner guests at their house. Wyman remarked: "I just couldn't watch that damned *Kings Row* any more." During the divorce proceedings, she contented herself with testifying that he was too absorbed in politics.

Our First Couple met cute— significantly, in a political context. Reagan first met the prudish and conservative young actress Nancy Davis when he helped her clear herself of the suspicion of Communist affiliations. Her name had turned up on the witch-hunters' lists. At that time, Reagan was the liberal President of the Screen Actors Guild. Their first date took place when he invited her to dinner and informed her that she had been cleared—it was another Nancy Davis who was listed as a Commie. They continued dating. The following year, Nancy gave the most uplifting performance of her tiny film career when, as a pregnant housewife in *The Next Voice You Hear,* she heard the voice of God on the radio. The next logical step was to marry Ronald Reagan. They were wed in 1952.

Ronnie is getting mighty fed up on those swell guy roles he's been getting. He wants to play a meanie for a change.
—RUTH ROMAN, *Movieland, April 1950*

Ronnie had been a leftish Democrat during his early career; if he became a Republican, and has since proven himself the country's most right-wing President since McKinley, the thanks may be in large part due to Nancy.

◄ Bunker mentality: Nancy and Ronnie

Patricia Neal, who starred with him in three films at Warners, opined: "When I knew Reagan he was very liberal. And I think he was liberal until he met his present wife."

Nancy regarded her stepfather, the Chicago surgeon Dr. Loyal Davis, as her real father. This gentleman is said to have been "intolerant of minorities." When Nancy was in Chicago in 1980 for a campaign fundraiser, she spoke to her husband on an amplified phone hookup and told him, while the assembled press listened, how much she wished he could be there to "see all these beautiful white people."

The only premiere I can think of this month was *Bedtime for Bonzo* at the Carthay Circle which was somewhat marred by the accidental death of its chimpanzee star the day before.

—GRACE FISCHLER, *Motion Picture, June 1951*

Subsequent to his second marriage, Reagan's career was confined to a handful of B turkeys. In 1954, he began a new career on television. Ann Sheridan says: "I remember Ronnie telling all of us not to join TV because it was the enemy of the movies. Next thing, he was on G.E. Theater with his contact lenses reading the commercials." In 1961, he spoke at a fundraiser for the re-election to Congress of John Rousselot of the John Birch Society. In 1962, Reagan became a full-fledged Republican. That same year, he was fired from the *General Electric Theater* because his off-the-tube political speeches were too far to the right even for that company's comfort.

He was a silly young kid. Everyone called him Little Ronnie Reagan.

—BETTE DAVIS

After his election as Governor of California, he promptly fired two of his staff members at Sacramento when he learned that they were gay. Reagan considers homosexuality "a tragic

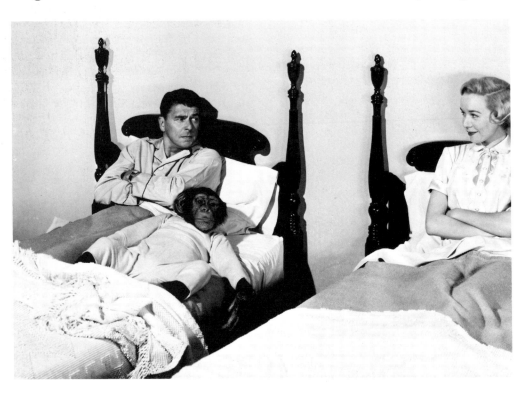

Strange bedfellows: *Bedtime for Bonzo* ▲

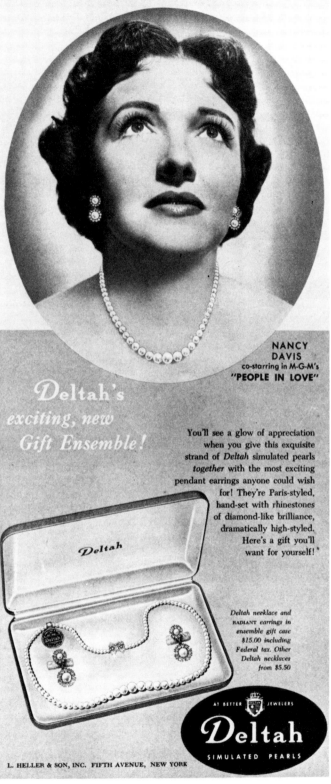
▲ Ronnie and Nancy: pitching for stuffed shirts and phony pearls

illness" which should remain illegal. "In the Bible," he told author Robert Scheer, "it says that in the eyes of the Lord, this is a great abomination." In the eyes of many Californians, his career as Governor was an even greater one.

When the Reagans set up housekeeping in the White House, they

Vol. 14 — No. 23   DECEMBER 25, 1967   Standard   ★★★ 15¢

Gov. Reagan Says:

SOME OF MY BEST FRIENDS ARE HOMOSEXUALS

Gov. Reagan's friends are not necessarily President Reagan's friends ▲   The First Lady gets friendly ▶

removed the portrait of Harry Truman, replaced it with one of Calvin Coolidge, and affairs of state permitting, set about inviting globs of Old Hollywood Cronydom to drop in and dine off Nancy's fancy Graustarkian plates. The wizened happy few have included Charlton (Moses) Heston, Jimmy Stewart, gung-ho Tough Tittie anti-Commie Ginger Rogers, Shirley Temple and Claudette (Cleopatra) Colbert who was said to be among the first to advise the President to invade Grenada—she was far from delighted at the prospect of an island full of Reds so near to her palatial Barbados estate. When President Ronnie calls, the old glamour pusses jump: ex-Democrat Frank Sinatra, Audrey Hepburn, and that evergreen ski-nosed pillar of reaction, Bob Hope. (One pious old star caused a tizzy when her colostomy can, concealed in the folds of her evening gown, set off security alarms.) It's a bit like the last volume of Proust, *The Past Recaptured*, in which all of the appealing creatures we had previously met in their younger heydays reappear at a party— as barely recognizable gargoyles.

Reagan is a major concern. I think we're headed for disaster. . . . I listen to a Reagan speech and want to throw up.
—HENRY FONDA, *Playboy, December 1981*

Alexis Smith enjoyed the signal honor of being the sole emissary from Tinseltown at an October 1982 White House State Dinner in honor of President Suharto of Indonesia. Alexis dined on beef *béarnaise* and molded pear sherbet, breaking bread with the statesman whose regime established itself by means of the execution of an estimated half-million human beings, whose Death Squads have summarily killed over 4,000 inhabitants of his capital in recent months and who is

practicing genocide in East Timor.

I never worked with Ronald Reagan. I'm not happy that he's President. I was willing to give him a chance. But he's destroying everything now I've lived my life for.
—MYRNA LOY, *on the TV show Legends of the Screen, 1982*

The ingratiating star of *Swing Your Lady* and *The Cowboy from Brooklyn* has slashed government programs that benefited the poor, depriving thousands of the country's underprivileged children, so that we can afford more nuclear bombs, while his cuts in corporate taxation have ensured that his rich supporters will get richer. His anti-environmental stance has made his the most "toxic" administration in America's history. (In a 1979 radio speech, Reagan maintained that most air pollution is caused, not by chimneys or auto exhaust, but by plants and trees.)

He has shattered the détente carefully built up by previous administrations and reinstated Uncle Sam as the world's policeman, using the CIA to foment war against Nicaragua; he instituted an unprecedented stifling of the press during his invasion of Grenada.

He has insulted vast numbers of loyal citizens by reiterating that the anti-nuclear power movement is Communist-inspired. His "devil theories" on the Soviet Union have put us on a collision course with Russia. In the light of his appalling nuclear policy, the titles of several of his movies take on a peculiarly somber afterglow—*Accidents Will Happen, The Killers, Dark Victory,* and *Nine Lives Are Not Enough. Hollywood Babylon* is moribund, dead, defunct, croaked, crowbait, finito, Kaput, Kaputissimo!—with Reagan at the helm, we're already watching the trailer of the ultimate picture show: Hollywood Armageddon.

☆ END OF REEL TWO ☆

☆ INDEX ☆

Acord, Art, 229
Adams, Abigail, 222, 229-30
Adams, Nick, 127, 230, *230*
Adrian, 227
Albee, E. F., 42
Alexander, Ross, 206, *206*
Allyson, June, 224
Ameche, Don, 183
Angeli, Pier, 195, 230-31, *231*
Annenberg, Walter, 61
Arbuckle, Fatty, 225
Armendariz, Pedro, 207, *207*
Atwill, Lionel, 87-103, *87, 88, 89, 90, 91, 94, 96, 97, 100, 102,* 251
Atwill, Louise Cromwell, 88, 90-96, 103

Bacon, Lloyd, 183
Baggett, Lynne, 231-32
Balaban, Barney, 65
Ball, Lucille, 72
Bankhead, Tallulah, 57, 111, 142, *142*
Banks, Monty, 210, 225
Barry, Donald "Red," 208-209, *209*
Barrymore, John, 63, *167,* 198
Barrymore, Lionel, 50, 56, 103
Barthelmess, Richard, 216
Bates, Barbara, 203, *203,* 218
Baxter, Anne, 91, 203
Bean, Roy, 87
Beckett, Scotty, 232, *232*
Beery, Wallace, 51, *262*
Belasco, David, 87, 211
Belushi, John, 297
Benchley, Robert, 198
Bennett, Constance, 56
Bennett, Joan, 56
Bennett, Richard, 25
Berkeley, Busby, 18, 71-84, *71, 72, 75, 78, 81, 84,* 97, 196
Bern, Paul, 209, *209*
Bernard, Lois, 224
Bing, Herman, 198, 209-10, *210*
Bioff, Willie, 65-69, *65, 69*
Bishop, Julie, 26
Blair, Linda, 296
Blandick, Clara, 232-33, *232*

Bogart, Humphrey, 26, 132
Borzage, Frank, 103, 206, 251
Bow, Clara, 30, 56, 108, 144, *144*
Bowers, John, 16, 198, *199*
Boyer, Charles, 183, 233, *233*
Brackett, Rogers, 127
Brady, Diamond Jim, 222
Brando, Marlon, 127, 205
Brooke, Tyler, 195, 196, *196*
Brooks, Louise, 108, 151
Brown, Clarence, 49
Browne, George, 65-69
Browning, Tod, 103
Bruce, Virginia, 71
Bruckman, Clyde, 210-11
Brulator, Jules, 67
Buckland, Wilfred, 211-12
Bunny, John, 15
Burke, Billie, 87, 224
Burton, Richard, *180*
Butterworth, Charles, 198, *198*
Buttons, Red, 220

Cagney, James, 26, 132, 209, 220
Cantor, Eddie, 15, 71, 195
Capone, Al, 66
Capote, Truman, *180*
Cardwell, James, 212
Carew, Arthur Edmund, 212, *212*
Carroll, Nancy, 16, 17, 22
Chaney, Lon, 40, 50, 189, 214, 216, *295*
Chaplin, Charlie, 8, 71, 78, 108, 111, *150*
Charters, Spencer, 195, *196*
Christensen, Benjamin, 218
Christian, Linda, 227-28, *228*
Clift, Montgomery, *287*
Colbert, Claudette, 56, *142,* 227, 312
Columbo, Russ, 25, 141
Connery, Sean, 272
Cooper, Gary, 26, 227, 252
Cooper, Jackie, 184
Coppola, Francis Ford, 138, 296
Cornell, Katharine, 87
Cortez, Ricardo, 72
Cowdin, J. Cheever, 202

Crawford, Joan, 49, *49,* 53, 57-58, *57, 113, 114, 121, 123,* 189, 200, 296
Crosby, Bing, 27, 251, 279
Crowley, Aleister, vii, 97
Crowther, Bosley, 189
Cukor, George, 49, 63, *63*
Cummings, Constance, 26
Cuneo, Lester, 212-13
Curtiz, Michael, 89, 103, 198, 205, 206, 207, 218

Damone, Vic, 231
Dandridge, Dorothy, 233-34, *234,* 237
Dane, Karl, 213-14, *214*
Daniels, Billy, 142
Darnell, Linda, *282*
Darvi, Bella, 204-206, *204*
Davies, Marion, 49, 51, 53, 56, 80, *150,* 151, 213
Davis, Bette, 26, 202, 203, 217, 220, 223, 233, 306
Davis, Joan, 210
Day, Doris, 81, 227
Dean, James, 127-38, *127, 129, 132, 135, 138,* 230, 231
De Havilland, Olivia, 49, 103, *261*
Dekker, Albert, 203, 220, *221*
De La Motte, Marguerite, 22, 198
Del Rio, Dolores, 72, 103, 227
De Mille, Cecil B., 26, 195, 211, 214, 217, 229, 244, 256
Derek, Bo, 141
Devine, Andy, 202
Dietrich, Marlene, 8, 89, 103, *142,* 221, 227, 233, *289*
Disney, Walt, 184, 186
Dodd, Claire, 71
Dolly Sisters, 221-22
Donnelly, Ruth, 25
Dougherty, Jack, 196
Douglas, Sharon, 103
Dreyer, Carl, 218
Dreyfuss, Richard, 296
Driscoll, Bobby, 183-86, *183, 184, 185, 186*
Duncan, Bob, 214
Dunne, Irene, 71, 103, 201
Dwan, Allan, 103

Eburne, Maude, 25
Ehrlich, Jake, 33
Emerson, Faye, 26
Entwistle, Peg, 224-25, *224*
Evans, Robert, 296

Fairbanks, Douglas, 198, 211, 252
Farmer, Frances, 185
Farrar, Geraldine, 211
Farrell, Glenda, 78
Fields, W.C., *162*, 210
Finch, Flora, 15
Fleming, Victor, 49, 63, 229
Flynn, Errol, 35, 78, 103, 111, *170*, 206
Fonda, Henry, 312
Fontaine, Joan, 183
Ford, John, 207, 215, 216, 256
Ford, Ruth, 26
Forman, Tom, 214
Foster, Jodie, 297
Foster, Preston, 25, 89
Fowler, Gene, 56
Fowley, Douglas, 103
Franco, Francisco, 8
Frazin, Gladys, 225
Freed, Arthur, 81
Freel, Aleta, 206
Frenke, Eugene, 99, *99*, 100
Fromkess, Leon, 103

Gable, Clark, 27, 49, 51, 54, 63, *63*, 141, 190-91, *192*
Gaby, Frank, 222
Garbo, Greta, 111, *141*, 202, 209, 212, 227, *267*
Garland, Judy, 26, 198, 218, 227, 232
Gaynor, Janet, 199, 215
Geisler, Jerry, 30-33, 35, 78-79
Gibbons, Eliot, 227
Gibson, Hoot, 229
Gilbert, John, 51, 53
Gillingwater, Claude, 214, *214*
Gioe, "Cherry Nose," 66
Girard, Bernard, 185
Gish, Lillian, 183, 216
Gleason, Jackie, 26
Gleason, Russell, 225, *225*
Glyn, Elinor, 56
Goddard, Paulette, 71
Goetz, William, 56
Goldwyn, Samuel, 40, 49, 69, 71, 99, 195
Grable, Betty, 71, 222
Grahame, Gloria, 26
Grange, Red, 42
Grant, Cary, *145*, *146-47*, *149*
Greene, Graham, 150
Griffith, D.W., *162*, 216, 244, 252
Grot, Anton, 89

Goulding, Eddie, 96
Guinan, Texas, 26

Haber, Joyce, 248
Hagen, Uta, 27
Haines, William, 15, 49-63, *49*, *51*, *54*, *57*, *61*, 215
Hale, Barbara, 183
Hale, Jonathan, 215
Hardy, Oliver, 210, 225
Harlow, Jean, 209, 244, *271*
Harrison, Rex, 235
Harron, Bobby, 215, *215*
Hathaway, Henry, 103
Haver, Phyllis, 227
Havier, Jose Alex, 216
Hawks, Howard, 195, 207
Hayes, Helen, 15, 87
Hays, Will, 42, 45
Hayward, Susan, 207, 221, *287*
Hayworth, Rita, 250, 279, *279*
Hearst, William Randolph, 51, 56, 90, 150-52, *150*
Hedren, Tippi, 157-58, *158*
Hellman, Jack, 189
Hepburn, Audrey, 157, 312
Hill, George, 213, 216
Hirohito (Emperor), 217
Hitchcock, Alfred, 155-58, *157*, *158*, 215, 220
Hitler, Adolf, 202, 220
Hoover, J. Edgar, *247*
Hope, Bob, 100, 279, 312
Hopper, Hedda, 127, 206, 305
Hughes, Howard, 205
Hunter, Ross, 189
Hutton, Barbara, 61
Hyams, Leila, 56

Indrisano, Johnny, 198, 222-23
Irene, 220, 221, 227, *227*
Ives, Burl, 184

Jessel, George, 222, 230
Johnson, Nunnally, 56
Jones, Marcia Mae, 103
Jorgensen, Christine, 223
Jory, Victor, 96, 192

Karloff, Boris, *141*, 198, 201, 230
Kaye, Danny, 203, 218
Kazan, Elia, 129
Keaton, Buster, 53, 204, 210, 211
Keeler, Ruby, 84
Keighley, William, 25
Kelly, Gene, 81
Kelly, Grace, 27, 155-57, *155*, 157
Kelly, Patsy, 142, *142*
Kelly, Paul, 15-27, *15*, *17*, *19*, *27*, 215

Kennedy, John F., 42
Kennedy, Joseph P., 35, 39-46, *39*, *40*, *43*, *46*
Kennedy, Merna, 71
Kent, Sidney, 66
Kern, Jerome, 201
King, Henry, 196, 206
Kirkwood, James, Jr., 22
Koenig, William, 72

Ladd, Alan, 183, 234, *234*
Laemmle, Carl, 201
Lake, Veronica, 72, 183, 234
La Marr, Barbara, 1, 2, 196, 296, *296*
Landis, Carole, 78, 235, *237*
Lane, Rosemary 256
Langlois, Henri, 8
Langtry, Lillie, 87
Lasky, Jesse, 40, 211
Lasser, Louise, 295, *295*
Laurel, Stan, 210, 225
Lehman, Trent, 223-24, *223*
Leisen, Mitch, 54, 141
Leroy, Mervyn, 78
Lewis, Christopher, 192-93
Lillie, Bea, 281, *281*
Lloyd, Harold, 210, *262*
Loew, Marcus, 40, 51
Lombard, Carole, 52-56, *54*, 141
Loy, Myrna, 103, 183, 224, 312
Lubitsch, Ernst, 67, 209, 233, 251
Luciano, Lucky, 66
Lugosi, Bela, 144, *144*, 150, *301*

MacArthur, Douglas, 88, 91, 103
McCullough, Paul, 259, *259*
McCutcheon, Wallace, Jr., 216
McDaniel, Hattie, 142-43, *142*, 184
MacDonald, Jeannette, 198
McDonald, Marie, 235, *235*
McDonald, Ray, 204
McDowell, Nelson, 217
McHugh, Frank, 26, 78
McIntyre, Robert, 49
Mackaye, Dorothy, 15-26, *16*, *17*, *22*, *25*
McNamara, Maggie, 235
McPherson, Aimee Semple, 144
Malden, Karl, 129
Mamoulian, Rouben, 103, 195, 196
Mannix, Toni, 218
Mansfield, Jayne, *269*
March, Frederic, 199, 227
Marx, Groucho, *275*
Mauch, Billy and Bobby, *152*
Mostel, Zero, *272*
Mayer, Louis B., 40, 50, 51, 53, 65

Maynard, Claire, 206
Miles, Vera, 157
Milestone, Lewis, 16, 22, 212
Miller, Ann, 72
Mineo, Sal, 127
Miranda, Carmen, 79, *267, 300*
Mitchell, John, 217
Mitchum, Robert, 78, 178
Monroe, Marilyn, 203, 237-44, *237-42, 246, 271, 279*
Moore, Colleen, 37
Moorehead, Agnes, 207
Moorhouse, Bert, 217
Morgan, Helen, 201
Morris, Chester, 196, 244, *244*
Morse, Terry, 103
Munson, Ona, *244*, 245
Murnau, F.W., 209
Murray, James, 199-200, *199*
Murray, Mae, 49

Nabokov, Vladimir, 108
Nagel, Anne, 206
Nazimova, Alla, 71, 87
Neal, Patricia, 306
Negri, Pola, 2, 51, 53
Negulesco, Jean, 198, 305
Newman, Paul, 231
Nitti, Frank, 66, 68-69
Noguchi, Thomas, 230, 244
Novarro, Ramon, 108, 217

O'Brien, Margaret, 183
O'Brien, Pat, 26, 78
Oliver, Edna May, *145*
Orr, William, 203
Ouspenskaya, Maria, *282*

Pacht, Isaac, 102
Pantages, Alexander, 29-37, *29, 35, 37, 40, 45, 78*
Parker, Dorothy, 199
Parsons, Louella, *180*, 190, 305
Pegler, Westbrook, 68
Perkins, Tony, 129, 297
Pickford, Mary, 49, *170*, 215, 216
Pollack, Ben, 224
Powell, Dick, 78, 207
Powell, William, 15, 53, *289*
Power, Tyrone, 227
Preminger, Otto, 234, 237, 247
Preston, Robert, 183

Quine, Richard, 204

Rambova, Natacha, 96
Ray, Nicholas, 127
Raye, Martha, 256
Raymond, Ray, 15-16, *16*, 23
Reagan, Ronald, 202, 207, 218,

305-12, *305, 306, 307, 308, 312*
Reeves, George, 217-18, *217*
Renoir, Jean, 220
Riesner, Charles, 72
Robeson, Paul, 201
Rogers, Charles R., 202
Rogers, Ginger, 18, 312
Rogers, Roy, 184
Rogers, Will, 150
Romero, Cesar, *267*
Rooney, Mickey, 1
Rosi, Francesco, 227
Roth, Lillian, 25, *168-69*
Rothafel, Samuel L., 42
Rousselot, John, 306
Russell, Gail, 245, *245*

Salinger, Conrad, 220
Sanders, George, 183, *195*, 202, 203, 245
Scala, Gia, 246-47, *246*
Schenck, Joseph M., 68
Schenck, Nicholas M., 66, 68
Schoedsack, Ernest, 221
Scorsese, Martin, 193
Seastrom, Victor, 49
Seberg, Jean, 237, 247, *247*
Seiter, William, 56
Seitz, John, 25
Sekely, Steve, 95
Selfridge, Gordon, 222
Selznick, David O., 49, 63
Shaw, George Bernard, 56
Shaw, Wini, 72
Shearer, Norma, 49, 51
Sheridan, Ann, 306
Sinatra, Frank, 81, 312
Slezak, Walter, 218-20, *218*
Sloane, Everett, 250, *250*
Sloman, Ted, 202
Smith, Alexis, 312
Spiegel, Sam, 231-32
Stanwyck, Barbara, 25, 26, 220, 223, 232, 233
Sten, Anna, 99
Stevens, George, 234
Stevens, Inger, 250-51, *251*
Stewart, James, 224, 312
Strickling, Howard, 51
Sullavan, Margaret, 103, 251-52, *251*
Swanson, Gloria, 13, *13*, 39-46, *45, 46*, 211, 214

Taylor, Elizabeth, 204, 227, *291, 296*
Tellegen, Lou, 225
Temple, Shirley, 150, 215, *272*, 312

Templeton, Alec, 99
Tetzlaff, Ted, 183
Thalberg, Irving, 50, 51, 200, 209, 216
Thomson, Fred, 42
Tierney, Gene, 281, *281*
Tilden, Big Bill, 105-111, *105, 108, 111*
Todd, Thelma, 9
Tone, Franchot, 57
Turner, Lana, 26, 227

Ungar, Arthur, 67

Valentino, Rudolph, 1, 2, 8, *8*, 25, 96, 108, 213, 256, *261*
Velez, Lupe, 79, 252, *252, 253*
Vidor, King, 49, 50, 56, 199, 213, 215, 216
Von Sternberg, Josef, 8, 89, 96, 103, 209
Von Stroheim, Erich, 43-45, 100

Walsh, Raoul, 26
Warner, H. B., 53, 256
Warner, Jack, 56, 81
Wayne, John, 26, 207, 216, 256
Weissmuller, Johnny, 253
Welles, Orson, 25, 99, 151, 250
Wellman, William, 190, 191
West, Mae, 167, 198, 209, 222-23, 227
West, Roland, 196, 244
Westmore, George, *253*, 256
Westmore, Perc, 256
Whale, James, 90, 103, 200-203, *201*, 207, 220
White, Pearl, 216
Wiggins, Mary 220
Wilde, Cornel, 183
Wilder, Billy, 53
Wilson, Carey, 57
Winchell, Walter, 26
Windsor, Duke of (*formerly* Prince of Wales) 222
Withers, Grant, 189, 256-59
Wood, Natalie, 127
Wood, Sam, 42, 305
Wray, Fay, 89, 229
Wyler, William, 229
Wyman, Jane, 246, 305

Young, Gig, *218*, 220
Young, Loretta, 184, 189-93, *189, 190, 192, 193*, 234, 256, 259

Zanuck, Darryl, 72, 204-205
Ziegfeld, Florenz, 71, 195, 221
Zucco, George, 281-82, *282*
Zukor, Adolph, 8, 40

Swinging silent star George O'Brien

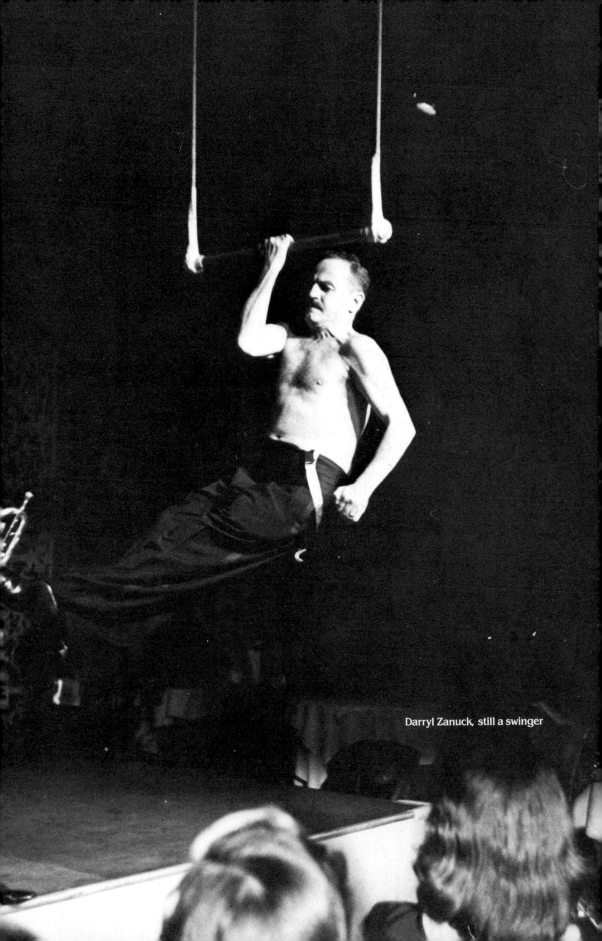

Darryl Zanuck, still a swinger

☆ CREDITS ☆

The author wishes to thank the following individuals and institutions for their generous assistance: Elliott Stein; Samson De Brier; David Frasier and William Dellenback, the Kinsey Institute for Research in Sex, Gender, and Reproduction; Olivia and Joel Baren; Anton Szandor La Vey; Ken Galente, Silver Screen; Carlos Clarens and Howard Mandelbaum, Phototeque; Marc Wanamaker, Bison Archives; Harriet Culver, Culver Pictures; Roy Schatt; David Del Valle; Jeffrey Goodman, *Oui*; Jay Padroff; Sandy Brown Wyeth; Pat Oliphant; Karen Larsen, UPI/Bettmann Archive; Fred Cantey, Wide World Photos; Spider Webb; Mary Corliss, Stills Collection, Museum of Modern Art Department of Film; Tom Luddy; Bob Chatterton; Walt Disney Productions; Bill Blackbeard, San Francisco Academy of Comic Art; Academy of Motion Picture Arts and Sciences Library; Lincoln Center Library for the Performing Arts; Bob Pike Photo Library; Cinema Shop.

Photographs:
Ken Galente Collection: i, viii, ix, xiv, xv, 2, 9, 27, 55, 67, 68, 83, 120, 121, 124, 128, 129, 130, 131, 132, 134, 135, 136, 137, 139, 143, 145 (bottom), 150, 151 (top), 157, 160, 166, 170, 172, 173 (top), 178, 180, 191, 193, 197, 209, 217, 219, 221, 228, 244 (left), 245, 257, 258, 262 (bottom), 280, 288, 292, 294; Phototeque: iv, v, 13, 48, 52, 54, 57, 70, 72, 81, 113, 115, 122, 142, 146, 147, 148, 149, 154, 155, 156, 158, 159, 175, 185, 191, 194, 196, 199, 203, 204, 206, 207, 210, 212, 213, 214, 215, 218, 223, 225, 226, 230, 231, 232, 233, 234, 235, 246, 250, 251, 263, 286, 287 (bottom left), 296 (bottom), 303 (Marvin Lichtner), 306, 307, 320; Sandy Brown Wyeth: 6, 10, 11; Wide World Photos: 12, 14, 151 (bottom), 238, 239, 240, 242, 243, 278, 279, 285, 290; United Press International/Bettmann Archive: 16, 17, 19, 20, 21, 22, 24, 25, 38, 40, 41, 43, 47, 69, 76, 77, 78, 80, 304, 309, 310-11; Bison Archives: 28, 30, 31, 32, 34, 35, 36, 37; Culver Pictures: 58, 59 (bottom), 64, 104, 105, 106-7, 108, 109, 110, 249; Elliott Stein Collection: 85, 308; Del Valle Archives: 91, 94, 95, 96, 97, 141, 145 (top), 167, 201, 301, 322; San Francisco Academy of Comic Art: 94, 98, 99, 281; Kinsey Institute: 101, 264, 265; *Oui*: 116, 117, 266; Page Wood: x, xi; Joel Baren: 110 (center), 118, 119; Ron Galella: 181; Roy Schatt: 126 (from *James Dean: A Portrait*, by Roy Schatt); Jerome Zerbe: 276 (left); Spider Webb: 276 (right); Guy DeLort/WWD: 291; Pat Oliphant: 313; Loomis Dean, *Life* © 1954 Time Inc., 321; other illustrations from the Kenneth Anger Collection.

ERTZNAY TO OUYAY